Eli J Sherlock

Memorabilia of the Marches and Battles in which the One

Hundredth

Regiment of Indiana Infantry Volunteers took an Active Part

Eli J Sherlock

Memorabilia of the Marches and Battles in which the One Hundredth
Regiment of Indiana Infantry Volunteers took an Active Part

ISBN/EAN: 9783337210175

Printed in Europe, USA, Canada, Australia, Japan

Cover: Foto ©ninafisch / pixelio.de

More available books at **www.hansebooks.com**

MEMORABILIA

OF THE

Marches and Battles

IN WHICH THE

One Hundredth Regiment

OF

Indiana Infantry Volunteers

TOOK AN ACTIVE PART.

WAR OF THE REBELLION,
1861-5.

TO THE READER.

I have in my possession at this date four books which I carried during the entire term of my service in the War of 1861-5.

In these books I made daily, in my own handwriting, chronological order, memorabilia of such occur... as came under my personal observation, and such as came to my knowledge from direct and authentic sources

The facts so recorded by me constitut' the basis of this book. In many respects I have embellished my own account of particular events with extracts from the Records of the Union and Confederate armies, published by the Government, and have it a the volume and page in support of the truthfulness thereof. The book has been prepared in great haste and many difficulties had to be overcome. There may be some errors in it, but and the errors must be shown to be such, by the Government records. No claim whatever is made for literary excellence. Doubtless the memory of many members of the Command will not coincide with some of the facts herein stated. If such should be the case, I only ask the reader to reserve his decision until he has examined the official records.

I have endeavored herein not to exalt one man above another, but to write the truth concerning each man's military record, as far as he has put me in possession of the facts relating thereto, and as far as I could learn the same from the Regimental Records. I feel grateful to my Comrades for the many expressions of kindness which I have received from them.

E. J. SHERLOCK.

Kansas City, Missouri, September, 1896.

Outbreak of the Rebellion.

For many years prior to the outbreak of the Rebellion the people of the North and South had been divided upon the question of human slavery. The latter favored its continuance in the slave states and its extension to the territories. To this the sentiment of the people of the North was not only opposed, but was in favor of the abolition of slavery within the slave states. Some of the leaders of the South for years had contemplated the withdrawal or secession of the slave states from the Union and the establishment of a separate government, whose corner stone was to be human slavery.

The agitation of these questions produced a state of sectional feeling and animosity between the people of the North and South, which eventually culminated in secession and the Civil War of 1861-5.

Including December 3, 1859, more than a year before hostilities actually began, there had been transferred, by order of President Buchanan's Secretary of War, one hundred and twenty-five thousand stand of arms from the armories and arsenals in the North to those of the South. The object was to disarm the former and arm the latter. This was so quietly done that but few persons knew of it at the time. The secretary had also sold about fifty thousand stand of arms to the Southern States and sundry individuals in the South, at $2.50 each, without the consent of the Congress.

Governor Gist of South Carolina, on October 5, 1860, addressed a confidential letter to the governors of the Southern States, in which he requested them severally to communicate to him their opinions in regard to the secession of their respective states from the Union, in case Abraham Lincoln was elected to the Presidency. In this letter, speaking for South Carolina, he said:

"If a single state secedes, South Carolina will follow." North Carolina answered, that the people of that state did not consider the election of Mr. Lincoln a sufficient justification for secession. Alabama answered, that it would not go out of the Union alone, but would, with two or more other states. Mississippi answered, that if any state moved for secession, it would follow her. The Governor of Louisiana answered, that he would not advise the secession of his state. The Governor of Georgia said, that the people of that state would await some overt act of the Lincoln government. The Governor of Florida answered, that his state was "ready to wheel into line, with the gallant Palmetto State, or any other cotton state or states."

On the 5th of November, 1860, the Governor of South Carolina sent a message to the Legislature of that State (then in session) recommending the purchase of arms and war material and the calling of a State convention; which, being called, convened at Columbia, December 17, 1860, from whence it adjourned to Charleston, and on the 20th of December, 1860, it passed an ordinance of secession in the following words:

"We, the people of the State of South Carolina in convention assembled, do declare and ordain, and it is hereby declared and ordained, that the ordinance adopted by us in convention, on the 23d day of May, in the year of our Lord, 1788, whereby the Constitution of the United States of America was ratified, and also all acts and parts of acts of the General Assembly of this State, ratifying amendments of the said constitution, are hereby repealed, and that the Union now subsisting between South Carolina and the other States under the name of the United States of America is hereby dissolved." (Ser. 1, p 110.)

On the same day the Secretary of War ordered one hundred and ten (110) Columbiads and eleven (11) thirty-two pounders to be shipped from the arsenal at Pittsburg to different points in the South, but this shipment was prevented by citizens of Pennsylvania. There were many forts and navy yards along the South Atlantic and Gulf coasts and on the rivers, and large arsenals were located in many of the cities of the South, which were all supplied with arms and munitions of war, by stripping those of the North, and the militia in the Southern States were organized into regiments and battalions, drilled, armed and equipped and were ready for the field in 1860, before any State had seceded.

On December 22d, the South Carolina convention made an order: "That three commissioners, to be elected by a ballot of the convention, be directed to proceed forthwith to Washington, authorized and empowered to treat with the government of the United States for the delivery of the forts, magazines, light houses and other real estate, with their appurtenances, within the limits of South Carolina, and also for an apportionment of the public debt, and for a division of all other property held by the government of the

United States, as agent of the Confederate States, of which South Carolina was recently a member, and generally to negotiate as to all other measures and arrangements proper to be made and adopted in the existing relations of the parties, and for the continuance of peace and amity between this commonwealth and the government at Washington." These Commissioners were elected and received their authority under the seal of the State of South Carolina and proceeded to Washington. (Ser. 1, p. 111.)

On the 26th of December, 1860, the garrison of Fort Moultrie, under command of Major Robert Anderson, moved into Fort Sumter, in Charleston Harbor. This did not please the Governor of South Carolina, and on the 27th he "courteously, but peremptorily," demanded that Major Anderson should transfer the garrison from Fort Sumter back to Fort Moultrie. This was refused. The Governor replied, that there was an understanding with President Buchanan that "no reinforcements were to be sent to any of these forts, and particularly to this one," and that Major Anderson had violated this agreement by moving to Fort Sumter. The Governor was reminded by Major Anderson that he had moved his command from one fort to another in the same harbor, which he had a lawful right to do.

During the afternoon of the 27th two steamers "took possession by escalade of Castle Pinckney" and of Fort Moultrie at night, both by South Carolina State troops. This was the first seizure of government property by the Confederates. (Se. 1, Vol., I. p. 3.)

On the 28th, after the seizure of these two

forts, the three Commissioners presented an address to President James Buchanan, declaring their readiness to "negotiate," "with the earnest desire to avoid all unnecessary and hostile collision." But which they then declared to be impossible, in the light of the events of the last twenty-four hours, because they said to the President:

That "since our arrival, an officer of the United States * * * not only without, but against your orders, has dismantled one fort and occupied another" (referring to Anderson's evacuation of Fort Moultrie and occupation of Fort Sumter). The Commissioners urged the President to immediately withdraw the United States forces from Fort Sumter and Charleston Harbor, because, they said, "Under present circumstances, they are a standing menace to South Carolina, which renders negotiations impossible and * * * threatens speedily to bring to a bloody issue questions which ought to be settled with temperance and judgment."

After three days President Buchanan answered the Commissioners, stating among other things, that his "position" as President of the United States "was clearly defined in his message to the congress on the 3d instant," a portion of which was:

That "apart from the execution of the laws, so far as this may be practical, the executive has no authority to decide what shall be the relations between the Federal Government and South Carolina," and that it was his duty to submit the whole controversy to congress in all its bearings, and that if any attempt was made to expel the United States authorities from the properties which belong to the United States in Charleston Harbor, the officer in charge has orders to act on the defensive, and the President informed the Commissioners that he had information dated the 28th, that "the Palmetto flag floated out to the breeze at Castle Pinckney, and that a large military force went over last night (the 27th) to Fort Moultrie" and that the South Carolinians have covered the Federal forts with their own flag, instead of that of the United States, and that he cannot conceive how a reinforcement of Sumter can be a menace to Charleston. (Ser. 1, p. 115.)

December 31, General Scott ordered the sloop of war Brooklyn, lying at Fort Monroe, to reinforce Fort Sumter with men, arms and ammunition, "as secretly and confidentially as possible," and on the same day Major Anderson reported great activity among the South Carolinians in Charleston harbor, and on the 28th a body surrounded the United States arsenal. On the 29th sentinels were placed around it, and on the 30th, before the President had made his answer to the Commissioners, the arsenal in Charleston, and all it contained was seized by the 17th Regiment Infantry S. C. M. "in the name of the State of South Carolina and by order of Governor Pickens," at 10:30 A. M. This was the second seizure of Government property. On the 1st day of January, 1861, the Commissioners replied at great length to the President's answer. The burden of their reply was to charge the President with acting in bad faith with South Carolina, and that his answer not only left them without any hope for the withdrawal of the troops from Fort Sumter, but that the garrison would be reinforced, and they endeavored to torture the action of Major Anderson, in removing the garrison from Moultrie to Sumter, into an act of war against the people of South Carolina. (Serial 1, part 1, page 124.)

On the second, Fort Johnson, in Charleston Harbor, was seized by South Carolina State troops. This was the third seizure of Government property. General Scott ordered the A. A. G. to reinforce Sumter with 200 men and three months subsistence, and directed that if any vessel carrying the same should be fired upon in Charleston Harbor, that the vessel should use her guns to silence such fire. On the 4th the "Star of the West" was engaged to carry the reinforcements to Fort Sumter, and on the 5th, two hundred men were ordered from Fort Columbus, under command of Lieutenant Charles R. Woods, to be shipped on board the "Star of the West" to reinforce Sumter.

On the 5th of January, 1861, a remarkable Council of Southern Senators was secretly convened at Washington, which at once assumed "the powers of a revolutionary Junta." It met in one of the rooms of the Capitol, on the night of the above date. It was composed of the senators from seven Southern States: Florida, Georgia, Alabama, Mississippi, Louisiana, Arkansas and Texas. Fourteen senators were present. It was decided at that meeting to recommend the secession of their respective States, and the holding of a convention at Montgomery, Alabama, February 15, 1861. The proceedings were secret. Complete orders and instructions were promulgated as to the manner in which all the forts and arsenals in the South were to be seized.

There is no doubt but that at this remarkable Council of Southern Senators it was determined that R. M. T. Hunter, of Virginia, was to be President of the new Confederacy and Jefferson Davis Secretary of War. The latter, by training and education, was supposed to be well fitted for that position. (Secret Hist. Confederacy, by Pollard, pages 61-2.)

The "Star of the West" reached Charleston Harbor on the morning of the 9th of January, 1861. She was fired upon when she attempted to enter the harbor, by the batteries on Morris Island. Major Anderson sent an inquiry to the Governor of South Carolina, asking if the vessel had been fired upon by his orders, and stating that if it be not disclaimed, the act would be regarded as an act of war. This was the first shot fired in the Rebellion.

Governor Pickens promptly answered at great length, reciting the new relations which he insisted South Carolina then sustained to the Federal Government from a Confederate standpoint, insisting that the attempt to reinforce Fort Sumter was an Act of War against South Carolina. The vessel on account of being fired upon did not reach Fort Sumter, and the fort was not reinforced or furnished with subsistence.

On the 11th a commission from Governor Pickens demanded the surrender of Ft. Sumter, which being refused, was modified, so as to have it understood that they desired to send a joint commission to Washington, which was also refused. The United States Government notified Major Anderson that the act of firing upon the "Star of the West" was an act of war, and that his forbearance to return the fire was approved

Abraham Lincoln.
(From an old war times photograph.)

by the President and the Secretary of War. This was the first demand for the surrender of Fort Sumter. So the first seizures of forts and other Government property, and the first shots were fired and the war was actually begun before Mr. Lincoln was inaugurated, and all through the month of January the South Carolinians were fortifying the harbor at Charleston,

The Confederate Convention assembled at Montgomery, Alabama, on the 15th. Mr. Hunter was indiscreet enough to broach the subject that there might yet be a peaceable and amicable settlement of the differences between the North and the South. This act on his part lost him the respect of the convention, and he was at once dropped as the prospective President of the new Confederacy and Jefferson Davis was elevated at once to the position of its champion. (Pollard's Secret History of the Confederacy, page 65.)

On the 17th of February the Confederate Congress assumed control of all questions relating to forts and arsenals. Major Anderson, in Fort Sumter, in obedience to orders, acted strictly on the defensive. All through the month of February work had been carried on night and day fortifying Charleston Harbor by the Confederates, and a constant watch was kept on Fort Sumter to prevent reinforcements being landed by small boats in the night time. Every act of the Government at Washington was observed by spies and quickly made known to the Southern leaders. All through the month of March the Confederate War Department was extraordinarily active. General Beauregard was in command at Charleston.

On the 4th of March, 1861, Abraham Lincoln was inaugurated President of the United States, and at once proceeded to discharge the duties of that great office under the most trying circumstances.

On the 8th of April, 1861, President Lincoln determined that Fort Sumter should be reinforced, and so notified Governor Pickens by messenger. The Confederate Secretary of War dispatched to Beauregard from Montgomery, that "Under no circumstances are you to allow provisions to be sent to Fort Sumter." "Diplomacy has failed, the sword must now preserve our independence."

A demand for the evacuation of Fort Sumter was made at 2 P. M. on the 11th, and the commandant was allowed until 6 P. M. to answer. Major Anderson refused to surrender the fort. At 4 P. M. on the 11th, the Confederate batteries were reported ready to fire on Sumter. At 3:20 A. M. on the 12th, Major Anderson was notified that the bombardment of Fort Sumter would begin in one hour. Accordingly the bombardment began at 4:30 A. M. on April 12th, 1861. The first shot was fired from the mortar battery on James Island, after which the fire soon became general from all the batteries. The total number of guns trained on Sumter was 30 and 17 mortars. The total available guns in Fort Sumter was 48. The fort was set on fire by the red hot shot and the quarters burned. The garrison surrendered on the 13th. One man was killed and four wounded. The surrender took place at 1:15 P. M. (Ser. 1, page 15, Et. Seq.)

Two days after the surrender of Sumter, President Lincoln issued a proclamation calling for 75,000 volunteers for three months. Under this call the States furnished 91,816 men, or an excess of nearly 17,000 men. In the meantime the Confederates were putting forth all their energy to supply men and means to carry on the war. On the 3d day of May the President called for an additional levy of 500,000. Under this call 700,000 men were furnished.

During the period from July 21st to December 20th, 1861, both parties put forth every effort in preparing for war. On the 21st of July the battle of Bull Run was fought. In that engagement the Union loss was 474 killed and 1,071 wounded. Total killed and wounded on the Union side, 1,545. The Confederates lost 387 killed and 1,582 wounded. Total, 1,969. The Confederate loss in killed and wounded exceeded that of the Union Army by 424. The Union Army had 87 more killed, but the Confederates had 511 more wounded. Although the Confederates suffered the greater loss in killed and wounded, yet the battle was a great disaster to the North. No military advantages resulted to either party, so far as position or territory was concerned, but the Union troops fell into disorder and retreated. The effect of the battle upon the Union Army and the Union cause was very depressing, and a corresponding feeling of buoyancy pervaded the Confederates.

Beginning with the bombardment of Fort Sumter in Charleston Harbor on April 12th and 13th by the Confederate batteries on that side, and the United States forces under Major Anderson on the other, and ending with the encounter on December 28, 1861, at Mount Zion, Missouri, there were fought during that year (156) one hundred and fifty-six engagements, the more important of which, together with the losses on each side respectively, were as follows:

	FED. LOSS.	CON. LOSS.
July 21, 1st Bull Run, Va., K.& W..	1,545	1,969
Aug. 10, Wilson's Creek, Mo.	1,235	1,095
Oct. 3, Green Briar, W. Va.	43	52
Oct. 21, Ball's Bluff, Va.	921	155
Nov. 7, Belmont, Mo.	501	641
Dec. 13, Camp Allegheny, W. Va.	137	144
Dec. 20, Dranesville, Va.	68	194
Total killed and wounded.	4,450	4,250

In the Bull Run disaster the Confederates took 1,789 prisoners.

The comparative net results of the fighting done during the year 1861 cannot be accurately estimated. In some quarters unimportant military advantages were gained by the Confederates, while in others the Federals had succeeded in about a corresponding degree. The Confederates lost more men in killed and wounded than the Federals, but the latter suffered the greater loss by capture; but both sides were assiduously employed in fortifying strategic points and in increasing and disciplining their respective armies, so that at the end of the year 1861, the available forces of the contending parties were very nearly equal on the score of numbers, but the Confederates were the better armed and equipped.

THE BATTLES OF 1862.

The Union Army in the Mississippi Valley did not go into winter quarters nor did it cease active offensive operations during the winter of 1861-2.

On the 2d day of July, 1862, President Lincoln issued a proclamation, calling upon the Governors of the several States for 300,000 men to serve three years or during the war. The number to be furnished by each state was based upon its military population. 421,465 men responded to this call. Indiana's quota was 21,250, but the State responded with an enlistment of 30,359.

The 100th Regiment enlisted under this call of July 2, 1862. Company "A," Captain Marquis L. Rhodes, from DeKalb County; Co. "B," Captain Gillespie, from Stuben County; Co. "C," Captain H.Crocker, LaGrange County; Co. "D," Captain R. M. Johnson, Elkhart County; Co. "E," Captain William Barney, Noble County; Co. "F," Captain Abram W. Myers, Whitley County; Co. "G," Captain G. O. Behm, Tippecanoe County; Co. "H," Captain John W. Headington, Jay County; Co. "I," Captain John N. Sims, Clinton County, and Co. "K," Captain Charles W. Brouse, Marion and Allen Counties; and there were men in the Regiment from other counties than those mentioned. The companies from the northeastern counties went into camp on the left bank of the St. Mary's River, on ground which is now embraced within the city of Fort Wayne.

After a short stay in camp at that place those companies were moved to Camp Morton at Indianapolis and thence to Madison, on the Ohio River, and for some time guarded the fords on that river to prevent the crossing of a body of Confederate cavalry, which rendezvoused in the vicinity of Carrollton, Kentucky. The 2nd Indiana Cavalry, Col. Isaac Gray, assisted the 100th Indiana in the performance of this service, which ended on the 10th of November, 1862.

At that date those Companies, "A," "B," "C," "D" and "E" returned to Indianapolis, and having joined the other companies of the Regiment, on the day following (the 11th) left Camp Morton for Memphis, Tennessee, by way of Cairo, Illinois, and the Mississippi River. On the 16th the command disembarked from the transports and was stationed in Fort Pickering, on the east bank of the Mississippi River, on the precipitous bluffs, at the then southern limits of the city, and was assigned to "The Second Brigade District of Memphis," commanded by Brig. Genl. John W. Denver, the "District of Memphis" being commanded by Genl. W. T. Sherman (S-17-pt. 2-340).

Soon thereafter, Col. J. A. McDowell was assigned to the command of our brigade and Genl. Denver was assigned to command the division (S-17-pt. 2-344). The brigade at that time was composed of the 100th Indiana, 40th Illinois, 46th Ohio, 6th Iowa and the 13th United States Infantry, 1st Batallion (Ser. 17, p. 340).

A Confederate Army under Genl. Sterling Price was then located in the Northwestern portion of Mississippi, against which Genl. Grant proposed to move. The plan of the campaign embraced the defeat of this army and the ultimate investment of Vicksburg, at that time regarded as the Gibraltar of the South by the Confederate Government.

The weather was extremely unfavorable for military operations; snow had fallen thus early, and the cold rains had made the roads in many places almost impassable, the exposure and change of climate, water and mode of living, caused very much sickness among the men and a great many died during the late fall and early winter months.

Preparations for the campaign against Price's army to be made in winter's rain and mud were quickly completed, so that seven days after we entered Fort Pickering (the 23d) we received marching orders.

Our baggage was reduced under orders to what was then supposed to be the lowest point attainable, but we learned better before the war ended. All the troops at Memphis by this order were directed to prepare for active field service.

The Yocna March.

On the 26th of November the army moved out of the city of Memphis, following Vance street. Our Division, the First, took the Pigeon Roost Road, the 100th Indiana leading the 2d

Brigade. We marched very hard until the column had crossed Nonconnah Creek, where we went into camp, having made our first day's real march of about fifteen miles. The men of the 100th stood the fatigue of the march fully as well as the other troops, many of whom had been in the service a year or more. The men of that regiment were men of brain and brawn, being of that class who had not inconsiderately rushed into the army under the influence of excitement or sudden impulse, nor to that class who had remained at home until a large bounty was offered, or until their names were drawn from the wheel of chance in the draft; they belonged to that intelligent, sober minded, brave, strong and intrepid class who left substantial interests, home, kindred and friends, because upon mature deliberation they had determined that their services were demanded of them by their country and they had yielded to that demand through patriotism alone. As the mere pittance paid to the common soldiers of the Union army, many of whom were well-to-do, was no inducement to them to expose themselves to the dangers of death by disease or in battle.

On the 27th we moved early, on the same road to Byhalia, Mississippi, fourteen miles, and encamped in line of battle. Our division formed the center, Smith's the left and Lauman's the right. That was our first night in line of battle. A confederate force of 30,000 was in our front, but it "retired" during the night to a new "position." Our forces numbered about 35,000.

On the third day we took a road leading from Byhalia to Chulahoma, marched twelve miles, crossed Pigeon Roost Creek and bivouacked in line of battle with Lauman's Division on our right and Smith's in the rear. On the 29th we marched into the town of Chulahoma, formed in line, with a division on each flank. During the 30th and the 1st of December we remained in camp.

On the 2d the rain, which had fallen incessantly for two days, continued. The roads had become almost impassable; the men were literally drenched; the weather was chilly; the ground covered with water; and many of the men had slept none for three nights. We moved from Chulahoma to a point near Wyatt, Mississippi, about twenty miles from Holly Springs, where we remained, on account of the condition of the roads, until the 5th, when we moved forward and to the left on the College Hill road. On the 9th, Major General James B. McPherson was assigned to the command of our "First Division" by General Grant, by special field order No. 18 (Serial 17, p. 396), and General Sherman took leave of the Army and assumed command of a force which was to operate in conjunction with us against Vicksburg, by going down the Mississippi River. Prior to this date Holly Springs, Oxford and Abbeville had fallen into our hands, as the Confederates "retired" when we advanced. As we approached the Tallahatchie River, the Confederates made some resistance with artillery and infantry. This was our first experience of that kind, though we were not actually engaged. By the 18th we had advanced to and were in position on the high ground on the Yocna Patufna Creek, or, as the soldiers called it, the "Yocna,‚" by which this march and campaign was afterward known. We had about 800 rebel prisoners, taken in several minor engagements at or near Coffeeville, Mississippi. These were the first we had seen.

McPherson's troops were all in position about Otuckalofa and Water Valley. On the 18th, President Lincoln divided the forces in this department into four Army Corps, the 13th General McClernand, the 15th General Sherman, the 16th General Hurlbut, and the 17th General McPherson, so that Abraham Lincoln was the author of the famous 15th Army Corps, and December 18, 1862, was its birthday and Mississippi its birthplace and General Sherman its first commander. (Serial 17, page 433.)

General Grant had made Holly Springs a supply depot, and all of the Commissary and Quartermaster's stores for the army, which had advanced beyond, were stored at that place. On the 20th the Confederate Generals, Van Dorn and Jackson, with about 6,000 cavalry, dashed in and destroyed all the supplies. We fell back to the Tallahatchie, and on the 23d encamped on the hills on the north side of that river.

We had little to eat except black beans, which were foraged from the plantations near by, and which were called by the soldiers "Nigger Beans." Very many of the men were sick at the time with rheumatism and other maladies, brought on by the use of bad water and constant exposure, and several died On the 26th the men present for duty were put on half rations of such supplies as we had. We remained in camp several days.

On the 4th of January, 1863, we marched to within a few miles of Holly Springs, and on the 5th we reached that place and encamped on the north side of the town, on a hill sloping to the south. During the few days that we remained there several of our men died, after a few hours illness, of what the physicians called spotted fever. All who were attacked died. On the 8th we marched to the town of Salem, Mississipi, and encamped, the 100th Indiana occupying the town, which was entirely deserted by the inhabitants. On the 9th, after a hard march along detestable roads, we reached Grand Junction, Tennessee, and went into camp half a mile northwest of that place.

The army had made a march of about one hundred and sixty miles, from Memphis to Water Valley and return to Grand Junction, covering a period of forty-five days, having accomplished but little and lost much in stores and supplies. The original plan of the campaign was to force the Rebel Army under General Price as far south as Vicksburg, and then, in conjunction with a force to be sent down the river, to invest the place. But the destruction of our supplies at Holly Springs forced us to make a retrograde movement to a line of communication in our rear.

By special field orders No. 18, the 100th and 12th Indiana, 6th Iowa, 40th Illinois and 46th Ohio composed the 2nd brigade, first division 13th Army Corps, Major General J. B. McPherson commanding right wing (Serial 17, p. 514).

On our arrival at Grand Junction we went into camp for the winter. During the time we remained at that place our duties were to picket the post and to perform the usual and ordinary post duties. Active operations for the year

1862 closed with our arrival at that place. There was much fighting done during the year 1862. Beginning with the action at Port Royal, Coosa River, South Carolina, on the 1st of January, 1862, and ending with the battle of Stone River, January 2, 1863. There were fought during that year five hundred and sixty-four (564) engagements. Some of the more important of which, with the losses sustained therein by the Federal and Confederate armies, respectively, were as follows, as nearly as will ever be known:

DATE, 1862.	ENGAGEMENT.	FED. LOSS.	CON. LOSS.
Jan. 19	Mill Springs, Ky	246	529
Feb. 8	Roanoke Island, N. C	264	2,608
Feb. 14-16	Fort Donelson, Tenn	2,832	15,829
March 6-8	Pea Ridge, Ark	1,382	5,200
March 23	Kernstown, Va	590	718
March 14	Newberne, N. C	471	578
April 6-7	Shiloh, Tenn	13,047	10,694
May 5	Williamsburg, Va	2,239	1,560
May 23-25	Front Royal and Winchester	2,019	214
May 31	Fair Oaks (Seven Pines)	5,031	6,134
June 8	Cross Keys, Va	684	495
June 9	Port Republic	1,018	615
June 16	Secessionville, S. C.	683	204
June 25-July 1	Seven Days' Battle	15,849	20,614
August 9	Cedar Mountain, Va	2,381	1,314
August 30	Richmond, Ky	5,353	451
Sept 11-20	Harper's Ferry	12,737	12,601
Sept. 16	Mumfordville, Ky	4,148	714
Sept. 17	Antietam, Md	12,410	25,899
Sept. 19	Iuka, Mississippi	790	693
Oct. 3-5	Corinth, Mississippi	2,520	4,838
Oct. 8	Chaplin Hills, Ky	4,211	8,396
Dec. 7	Hartsville, Tenn	2,096	139
Dec. 7	Prairie Grove, Ark	1,251	981
Dec. 13	Fredricksburg, Va	12,653	5,315
Dec. 26-28	Chickasaw Bluffs, Mississippi	1,776	187
Dec. 31	Stone River, killed and wounded	8,778	9,000
Dec. 31	Guerrilla Campaign in Missouri	580	2,866
Total Losses		118,041	132,486

The foregoing figures are compiled from various sources, but principally from the archives of the Union and Confederate armies published by the Government. The casualties in the engagements mentioned show a total on both sides of over a quarter of a million, and that the Confederate loss was nearly fourteen thousand more than the Union.

The net results of the fighting done during the year 1862 were very much in favor of the Unionists. In addition to a greater loss in killed, wounded and missing, the Confederates lost a vast amount of territory as well as several forts and arsenals.

The 100th Indiana.
Operations as Guards and Scouts During 1863.

In January, 1863, by order of General Grant, General McPherson stationed six regiments between Grand Junction and Memphis, Tennessee, to act as scouts and to guard the line of the Memphis and Charleston railroad between those places, one of which was the 100th Indiana, then lying at Grand Junction. Nearly all other troops were sent down to Vicksburg to operate against that place.

We were encamped on low, wet ground at Grand Junction. The winter was severe on the men; we had some snow, but much more rain. Very many of the men fell sick and died of disease. On the 7th of March we received orders to move on the 9th, which we did, arriving on the 10th at Collierville, twenty-four miles east of Memphis, and encamped in the town.

We soon made an attractive parade ground and a clean and very pretty camping ground. There we did duty as guards, and soon had erected a fort and lines of entrenchments. Some of our companies occupied stockades on the railroad to the east of Collierville. If space would permit, enough ludicrous and amusing incidents of our camp life at these places could be related to fill a volume.

We foraged pretty liberally "on the country" at times while performing this service, captured a good many Rebels and Guerrillas, and a great many fine mules and horses, which were turned over to the quartermaster. These were very valuable to the government as train mules. Although the health of the men was much better at Collierville than at Grand Junction, yet a good many died of disease there also.

On the 9th of May, in obedience to orders, we started on a scout at sundown, marched northwardly all night, crossed Wolf River at 2 A. M. on fallen trees. Lieut. Boyd, Co. "C," fell into the river but was rescued. We rested until three hours after day light, then moved against a body of Rebels, in our front. They fled on our approach, leaving their camp fires burning, and some arms. We captured some prisoners, and breaking up into squads, we captured and brought in about seventy horses. The writer made an important capture of a Rebel officer and a fine horse, in the presence of Capt. (now Colonel) Johnson, and under his direction.

Major Parrott and his detail and Charlie Pearce and others of Company "E," as well as quite a number of squads from other companies, which I cannot now name, all made captures and brought everything safely into camp, having made a march of sixty miles without sleep.

On the 20th of May the 100th Indiana started at 2 A. M. on a scout southward, across Coldwater River into Mississippi. We drove the Confederates away from Quinn's Mills and secured a great many good horses and mules for the trains. We returned to our camp through Nonconnah, Mississippi, and while mounting guard that evening were attacked by the Rebels. We repulsed the enemy, who had followed us from the Coldwater River close in our rear. We lay in line all night. Our casualties were two killed and ten missing: Capt. O. J. Fast was wounded.

The following is an extract from the official report of Col. Loomis:

"Collierville, May 21, 1863.

"The attack of yesterday evening was made * * directly in our front in three columns, by different roads and of larger force than I supposed last night. * * My loss was one killed and nine missing. * * The pickets fought well and held their posts until they were surrounded and unable to retire. * * Citizens who saw the fight * * speak in praise of the conduct of the men."

The following is the Rebel official report of this affair:

"Senatobia, Miss., May 21, 1863.

"General Chalmers: The enemy advanced yesterday from Collierville, 1,000 strong, to Coldwater, returned in the evening, followed by Captains White and Cousins and Lieut. Jennings, who killed two and captured ten Federal prisoners." (S. 34, p. 425.)

On the 31st of January, 1863, the army was reorganized and after that date our Brigade embraced the 40th Illinois, 12th and 100th Indiana, 6th Iowa, 15th Michigan and 46th Ohio, 1st Brigade, 1st Division, 16th Army Corps, Genl.

General Grant.
(From a war times photograph.)

Denver, commanded the Division and Col. Walcutt, the Brigade (Ser. 28, p. 24).

On the 30th of April the Brigade was composed of the 26th and 90th Illinois, 12th and 100th Indiana. Col. Loomis commanded the Brigade and W. S. Smith the Division. (Serial 28, p. 253.)

From the 9th of January until the 7th of June, 1863, the 100th Indiana did active service every day. There was much to do to guard our line of communication and to hold off and drive out the many detachments of Rebel cavalry, as well as large bodies of Confederates who sought to sever our lines of communication and to recover the country.

On the 30th of May the troops stationed between Memphis and Corinth, which numbered about fifteen thousand, began to move to Memphis, having been ordered to reenforce Grant's army at Vicksburg.

The Siege of Vicksburg.

On the evening of the 3d of June, 1863, the 100th Indiana received orders to be ready to march at any moment. We at once began to make ready. During the night of the 4th a severe storm of wind and rain came up and we were literally soaked with torrents of rain and almost blown away.

On the 7th we left our old camp at break of day. The weather was intensely hot. We marched twenty-two miles and went into camp about two miles east of Memphis. During the night the rain fell again in torrents. On the 8th we marched to the steamboat landing and went on board the steamer "Adams." It rained very hard all night.

On the morning of the 9th we left for Vicksburg. On the night of the 10th we lay up at Lake Providence, Louisiana. In the middle of the night a hurricane came up, which crushed nearly all the glass in the windows and doors of our boat and almost capsized us; a season of storms seemed to have overtaken us. On the 11th we came in sight of Vicksburg. We ran down to and beyond "Young's Point," whereupon the Rebel batteries in Vicksburg began to throw shells at us. We at once steamed up the Yazoo River to Haine's Bluff, where we disembarked about twelve miles above Vicksburg.

The Yazoo River was blockaded at this point with timbers, torpedoes and other obstructions. Nearly all the reinforcements for the Vicksburg army were landed at this point, as well as arms and army stores.

For several days after our arrival we, together with a very large force, were engaged in strengthening the fortifications at this point. The weather was extremely hot and almost every night we had a terrific rain. The water was very bad and a great many men suffered with camp diarrhœa and other complaints. On the 19th we were employed, in common with many other regiments, in making roads leading to the rear of Vicksburg.

On the 21st we were engaged in mounting cannons of large caliber on the heights, where we had made additional works. On this day, the 9th Army Corps, consisting of about 8,000 men, landed at Haines' Bluff and moved out about twelve miles towards Pearl River and the rear of Vicksburg, General Parke commanding. We marched from midnight on the 22d until morning, got breakfast after sunrise, and then, with three days' rations, marched to Oak Ridge, on the east of Vicksburg, having passed the 9th Army Corps during the day and night. We occupied here a position directly between Vicksburg and a Confederate army of 40,000 infantry and 4,000 cavalry under General Joseph E. Johnston, who were on Black River endeavoring to aid the garrison of Vicksburg, if an opportunity offered. The object in placing us in this position was to prevent Johnston's army from in any manner aiding Pemberton's, which was shut up in Vicksburg, and to prevent the latter from escaping from the besieged city. The Rebels were, at this date, reported to be tearing down houses and building boats in Vicksburg to escape by the Mississippi River. We were liable also to be attacked at any moment by General Johnston. Generals Dennis, Herron, Logan, McPherson and Admiral Porter were so notified in orders by General Grant, and the entire command was ready to do battle at a moment's notice. (No. 38, p. 427.)

All the roads between Black River and Vicksburg were blocked. Deserters from the latter place reported that the Rebels were eating mule meat and parched corn, and that at Port Hudson the principal ration was parched corn. We, the 100th, captured some Rebel officers on this date, and killed some beeves which were so poor we could hardly skin them. (No. 38, p. 435.)

On the 24th there was heavy firing at Vicksburg all day. We received orders to march at 4. A. M. on the 25th. At that hour the 100th was ordered to perform the special service of feeling to the east for Johnston's line of battle. We passed our outer picket line, destroyed the bridge over Black Creek, moved nearly to Black River, ascertained definitely that Johnston's army was not west of the Big Black, then returned to camp at 11 P. M., with nothing to eat. The men were tired and mad. We all went to sleep very hungry and very tired. We took some Rebel deserters who said that they had no bread in Vicksburg except what was made of rice and flour mixed, and that corn was worth forty dollars a bushel, Confederate money (Serial 38, p. 439).

On the 26th we got some rations. On the 27th we all slept under arms.

The 29th of June was intensely hot. There was but little firing on the lines. On the 30th we were paid and a large amount of money was expressed home by the men, as money was of little use in the intrenchments. On the 3d we learned early that negotiations were pending for the surrender of Vicksburg, and we were all happy. On the 4th the news came along the lines early that the garrison of Vicksburg would march out and stack arms and then march back again as prisoners of war.

All the Generals, great and small, were exchanging congratulations and letters, and new orders were being issued. The whole army enjoyed that 4th of July, and even General Sherman was delighted at the shouts of his old command and said he would punish no soldier for getting "uncohappy" on that day (Serial 38, p.

472). By this surrender we took 31,000 prisoners and a vast amount of arms and military stores. We had now cut the Confederacy in twain, separated Arkansas, Louisiana and Texas from the states east of the Mississippi and had secured the navigation of that stream and many of its tributaries. The blow to the Confederacy was irreparable. Rations were issued to the Confederate prisoners by order of General Grant, which was a great treat to them, indeed. The military advantages gained by the surrender of Vicksburg were very great, and each officer and soldier of the 100th Indiana is entitled to take to himself a full share of the honor which attached to that achievement.

Siege of Jackson, Mississippi, and Return to Camp Sherman.

A few hours after the surrender of Vicksburg we received orders to march, which we did at 5 P. M., toward Black River and Johnston's army. Our course took us over high hills and through the woods and cane brakes. The night was very dark. We crossed Black Creek (or Bear Creek) and went into camp on a high hill at sunrise, having marched all night and made about ten miles. We remained here all day and until 8 P. M. of the 5th, when we again marched, in Egyptian darkness, all night and only made about ten miles, to a point near Birdsong's Ferry on the Big Black River.

We crossed that stream on the 6th in the evening on a small boat. The weather was very hot and the roads dusty. We could trace the route of the retreating Rebel cavalry by the columns of dust seen at a distance across the valley. We went into camp on the east bank of the river. On the 7th we marched about eight miles in the night time, during which a terrific rain and wind storm came upon us. The mud was deep, the men wet and teams mired down in the sand.

On the 8th we marched about ten miles, passed the farm of Joseph Davis, a brother of Jefferson Davis. We were unable to obtain any water to use, except such as we took from the ponds and wagon ruts along the road. There were no wells or cisterns and no springs. The Confederate army retreated in our front toward Jackson and we went into camp in line of battle. On the 9th we marched about eight miles, all the way in the woods; the weather was very hot. We lay on our guns all night, and on the 10th we moved to the left of our line and to the north side of Jackson, and encamped in line of battle, on the plantation of the Rebel General, R. Griffith. The 90th Illinois had a brisk skirmish with the enemy, for which it received a compliment by the Brigade Commander. (Serial 37, p. 629.)

On the 11th we moved by the left flank as far as the railroad running north. About 10 o'clock we moved to the insane asylum north of the city and from there, in line of battle, directly toward the Rebel batteries in our front. J. P. Farden of Company "G" was wounded. There was sharp firing all day around Jackson. On the 12th we remained under our batteries, the 100th directly in front of a 12-gun Confederate battery. Our skirmishers fired continually into the embrasures of the Confederate works and thus prevented the gunners from using their guns.

During the night of the 11th the 100th Indiana planted a sunk battery within short range of the Confederate fort in our front, and at about 7 A. M. on the 12th four batteries of the First Division opened fire on the enemy with twenty-four guns. The 100th Indiana lay in line directly in front of these batteries, and every shot, including such replies as the enemy were able to make, passed only a few feet directly over their heads.

The screech of those elongated shot and shell in such close proximity to our heads was simply indescribable. Fragments of shot and shell fell all around us. Charles Munroe, Company "E," and John P. Armstrong, of Company "K," were wounded. On the 12th and 13th heavy details were made to fortify, and on those two days our batteries threw three thousand rounds into the city, mostly from ten and twenty pounder Parrotts and twelve pound Napoleons. The Rebels were seen to fly in all directions to escape the shot and shell from our batteries. (Serial 37, p. 629.) The enemy replied sharply and shelled us all day.

On the evening of the 14th the 100th Indiana went on the skirmish line and advanced the right 150 yards, so close that we could hear the Rebels talking. From this position we fired upon the Rebel cannons continually and kept them silenced, while our own batteries were being planted.

William Avery, of Company "D," was killed.

We were relieved on the morning of the 16th by the 97th Indiana Regiment which took the same position we occupied and suffered a loss of five killed and twenty-eight wounded, by an attempt to advance the line. (See serial 38, p. 641.) Corporal O. S. Davis, of Company "A," was wounded. During the time we were in this critical and dangerous position every officer and man of the 100th displayed coolness and courage, and cheerfully bore the hardships of the severe test of heat and Rebel shot and shell. "It is sufficient praise to the officers and men of my command to say, that when pelted with shot, shell, canister and bullets, I have never seen either officer or man falter or quail." (Official report Genl. W. S. Smith, commanding 1st Division 16th A. C., Serial 37, p. 630.)

During all the night of the 16th we could hear the rumbling of wagons and other ominous sounds, which indicated that the Rebels were evacuating, and at daylight on the morning of the 17th we entered the capital city of Mississippi.

At this time we were in the First Brigade, First Division, Sixteenth Corps, composed of the 12th and 100th Indiana, and the 26th and 90th Illinois. (Serial 37, p. 544.) The following is an extract from the official report of Lieut. Col. Albert Heath: "The 100th Regiment was equidistant from our own and the Rebel batteries." "Pieces of lead from our own rifle shells and solid shot from the enemy fell continually around us. * * During the three days we lay in line not less than fifty shells exploded around my men. * * The solid shot would strike the ground and ricochet over the men, covering them with earth. * * I know of no instance where either officer or man failed to stand by his gun day and night. Joseph Farden, Charles Munroe, John P. Armstrong and Oliver S. Davis were wounded, and William Avery, of Company "D," was killed. The officers and men of the 100th displayed courage and coolness." (Serial 37, p. 634.)

The Division had two officers and thirty-two men killed, fourteen officers and two hundred and fifteen men wounded, and three officers and twenty-five men missing; total casualties at Jackson, 291. (Serial 37, p. 544.)

Loring's Rebel Division was on the Confederate right and in our front, Walker's and French's in their center and Breckenridge on their left; about 32,000 in all. We took more than 1,200 prisoners. The total Federal loss—killed, wounded and missing—was 1,122. The Confederate was twice that number. (Serial 37, p. 550.)

A great many buildings were on fire when we entered and the citizens had nearly all left the city, which was occupied by the 15th Army Corps and other troops. A great many prisoners were taken, of whom 1,150 were paroled that afternoon. Many dwellings contained fine furniture, libraries and the clothing of the occupants who had fled. There was evidence on every hand of the terrible effect of our artillery on the buildings in the city.

The fruits of the victory were the expulsion of Johnston's army from the Mississippi River Valley, the entire destruction of about one hundred miles of railroad and two hundred railroad cars, four thousand bales of cotton, several pieces of artillery and an immense quantity of shot, shell and other munitions of war, besides about 1,200 prisoners.

General Sherman turned over to a committee of citizens two hundred barrels of flour and one hundred barrels of mess pork, as they were entirely destitute of provisions. The condition of the country from Vicksburg to Jackson, Mississippi, was one of utter ruin and destruction (Serial 37, p. 539). The railroad bridge over Pearl River was knocked down by firing 388 solid shot against the piers (Ib. p. 542).

On the 22d we again received orders to march, and at 3 o'clock A. M. we moved toward Vicksburg on the same road we came. We passed to the right of the town of Clinton, which was burning at the time, and encamped.

On the 23d we marched at 3 A. M., very hard. Weather very hot; roads very dusty; water very scarce. The men and animals suffered intensely. We went into camp on the Champion Hill battle field.

On the 25th we marched at 3 A. M., crossed the Big Black River, marched about a mile and a half and went into camp on the ground, which was then named Camp Sherman, eighteen miles east of Vicksburg, where we remained until September 28, 1863.

On the 27th we received our knapsacks and tents form Haine's Bluff, where we had left them in June. We had several heavy rain falls while in this camp.

The campaign to Jackson and return was made in twenty days; the distance marched, a little over one hundred miles. We frequently had religious services in Camp Sherman. There was considerable sickness among the men and several of the 100th died. We drilled but little, but were reviewed several times. It was said that the 100th lost fewer men by death, in this camp, than any other Regiment. Our men were all well supplied. We got the newspapers daily. During the month of August the mercury frequently registered 113 deg. Fahrenheit in the shade.

In September we were transferred from the 16th Corps to the 15th, then commanded by General F. P. Blair, becoming the 4th Division of the 15th Corps, Brigadier General Hugh Ewing commanding the Division. (Cox, p. 95.)

On the 4th of July, 31,270 Rebels had surrendered to us, or were killed or wounded here. On the same day was fought the battle of Gettysburg, in which the Confederates lost 20,448 men, or 31,620 according to another authority, and were decidedly defeated. On the same day at Helena, Arkansas, the Confederate army under Price and Holmes was defeated by Prentiss, with a loss of 2,000 killed, wounded and prisoners. Thus the Confederates lost essentially in a day 65,000 men, besides the seceded states were severed; valuable territory was lost; railroad and river commuincations wrenched from them, and a vast amount of stores and munitions of war fell into the hands of the Unionists.

The whole North was convulsed with rejoicing, while a corresponding depression was felt all over the South. In the midst of this period of rejoicing, General Rosecrans attempted to demolish Bragg's army at Chicamauga, which had been reinforced with Longstreet's Corps from Virginia without Rosecrans' knowledge. One of the fiercest battles of the war was fought on the field of Chicamauga, both sides displayed the most surprising valor and many deeds of bravery and daring were done. Rosecrans was outnumbered and possibly outgeneraled, but he had an army of brave and heroic men, who, under the General who never lost a battle, George H. Thomas, saved the army. The battle was stubborn, the Federals lost heavily and retired to Chattanooga. The Confederates pursued the Union Army to the valley of the Tennessee at Chattanooga; and occupied Lookout Mountain and the heights of Missionary Ridge. They were so badly punished that they could do no more than this. No particular military advantages were gained or lost by either side as a result of that battle beyond the losses sustained. It is true that Bragg's army occupied the heights around Chattanooga, but when he massed his army in front of Sherman at Mission Ridge, on the 25th of November, the same army that fought him at Chicamauga broke through his weakened center and routed his forces. The news of the battle of Chicamauga came to us at Vicksburg on the 23d of September. Two days after that we had marching orders.

The March From Vicksburg to Chattanooga.

On the 27th the 100th Indiana left Camp Sherman and marched to Vicksburg, where many river crafts were lying, to be used in transporting us back to Memphis, which place we had left but little more than three months before, but these had been eventful months to the men of the 100th, who boarded a transport on the 28th and started to Memphis, 425 miles distant, at low water.

The passage was slow and tedious. We ran aground every day. No incident worthy of note occured to break the monotony of the tiresome journey. On the 9th of October the 100th arrived again at Memphis. A good many of our men fell sick during the trip and were left in hospitals at that place.

On the 11th General Sherman and staff and some other officers were going east in a special train, on the M. & C. R. R. They ran into Collierville just as General Chalmers, with a Confederate cavalry force of 3,000 men and eight pieces of artillery were making an assault on the place, which was garrisoned by the 66th Indiana, Col. Anthony. That Regiment occupied the same works which the 100th Indiana had built about three months prior.

Demand was made by Chalmers for the surrender of the post; this was refused and the attack began. At this time we were about fourteen miles away, at Germantown, only eight or ten miles east of Memphis. General Sherman got a message to us at Germantown, before the wires were cut by the Rebels at Collierville, and we double quicked nearly all the way from the former place to Collierville. As we approached the place the Confederates retreated to the south. They had cut the wires and torn up the railroad both east and west of the town. A detachment of the 13th regulars and the officers and men on the train all joined in the defense, and the old works built by the 100th probably on that day prevented the capture of General Sherman and his staff.

On the next day the damage to the railroad was repaired and we moved on. Our Division was the only one of the 15th Corps that marched through from Memphis to the Tennessee River. Osterhau's and Morgan L. Smith's Divisions went by rail and on their way to Stevenson followed the line of the M. & C. railroad south of the Tennessee River. We crossed that stream at East Port about the 27th and marched thence to Florence. Our 4th Division bore to the northeast and struck the Nashville and Chattanooga railroad at Decherd, and then crossed the mountains by way of Cowan to Stevenson, Alabama, where we arrived on the 14th of November.

On the 15th we marched to within one mile of Bridgeport and encamped. On the next day we drew some clothing and three days' rations and on the morning of the 17th we left our tents and all our baggage, crossed the Tennessee River on pontoons, just below the railroad bridge, at Bridgeport, Alabama, and marched beyond Nicka Jack cave, turned to the right and encamped on the side of Sand Mountain in the timber. The mountain road was very rocky and very steep. On the 18th we marched only eight miles. We drew the artillery up some steep places on the mountain side by hand. On the 19th we marched to Wincher's Gap, in the Sand Mountains, about fifteen miles southwest of Chattanooga. The 100th Indiana went forward to picket the Gap. We were relieved at noon the next day and moved down the mountain at six feet apart, with colors flying, which of course could be seen by the Confederates from the top of Lookout, the object being to deceive them as to our real strength. We went into camp three

Col. John Mason Loomis.
Commanding 1st Brigade, 4th Division, 15th Army Corps, and who led the Assault on Missionary Ridge.

miles south of Trenton, Walker County, Georgia. On the 20th we marched in a southwesterly direction three and one-half miles and went into camp. Rain fell most of the day. We captured twenty-five hogheads of wheat at this place and a mill near by was running in which we ground it. We knew nothing of the whereabouts of our train.

We marched at 6:30 A. M. on the 21st in a heavy rain and very deep mud in the direction of Chattanooga. We halted at Trenton, during which time the court house was burned. We marched very late, the night was very dark and the rain fell in torrents. We could see the fires of the Confederate army above us on our right, all along Lookout Mountain, as we traversed the valley below. On the 22d we moved early, down Trenton valley, to the junction of the Trenton and M. & C. railroad. We halted under the Rebel guns on Lookout, in plain sight of the Rebel army. The roads were almost impassable. Here we drew a few rations and 100 rounds of ammunition to each man, then we marched again late and hard, in the dark, wading in the mud, crossed the Tennessee River below Point Lookout on a pontoon bridge, which parted just as the rear of the 100th had cleared the river and left our train and part of our Division on the other side and we had nothing to eat. We were wet, muddy, tired, sleepy and hungry but every man was full of grit and energy, and few, if any, complaints were heard. When we were within a mile or two of Chattanooga on the north side of the Tennessee River we all lay down on the cold, muddy ground, hungry and without a ration, and without shelter of any kind. And this ended the long and tedious march from Vicksburg to Chattanooga, more than 700 miles by the route our Division followed.

The Battle of Missionary Ridge, November 25, 1863.

On the 24th of November we were aroused at 2 o'clock A. M. At that hour the 100th Indiana drew a few rations, and four hours later the entire command moved eastwardly over the hills, on the north side of the Tennessee River, to a point at its north bank, opposite the mouth of South Chicamagua River, where we crossed the Tennessee on the steamboat "Dunbar."

Giles A. and John E. Smith's divisions of our 15th Corps had crossed over in advance of us and captured the entire line of Rebel pickets, seventy-three in number, without firing a gun, and had erected earthworks some distance out from the south bank of the Tennessee River.

Shortly after noon our fourth division, commanded by General Hugh Ewing, having crossed the river, formed in line of battle. The Second Division, General Giles A. Smith, formed the left of our line, General John E. Smith's 3d Division the center, and the 4th, General Hugh Ewing, the right. General Osterhau's First Division having been sent to the assistance of Hooker in taking Lookout Mountain. We moved forward in echelon over low swampy ground until we reached the western base of the hills forming the north base of Missionary Ridge, a distance of about a mile and half from the south bank of the

Tennessee river, or, perhaps, more properly, the southeastern bank.

The western side of the first hill of Mission Ridge, in our front, was stony and steep near its summit, but we ascended with such rapidity that at about 4 P. M., and before the Confederates were aware of it, we occupied the summit of the first hill and were fortifyng. The 100th Indiana ascended and occupied the summit of the second hill north and northwest of the railroad tunnel.

The Confederates had a battery on the first hill, to the north of the tunnel. Thus the 100th was the extreme right of that part of Sherman's army, which occupied the *summit* of Missionary Ridge, and was the first regimental organization that reached the summit of the ridge, and was nearer the Rebel line on the 24th than any other command.

We hastily constructed some trenches on the very summit of the hill spoken of, and although there was more stone than earth on the top of the hill, yet we threw up some works, by hard work, sufficiently high to protect a battery, and then drew our cannons up the hill by hand and placed them in the works we had built. There was some skirmishing during the time. The night, though cool, was nevertheless a very beautiful one. About 11 P. M. an eclipse of the moon occurred, which some of the men, who were still erecting works, said was an ill omen, but it was not, for just at that hour we learned that the Rebels had been driven from Lookout Mountain. The morning of the 25th of November was frosty on the hills and smoky and foggy in the valley below us. We moved from the top of the hill, which we occupied, next to Bragg's right battery, early in the morning, to the level plain below, and formed in line of battle, our left, the 90th Illinois, facing toward the railroad tunnel and the western slopes of Mission Ridge. This was about 8:30 or 9 A. M. It was still foggy on the low land, where we were formed, but it was clear and the sun shone brightly on the top of Missionary Ridge so that the Confederates could not look down into the fog and see us, but we could look up through it and see one long column of Rebels after another moving from the Confederate center to their right and being massed directly in our front, as if it required the whole Rebel army to prevent the four Regiments of our brigade from scaling the heights in front. We looked up through the fog and saw the thousands of bright gun barrels of the Rebel soldiers flashing in the sunshine as they moved in column after column from their center to their right. The polished brass cannons were seen by us glistening in the sunshine as they moved along the top of the ridge and also took position in our front, and so long did this continue that it seemed as if their entire force was being placed in position on the top and sides of the ridge in our front. About 9 or 9:30 A. M. we sent forward across the level ground to the west of the tunnel, a strong skirmish line. The Confederates being above us were compelled to fire downward upon us at an angle of 20 to 40 degrees, and we fired upward at them at the same angle.

From the place where Loomis' Brigade formed in line of battle that morning to the railroad track leading along the base of the hill to the tunnel is about one-third of a mile, almost perfectly level, with nothing whatever to protect our line from the plunging shot and shell of the Confederates, delivered at short range by several batteries and lines of infantry. As we moved in line of battle across the level land we lost a great many men in killed and wounded from the fire of the Confederates, who literally swarmed on summit and slopes of the hills.

The 90th Illinois, Colonel O'Meara, the Irish Legion, was on the left, nearest to the tunnel, then the 100th Indiana the left center, the 12th Indiana, and the 26th Illinois on the right of the Brigade. During the battle, which raged nearly all day, the 90th Illinois lost 117 men and the 12th Indiana 62, the 26th Illinois lost 95 and the 100th Indiana 137.

Only three Regiments in the entire Federal army lost as many men as the 100th on that day. Those were the 97th Ohio 149, the 40th Indiana 158 and the 15th Indiana 199, all three of which were in Sheridan's Division of the 4th Army Corps. These figures show, that as far as hard fighting and heavy losses are concerned, the Indiana soldiers stand at the head of the Roll of Honor, the 100th Regiment occupying the pinnacle of fame in that behalf, having lost a larger proportion of the number engaged than any of the others. It took into action 320 men, an average of 32 men to each company. The killed and wounded numbered 135; only two were missing. This shows a loss of 43 per cent, which is 7 per cent more than the loss sustained by the celebrated Six Hundred in the charge made by it at Balaklava.

The Advance of the Fifteenth A. C.

On the 24th the Second Division crossed the Tennessee River first and moved forward, following the main line of the Chicamagua River eastwardly and was the column of direction. The Third Division, General John E. Smith, formed the center, and the Fourth Division, General Hugh Ewing, the right, in which was the 100th. A heavy line of skirmishers were thrown forward, and the three Divisions, which were formed in echelon, moved forward in that manner, almost directly east, toward the group of hills which form the north end of Missionary Ridge, which we occupied as stated. On the 25th while we were moving forward across the level ground in our front, and when we had reached a point within short range of the Confederate masses on the slopes above us, we were exposed to a heavy cross-fire of infantry and artillery, the enemy being on our left and front. About 10:30 A. M., General Corse commanding the 2d Brigade of the 4th Division, charged the Rebel batteries and line of battle occupying the fort and entrenchments on the summit of the first hill west of the railroad tunnel, advancing right up to the Rebel works. Being unable to take the works, the Brigade took a position on the hill side and held it firmly until nightfall, having driven the enemy from his outer works and taken possession. (Serial 55, p. 631.)

As to what the 100th did during the battle, General Ewing says, in his official report, that "Loomis moved his Brigade in line of battle across the open fields under a trying artillery and infantry fire, drove the enemy up the tunnel road and hill south and took and maintained the position assigned him, threatening and opening the way to the tunnel from the flank and rear. The steadiness with which this movement was made, and the tenacity with which the postion was held, is deserving of high commendation, the attempts of the enemy to dislodge us being signally repulsed." (Serial 55, p. 632.)

The First Brigade, the 100th and the 12th Indiana and the 26th and 90th Illinois were reinforced by Bushbeck's Brigade of the 11th Army Corps. This Brigade did good fighting; its commander, Col. Taft, was killed. Later on the Brigades of Loomis and Bushbeck were reinforced by the Brigades of Matthies and Raum from John E. Smith's Division. The Rebels retreated during the night and at daybreak on the 26th the 15th Army Corps pursued them towards Graysville. (No. 55, p. 632.)

The losses in the First Brigade, as reported by the regimental commanders, were as follows: The 26th Illinois had 10 men killed, 6 officers and 76 men wounded and one missing; total 93. The 90th Illinois had one officer and 9 men killed, and 6 officers and 88 men wounded, and 13 missing; total 117. The 12th Indiana one officer and 9 men killed, and 7 officers and 43 men wounded and 2 missing; total 62. The 100th Indigna had one officer and 19 men killed, and 8 officers and 107 men wounded and 2 missing; total 137. The above figures are from the report of Col. Loomis, as to the 26th, 90th and 12th, but none are counted in the estimates above given except such as were disabled; those Regiments all had more casualties than as above given. The report as to the 100th is correct, but does not embrace such wounds as were slight and caused the soldiers no inconvenience. Total loss in the Brigade, 409. The loss in the 100th, as given by General Ewing, is manifestly wrong, as the killed and wounded have been counted name by name by the author and found to be 137, excluding those who were only very slightly wounded. General Ewing's report was made the second day after the battle, before the extent of our losses were known. Some of those reported missing, in all the Regiments, are now known to have been killed.

We remained on the field until about 4:30 P. M. when we were withdrawn by Col. Loomis, by order of General Ewing, having been engaged in battle about eight hours.

"During the night large parties were kept on the field to bring off the dead and wounded; all of the latter were removed before morning." Col. Loomis, after giving the movements of the Brigade in detail, closes his report by saying:

"I have the honor to mention for gallant conduct a few of the many who deserve it: Capt. Joseph W. Gillespie, Co. 'B,' and Capt. Charles W. Brouse, Co. 'K,' 100th Indiana Infantry * * on the line of battle the gallantry of the officers was beyond praise. I particularly desire to mention my regimental commanders, for spirited and splendid performance of duty. * * Also Lieut. Henry G. Collis, 100th Indiana, A. A. A. G. on my staff. * * Every color bearer in my Brigade was shot down and four-sevenths of the entire color guard; but men were thick to raise up and bear to the front the flags of their Regiments. For my gallant dead and wounded I have no language to do them justice." (Serial 55, p. 635.)

The 100th Indiana in the Battle.—Names of the Killed and Mortally Wounded.

Inasmuch as I have contradicted the official reports as to the number killed and mortally wounded, I will state their names:

Company "A" had sixteen men wounded during the engagement, but not a man was killed, although on that day it was the right color company in the line and had one-half of the number it took into the battle wounded. That none were killed is simply inexplicable.

Company "B" suffered severely in wounded but like Company "A," providentially none were killed, though a large proportion were severely wounded.

Company "C"—Edward Whitney killed.

Company "D"—Oaks, Knapp and Leedy killed or mortally wounded.

Company "E"—Wm. Calkins, George Hines and Lucius H. Knapp killed or mortally wounded.

Company "F"—William F. Keeney, Boyer, Pitman and James Samuels killed or mortally wounded.

Company "G"—George Doty, Abram Hight, William D. Little and Nathan Snyder killed or mortally wounded.

Company "H"—John Fluding and James Walker killed or mortally wounded.

Company "I"—Captain James Harland killed.

Company "K"—John Nerhood, David Tucker and Columbus Duke killed or mortally wounded.

(Official report Major R. M. Johnson, Commanding Regiment.)

Col. Heath was wounded severely early in the engagement and Major Johnson took command of the Regiment and achieved an enviable reputation for himself by his bravery and efficient conduct in the face of the enemy. The conduct of the brave officers and men of the 100th Indiana and its brave commander in taking and holding their position in the face of the enemy's batteries and lines of battle was observed and highly commended by many officers of high rank, who saw the resistless impetuosity with which the Regiment rushed upon the Rebel lines and drove them up the hills, over and to the right of the tunnel, while the main portion of Bragg's army was massed in their front and batteries supported by long columns of infantry fired on the men from the sides and tops of the hills above them. Their conduct under a murderous and plunging fire from the enemy above their heads was an example of courage unsurpassed and probably unequalled by the conduct of any troops during the Civil War or those of any other time. The Regiment established a reputation on that day which commanded the respect and admiration of the whole army, and of which every man who belonged to it ought to be proud.

On the 26th we pursued the retreating Rebel army toward Graysville. The roads were strewn with broken wagons, caisons, dead horses and mules, guns and accoutrements, knapsacks, cast off clothing, pots, skillets, ovens, camp kettles, piles of corn and corn meal and many other things, all indicating that their retreat must have been one of indescribable confusion.

Bragg's Official Report.

For the purpose of showing the Confederate side of this battle, the following is extracted from General Bragg's report to the Rebel Secretary of War: "On Tuesday, the 24th, they threw a heavy force over the river at the mouth of Chicamauga. I visited our right and made dispositions to meet the new development in that direction. I returned to the left and found heavy cannonading going on on the slope of Lookout Mountain. A heavy force soon advanced. Walthall's Brigade made a desperate resistance but was forced to yield.

"On the 25th I visited the extreme right, commanded by General Hardee. A heavy force in line of battle confronted our left and center. * * The enemy formed their lines with great deliberation, just out of range of our guns and in plain view. Though we were outnumbered, such was the strength of our position that no doubt was entertained of our ability to hold it." (Serial 55, p. 665.)

"Several attempts on our extreme right had been handsomely repulsed. About 3:30 the Federals in front of our left and center advanced in their lines. Our batteries opened upon them. In a short time the roar of musketry became very heavy and it soon became apparent that they were repulsed. While riding along the crest, congratulating the troups, intelligence reached me that our line was broken on the right and that the enemy had crowned the ridge. Assistance was dispatched. General Bates found the disaster so great that his small force could not repair it. About this time the extreme left gave way and my position was almost surrounded. Cheatham formed and checked the enemy." (Serial 55, p. 665).

"All to the left was entirely routed and in rapid flight, nearly all the artillery having been shamefully abandoned by its infantry support. * * A panic, such as I never before witnessed, seemed to have seized upon officers and men, and each seemed to be struggling for his personal safety, regardless of his duty or his character. * * In this distressing and alarming state of affairs, orders were sent to Hardee and Breckinridge to retire upon the depot at Chicamauga, * * which they did in good order, * * the routed left made its way back in great disorder." (Serial 55, p. 665.)

"No satisfactory excuse can possibly be given for the shameful conduct of our troops. * * The position was one which ought to have been held by a line of skirmishers against any assaulting column." (Official Report Braxton Bragg, Serial 55, p. 666).

The abuse of the Confederate soldiers by General Bragg, contained in the above extracts from his official report, was probably made to draw the attention of his government away from the fatal mistakes he had made in sending his cavalry away, detaching Longstreet's Corps of 23,000 men, and in massing his whole army in front of the 4th Division of the 15th Army Corps, thus weakening his centre so that it was no match for the veterans of the 4th and 14th Army Corps, who broke through the lines at that point and routed his army.

The March From Chattanooga to Knoxville.

On the 29th of November, 1863, we received orders to march to Knoxville, Tennessee, distant about 125 miles, to relieve the army commanded by General Burnside, it having been officially reported that Longstreet's Corps of the Confederate army had laid siege to that place on its return from the field of Chicamauga to Virginia, and that the garrison was in a starving condition and could hold out but a few days longer.

Accordingly, on the morning of the 29th, two Divisions of the 15th Army Corps, under General Blair, marched from our camp, near Graysville, Georgia, by way of Julien's Gap and Oltewa to Cleveland, Tennessee, a distance of thirty miles. The 4th Army Corps, under Gen. Howard, and General Davis' Division of the 14th Army Corps made substantially the same march, and we all encamped at Cleveland that night, which was cold and frosty. We halted where rails were plenty, and suffered but little from the cold.

On the next day we destroyed railroad ties and iron until 11 A. M., at which time we marched toward Knoxville until we had crossed the Hiawassee River and encamped near Charleston, Tennessee, on the East Tennessee and Virginia railroad.

On the 1st of December we marched from Charleston to Athens, Tennessee, about sixteen miles; the whole army moved early on the 2d. The 100th Indiana passed the entire army and took a position in advance, marched all day and until midnight, when we made some coffee and rested until break of day, when we again took the advance as far as the Holston River at Morgantown. There was some cannonading at Lowdon that day, some miles below. The Rebels had burned the ferry at Morgantown, the current was swift, the water from two to five or six feet deep and perhaps 500 feet wide. We tore down some houses in the town, and a large force began to build a bridge across the river.

The men worked all night, and at 2 P. M., on the 4th, the 100th Indiana had crossed over on the bridge and bivouacked on the high hill above the village. Batteries, teams and troops were passing over the bridge nearly all night. By morning the 15th Corps was over, and on the 5th we marched early, the 100th Indiana in advance. We marched at a lively pace. Never saw a Rebel during the day, although we passed their burning camp fires.

The first halt worthy of note was at Maryville, Blunt county, 17 miles from Morgantown and 13 miles from Knoxville. Here we learned that Longstreet had suffered a disastrous defeat and had raised the siege and fled toward East Tennessee and Virginia, from whence he came.

No account of the siege of Knoxville can be given here for lack of space, except an extract from the official report of General Burnside, describing the assault on Fort Sanders.

The besieged army numbered about 12,000, the besiegers about 23,000. On the 24th of November, 1863, Longstreet crossed his forces to the south side of the Holston River. On the 28th he was active on both sides of that stream. At 10 A. M. he drove in the Union pickets and eslished his line within eighty yards of Fort Sanders.

"On the 29th, at about 6:30 A. M., the enemy opened a furious fire on the fort. Our batteries remained silent and the men quietly awaited the attack. * * In twenty minutes the cannonading ceased and a fire of musketry was opened by the enemy. * * A heavy column charged on the bastions at a run. Great numbers of them fell in passing over the entanglements. * * In two or three minutes they had reached the ditch and attempted to scale the parapet. Our guns opened on the men in the ditch with tripple rounds of canister, and our infantry shot or knocked back all those whose heads appeared above the parapet. * * The first column was reinforced by a second, which pushed up to the fort as desperately as the first, but were driven back with great slaughter; most of those who reached the ditch were killed or mortally wounded. * * The ground between the fort and the crest was strewed with the dead and the wounded, who were crying for help. After the repulse was fully established, I tendered to the enemy a flag of truce for the purpose of burying the dead and caring for the wounded. His loss was certainly a thousand. Ours but thirteen." A. E. Burnside. (Serial 54, p. 277.)

The March From Knoxville, to Alabama via Chattanooga.

At this date the 100th Indiana and many other Regiments in the 15th Army Corps had drawn little or no rations since the 23d of November. On the 7th we received orders to march, which we did early, making twelve miles by noon, on the same road back to Morgantown, at which time we halted for dinner, and ate up all the provisions we had; every haversack was empty.

After this rest we sent out some foraging parties and marched on to Morgantown, five miles and bivouacked for the night on the north side of the Holston. The foragers brought in some chickens, some beans and meal. On the 8th we crossed the river on *our* bridge, as the soldiers called it. We then bore to the left toward the Chiliko and strawberry plains. The men of the 100th said they owned some farms over in that country which they had not seen for a long time and were going over there to collect the rent of some Johnnies they had rented to. It rained very hard during that day, but the men secured some flour and other provisions, so that each company had something to eat. On the 9th we moved slowly, encamped four miles north of Madisonville, Tennessee. Our foragers went east toward the Smoky Mountains, which were in plain view, and secured flour and corn meal and some fine pigs, and then we did have a feast. Although we did not have enough to satisfy the men, yet any quantity under the circumstances would have been a feast. On the 10th we came to a farm which had apparently escaped the ravages of the Confederate cavalry. We drove away all the sheep and cattle the Rebel (he was a Reb.) had, and Col. Johnson detailed Company "A" to drive the stock. Before leaving the place the men of that Company loaded themselves with chickens and turkeys. The other

Regiments in the Brigade got no forage and an order was made that our forage should be divided with them, under the supervision of the provost marshall, who ordered Company "A" to turn in their load of poultry. About a mile from camp we halted and every soldier of Company "A" picked all the feathers off and cleaned his poultry, rolled it up in his poncho, slung this over his shoulder and marched in. On our arrival at camp no poultry was visible and that Company and not the provost marshall ate those chickens and turkeys that night and the next day. We marched sixteen miles that day and went into camp at Athens, Tennessee. On the 11th we remained in camp. We looked the country over for forage but it was barren of everything, and we were again short of rations. During the day Sergeant James L. Drake, of Company "E," died. On the 12th the men were all hungry. We remained in camp. The cold rain poured down incessantly. We tore down some houses and made long sheds to keep the rain off.

We obtained some wheat bran at a mill and this was divided up among some of the companies—a tin cup full to each man. We boiled this in tin cans and ate it. On the 13th we still remained in camp. The foragers brought in some flour and pork. The cold rain fell all day. On the morning of the 14th, at 8 A. M., we marched to Charleston, Tennessee, on the Hiawassee River. The foragers got some corn meal which helped us greatly. On the 15th we marched one mile west of Cleveland and went into camp. It rained hard all day; the men were all cold, wet and hungry. On the 16th we marched through Oltewa and went into camp.

Most of the men were in the rain all night. On the 17th we marched in the deep mud down to the bridge near the mouth of Chicamauga Creek. Several trains of army wagons were waiting to cross. A great many teams were mired down. We moved over and encamped near the place where we formed in line to make the assault on Missionary Ridge, across the open plains, on the 25th of November. Along the line occupied by the 100th Indiana, near the railroad track, between the old water tanks and the 90th Illinois on our left, there were spots of coagulated blood all along in the short grass on the ground, making the line very plainly visible all along. Shells and shot were lying over the ground, and many holes were in the surface, where the plunging shells of the Confederates had entered the ground and exploded, leaving great holes. Besides there were many other evidences of the dreadful struggle which took place on that bloody field. On that evening we drew half rations for three days; the first regular issue of rations we had had for twenty-three days. On the 18th, at 9 A. M., we marched through Chattanooga, passed under Point Lookout, followed the line of the M. & C. railroad to Whiteside tunnel and encamped there. That evening Christian Cramer, of Company "A" by permission dropped out of the ranks and was never afterwards heard of. On the 19th we marched to Bridgeport, Alabama, and drew some clothing, which the men needed very badly. We also received our mail, the first for more than a month, drew our pay, and on the 24th we marched to Stevenson and on the 26th to Scottsboro, Alabama, and went into camp.

The 26th Illinois and the 100th Indiana were on the left, and the 90th Illinois and 12th Indiana on the right. One week later the 100th moved to Bellefont Station, Alabama. This closed a march of more than 350 miles since the battle of Missionary Ridge, on half rations or less all the time, in cold or rainy weather, in a country stripped of all kinds of products, and upon roads which with any other army or any other commander would have been deemed impossible.

By an order of the General commanding, the 100th Indiana was directed to place "Knoxville" on its flag, because the regiment marched to the relief of the besieged garrison.

Recapitulation, 1863.

Beginning with the engagement on January 1st, at Galveston, Texas, and ending with the four engagements of Greenville, North Carolina, St. Augustine, Fla., Waldron, Arkansas, and Matagorda Bay, Texas, on December 30, 1863. There were fought during that year six hundred and twenty-seven (627) battles and skirmishes, the more important of which, together with the losses on each side are as follows:

NAMES OF BATTLES.	LOSS FED.	LOSS CON.
Stone River, Dec. 31, '62, to Jan. 2d	13,249	10,270
Arkansas Post, Jan. 11, 1863.	1,060	5,500
Port Gibson, Miss., May 1, 1863	875	1,050
Chancellorsville, May 1st to 4th, K. & W.	11,368	12,764
Champion Hill, Miss., May 16, 1863	2,441	4,300
Vicksburg, Miss,. May 18th to July 4th	4,536	31,227
Port Hudson, Miss., May 27th to July 10th	3,000	7,208
Gettysburg, Pa., July 1st to 3d.	23,186	31,321
Chicamauga, Ga., Sept. 19th to 20th	15,851	17,804
Mission Ridge and Lookout Mt., Nov. 23-25	5,382	8,684

The following Regiments of the 15th Army Corps sustained the greatest loss in the Battle of Missionary Ridge. The First Brigade, Col. John Mason Loomis, of the 26th Illinois, commanding, as follows:

	KLD.	WND.	MISS.	TOTL.
100th Indiana	20	115	2	137
90th Illinois	10	94	13	117
26th Illinois	10	82	1	93
12th Indiana	10	50	2	62
Totals	50	341	18	409

Second Brigade, 4th Division, 15th A. C., General Corse.

	KLD.	WND.	MISS	TOTL.
103d Illinois	15	75	0	90
40th Illinois	7	43	1	51
46th Ohio	4	35	1	40
6th Iowa	8	57	0	65
Totals	34	210	2	246

The greatest battles of the year 1863 were: Stone River, Chancellorsville, Vicksburg, Port Hudson, Gettysburg, Chicamauga and Missionary Ridge. In these seven engagements the Confederates lost a total of 119,578 men. The losses sustained in the same engagements by the Federal army were 78,572, a difference of 41,006 in favor of the latter. The Confederates lost at Arkansas Post, 5,500; the Federal loss in that engagement was 1,060. This single item equals the number of Federal prisoners captured at Chancellorsville. Many other sanguinary conflicts took place between the contending armies, in which military advantages were lost and won.

In many of these the Confederates were the victors, but upon the whole they lost severely in strength and position. As to the latter, when they were driven from one fortress they could easily retreat to another, but when they lost in strength, the loss was irreparable, for nearly all the men of the South, who were liable to military duty, were in their armies already. A vast amount of territory was wrenched from the Confederates during the year 1863, but the loss of territory was not so serious to them as the loss of men. There was little or no hope for the Confederate cause after Vicksburg and Gettysburg. The result of the latter was the forerunner of ultimate defeat.

Winter Quarters, 1863-4, at Bellefonte, Alabama.

During the time we were in camp at Bellefonte, Alabama, perhaps no Regiment in the United States service led a more strictly military life. The duties we had to perform were to patrol the M. & C. R. R. half way to Scottsboro and Stevenson respectively, and to keep a general lookout for predatory bodies of the enemy.

We had large, beautiful parade grounds, kept perfectly clean and covered with fine cedar trees, in regular rows; had good water, plenty to eat, mails and newspapers regularly; quarters artistically arranged and kept scrupulously clean. Revielle at 5:15 A. M., which in the winter time was long before daylight. At this hour every company came to the color line on the double quick and in the darkness. The Regiment was then put through battalion drill for one hour by Col. R. M. Johnson, who was a consumate drill master.

The Regiment became so proficient that it could perform every field evolution in the tactics in the dark better than any Regiment in the United States service and was probably second to none, in a daylight drill. These evolutions were performed on the double quick, in answer to the commands of Col. Johnson, given from

Maj. Gen'l W. T. Sherman.
(From a war times photograph.)

any part of the field, whether the Regiment was in sight or not.

It must be admitted that such a camp life was rather heroic and exacting upon the men, yet it was eminently proper; the exercise kept the men in health—we had no sick. It greatly increased the efficiency of the Regiment and was for the good of the service.

Nothing creates a disposition in a soldier not to move any quicker than idleness and inaction. The efficiency of all the Federal armies were greatly increased during the winter and the Confederates put forth the utmost exertions to to increase their armies in number and discipline, for the struggle which was sure to come during the summer of 1864.

Strength and Position of the Federal Army, May 1, 1864.

As the great struggle for supremacy was to take place during the summer of 1864, the reader ought to possess some information relating to the location and position of the two armies and their respective strength to enable him to form correct conclusions as to the military results, of the battles fought during that year, to understand the strategy pursued beyond, or the tactics within the reach of each others guns by the commanders respectively, and to judge of the merits of any officer or the troops under his command; and of the advantages which the field gave to the one and the difficulties to be overcome by the other, it is deemed proper for this purpose to insert in this place an extract from the official report of General Sherman wherein these matters are fully set forth (Serial 72, p. 63), also an extract from the official report of General Joseph E. Johnston, C. S. A., for the same purpose (Serial 74, p. 615), the former being as follows:

"During the month of April I received from Lieutenant-General Grant a map, with a letter of instructions. Subsequently I received from him notice that he would move from his camp about Culpepper, Virginia, on the 5th of May, and he wanted me to do the same from Chattanooga. My troops were still dispersed and the cavalry, so necessary to our success, was yet collecting horses at Nicholasville, Kentucky, and Columbia, Tennessee.

"On the 27th of April I put all the troops in motion towards Chattanooga, and on the next day went there in person. My aim and purpose was to make the army of the Cumberland 50,000 men, that of the Tennessee 35,000, and that of the Ohio 15,000. These figures were approximated but never reached, and the Army of the Tennessee failed to receive certain Divisions that were still kept on the Mississippi River, resulting from the unfavorable issue of the Red River expedition. But on the 1st of May the effective strength of the several armies for offensive purposes was about as follows:

"Army of the Cumberland—Major-General Thomas, commanding. Infantry, 54,568; artillery, 2,377; cavalry, 3,828. Total, 60,773; guns, 130.

"Army of the Tennessee—Major-General McPherson, commanding. Infantry, 22,437; artillery, 1,404; cavalry, 624. Total, 24,465; guns, 96.

"Army of the Ohio—Major-General Schofield, commanding. Infantry, 11,183; artillery, 679; cavalry, 1,697. Total, 13,359; guns, 28.

"Grand aggregate—Troops, 98,797; guns 254. About these figures have been maintained during the campaign, the number of men joining from furlough and hospitals about compensating for the loss in battle and from sickness.

"These armies were grouped on the morning of May 6, 1864, as follows: That of the Cumberland at and near Ringgold; that of the Tennessee at Gordon's Mills on the Chicamauga, and that of the Ohio near Red Clay, on the Georgia line, north of Dalton. The enemy lay near and in Dalton, superior to me in cavalry, and with three corps of infantry and artillery, viz: Hardee's, Hood's and Polk's and the whole commanded by General Joe Johnson of the Conferate army. I estimated the cavalry under Wheeler at about 10,000 and the infantry and artillery about 50,000 men. To strike Dalton in front was impracticable, as it was covered by an inaccessible ridge, known as the Rocky Face, through which was a pass between Tunnel Hill and Dalton, known as the Buzzard Roost, through which lay the railroad and wagon road. It was narrow, well obstructed by abatis and flooded by water, caused by dams across Mill Creek. Batteries also commanded it in its whole length, from the spurs on either side, and more especially from the ridge at the farther side, like a traverse directly across its debouche. It was, therefore, necessary to turn it. On its north front the enemy had a strong line of works behind Mill Creek, so that my attention was at once directed to the south. In that direction I found

Snake Creek Gap affording me a good practicable way to reach Resaca, a point on the enemy's railroad line of communication, eighteen miles below Dalton. Accordingly I ordered General McPherson to move rapidly from his position at Gordon's Mills, via Ship's Gap, Villanow and Snake Creek Gap, directly on Resaca, or the railroad at any point below Dalton, and to make a bold attack. After breaking the railroad well, he was ordered to fall back to a strong defensive position near Snake Creek, and stand ready to fall on the enemy's flank when he retreated, as I judged he would. During the movement General Thomas was to make a strong feint of attack in front, while General Schofield pressed down from the north." (General Sherman's Report; Serial 72, p. 63.)

Strength and Position of the Confederate Army, May 1, 1864.

On December 18, 1863, less than one month after the defeat of the Confederate army by us at Mission Ridge, General Bragg left it and General Joseph E. Johnson took command, and the following is an extract from his official report, from that time until we moved against him about May 1st to 7th, 1864, showing the position and strength of the Rebel army made to General S. Cooper, Richmond, Va., the Confederate Secretary of War, as follows:

"I have the honor to make the following report of the operations of the Army of the Tennessee while it was under my command. Want of the reports of the Lieutenant-Generals, for which I have waited until now, prevents me from being circumstantial. In obedience to the orders of the President, received by telegraph at Clinton, Mississippi, December 18, 1863, I assumed command of the Army of the Tennessee at Dalton on the 27th of that month. Letters from the President and Secretary of War, dated, respectively, December 23d and 20th, impressed upon me the importance of soon commencing active operations against the enemy. The relative forces, including the moral effect of the affair at Missionary Ridge, condition of the artillery horses and most of those of the cavalry, and want of field transportation, made it impracticable to effect the wishes of the Executive.

"On December 31st, the effective total of the infantry and artillery of the army, including two Brigades belonging to the Department of the Mississippi, was 36,826. The effective total of the cavalry, including Rodney's command at Tuscumbia, was 5,613. The Federal force in our front, inclusive of cavalry and the Ninth and Twenty-third Corps at Knoxville, was estimated at 80,000. The winter was mainly employed in improving the discipline and equipment of the army and bringing back absentees to the ranks. At the end of April more than 5,000 had rejoined their Regiments.

"On the 1st of May I reported the enemy about to advance. On the 2d Brigadier-General Mercer's command arrived—about 1,400 effective infantry. On the 4th I expressed myself satisfied that the enemy was about to attack with his united forces, and again urged that a part of Lieutenant-General Polk's troops should be put

at my disposal. I was informed by General
Bragg that orders to that effect were given.
Major-General Martin, whose Division of cavalry
coming from East Tennessee, had been halted on
the Etowah to recruit its horses, was ordered
with it to observe the Oostenaula from Resaca
to Rome. Brigadier-General Kelley was ordered
with his command from the neighborhood of Resaca to report to Major-General Wheeler. The
effective artillery and infantry of the Army of
Tennessee, after the arrival of Mercer's Brigade,
amounted to 40,900; the effective cavalry to
about 4,600. Major-General Sherman's army
was composed of that of the Missionary Ridge,
then 80,000, increased by several thousand re-
cruits; 5,000 men under Hovey; the Twenty-
third Corps (Schofield's) from Knoxville, and
two Divisions of the Sixteenth from North Alabama. Major-General Wheeler estimated the
cavalry of that army at 15,000.

"On the 5th of May this army was in line
between Ringgold and Tunnel Hill, and after
skirmishing on that and the following day, on
7th pressed back our advance troops to Mill
Creek Gap. On the same day Brigadier-General
Cantey reached Resaca with his Brigade and
was halted there." (Official report of General
Joseph E. Johnston, Serial 74, page 615.)

The 100th Indiana in the Atlanta Campaign, 1864— 120 Days Constant Fighting.

On the morning of May 1st the 100th Indiana left its beautiful camp at Bellefonte and on

the 2d joined the 26th and 90th Illinois and the 12th Indiana, composing the First Brigade, Col. Reub Williams, 4th Division, General Harrow, 15th Army Corps, General John A. Logan, destined for the front. The 100th had at that time 450 men. The Brigade marched through Stevenson, Alabama, on the 2d and encamped at noon on Crow Creek. At this point Col. John Mason Loomis, who had commanded us for about a year and a half, and who had been with us so long under such trying conditions, that we had all learned to love him, took a final leave of us and Col. Reuben Williams took command of the Brigade. On the 3d we had reveille at 3 A. M., marched at 4, crossed the Tennessee River and encamped. On the 4th we marched at 7 A. M. to Whiteside, over a rough, mountainous road and encamped at 2 P. M. On the 5th our Brigade brought up the rear. We marched on the railroad under Point Lookout, then we bore to the right, passing between Mission Ridge and Lookout Mountain and encamped near Rossville, Georgia. Here we sent our tents and baggage to the rear. On the 6th we marched over roads, which were fairly good from Rossville, directly to Crawfish Springs. On the 7th the 100th Indiana took the advance. We crossed the South Chicamauga at Glass' Mill, at 10 o'clock. and at 11:30 A. M. we went into camp, and the 2d Division and other troops passed to the front, where an engagement was then going on.

On the 8th the 100th remained in camp until noon, to allow the trains to pass. We then covered the rear, crossed Taylor's Ridge at 6 o'clock that evening and encamped in Chestnut

Valley. During the day the 4th Corps engaged the Rebels under Reynolds and Granberry, on the heights of Buzzard Roost and Rocky Face Ridge and a portion of the 15th Corps drove the Rebel cavalry out of Snake Creek Gap. (Serial 72, p. 63.)

The battle of Dalton was fought on the 9th. On that day we made no move, but the 23d Corps drove the Confederates nearly to Dalton and the 4th and 14th Corps pressed them very hard on Rocky Face Ridge. The whole country is very rough and the Confederates were occupying the passes, gaps and fastnesses, some of which were so strongly fortified as to be almost impregnable.

On the 10th the 100th Indiana marched to Sugar Valley and on the next day took a position assigned us, on the front and fortified all night and until daylight on the 12th, when we found that we were in front of the enemy's line of heavy works, in Snake Creek Gap, to the northwest of Resaca.

The 100th Indiana in the Battle of Resaca.

On information that the Rebels were evacuating their front several miles to the north and massing in our front, at 5 A. M. on the 13th, we moved against him to a cross-road in his front and near Resaca. The 2d Brigade was placed on the advanced line and our Brigade on a line in its support; but the 100th Indiana was quickly ordered to take a position in line of battle with the first Division. Some firing was then going on in our front. The movement was performed by the 100th with alacrity. Company "B," about fifty men, were then sent forward as a strong skirmish line, under Captain Fast, and joined in with the Brigade skirmish line, under Major Johnson of the 100th Indiana, who had command of the entire Brigade skirmish line at that time. (74, p. 278.)

Behind this line of skirmishers the movement ordered was successfully made. About noon an order came to move forward in line of battle. This was done in a perfect manner, through a wooded thicket, to an open field directly in front of the first line of Confederate works. The 100th, in common with the general line of battle, formed in the edge of the wood, at the edge of the field, right at the crest of the hill. The skirmish line under Major Johnson, in the mean time, kept driving the enemy's line of skirmishers before them.

During all this time the enemy kept up a furious canonade with both shot and shell, not only on General Osterhaus' line, but the entire length of the 100th Regiment. But notwithstanding that, our line of skirmishers continued to advance and finally drove the Rebels from their outer line of works without the line of battle proper becoming engaged. Seeing this, the Brigade commander ordered the line of skirmishers of the 100th, which was Company "B," to be reinforced. Companies "C" and "D" deployed and the three Companies advanced, and the Regiment followed, in line of Battle, across the open field, drove the Rebels from the wood covered hill, on the right of the works we had just taken, and took a position some distance to the left and facing the enemy's works, which was quickly accomplished and was held until about 6 P. M., when the 100th was relieved and ordered to face back, having successfully performed every duty required of it throughout the day and under a severe artillery fire. The officers and soldiers bore themselves bravely during the time. We went into camp, in the field we drove the enemy from, and at 7 A. M. on the 14th we moved to the right to support the 2d Division, if need be, where we remained in line during the night of the 14th and 15th. The Rebels had about 70,000 men engaged in this battle. The 4th, 14th and 20th Corps, and the 15th, 16th and 23d Corps were all more or less engaged, and there was some severe fighting. The Confederates retreated during the night of the 15th across the Oostenaula River.

Captain Fast was the first one who entered the enemy's works. All of the officers of the Regiment conducted themselves gallantly and discharged their whole duty. The following is a list of "casualties" in the regiment before Resaca, Ga.:

MAY 13, 1864.

Hammond Frees, ———, "A," wounded in thigh; severe.
John D. Vanlear, — , "A," wounded in arm; slight.
Benjamin F. Bolinger, — , "A," wounded in leg; slight.
Henry M. Scott, Corporal, "B," wounded in arm; severe.
George French, Private, "B," wounded in leg; severe.
William Davis, Private, "B," wounded in hand; slight.
Isaac Myers, Private, "D," wounded in arm; severe.
Samuel Gerrard, Private, "G," wounded in hand; slight.
Con. Bowen, Corporal, "G," wounded hip; slight.
James Hillis, Private, "I," wounded in back; slight.
John Murphy, Private "I," wounded in hip; slight.
Noah T. Catterlin, 1st Lt.. "I," wounded in breast; slight.
David N. Pugh, Private, "K," wounded in shoulder; slight.
Zachariah Pollard, Corporal, "K," wounded in wrist; slight.

On the morning of the 16th we moved with

the army in pursuit. During this engagement, the 100th had 14 men and one officer wounded. In this engagement the Confederates lost 3,000 men. The fighting in front of the 4th Corps was very determined. Our loss was 2,600. The Confederates fought mainly from behind breastworks. The 100th Indiana marched in pursuit at 11 A. M., and went into camp at 8 P. M., on Oostenaula Creek. The strength of the Confederate Army at the battle of Resaca, was as follows:

Confederate Army, as at Dalton........52,990
Additions to Hardee's and Hood's Corps.. 5,000
Arrival of Mercer's Brigade, May 2d.... 2,800
Arrival of Loring's Division, May 12th.. 5,145
Arrival of Cantey's Division, May 8th.. 5,300

 Total...... 71,235

We had now driven the Rebels out of the gaps and passes and from the hills and mountain tops, which they had been fortifying for half a year and which they deemed impregnable.

On the 17th the 100th guarded the wagon train, and went into camp at midnight, having marched twelve miles.

On the 18th it joined the Brigade early in the morning, marched fourteen miles and encamped on the Burnley plantation at 7 P. M. The men were all very tired; sun very hot.

On the 19th we marched with the column nine miles and encamped at Kingston, where we remained in camp, on the 20th, 21st and 22d, during which time the 20th A. C. engaged the Confederates at Cassville, Georgia, and on that day they retreated across the Etowah River.

On the 23d we broke camp early and marched in the direction of Dallas, about twenty miles. The weather was very hot, but the men were healthy. On the 24th we continued in the same direction about eight miles and encamped in the mountains.

On the 25th the Brigade acted as train guards. We marched all night, over very bad roads and went into camp on Pumpkinvine Creek at 3 A. M., having marched only ten miles.

On the 26th the 100th guarded the train during the day and marched all night; only made five miles. We halted within one mile of Dallas, Georgia, where we arrived at 4 A. M. on the 27th, and at 7 A. M. we were ordered to take a position on the advance line of battle, directly in front of the enemy. We moved out promptly for that purpose and took the position assigned us. We were placed on the right of, and refused to a horizontal line, with the 6th Iowa and Companies "A," "I" and "F" were deployed as skirmishers in front of the Regiment

The 100th Indiana in the Battle of Dallas, Georgia.

At noon there were indications of an assault on our line by the enemy. The Regiment was without any works, for which reason the skirmish line was reinforced by Companies "B" and "C." At one o'clock the Confederates sent forward and attacked us with a heavy skirmish line. This was repulsed by the above named companies on the skirmish line, during which we had seven men and one officer wounded.

After this assault the Regiment fortified itself strongly, and on the 28th the skirmish line was made still stronger. About half past 3 P.M. the enemy raised a yell on his front and charged our line of skirmishers with a heavy line of battle, and steadily pressed them back until they had reached our main line, which they then attacked with great spirit and charged upon us with deafening yells. The men of the 100th fought gallantly in this action and repulsed the Rebels with great loss. Being protected by works, we only lost three killed and fourteen wounded. The Confederates carried away most of their dead and a great many of their severely wounded, but we hastily buried a large number in our front.

The attack lasted half an hour. This is what we usually call the Battle of Dallas. The Confederates met with a bloody repulse in the engagement. The brunt of this battle was borne by the 100th Indiana, as it occupied the only ground over which a charge could be made by the enemy.

On the 29th of May there were some indications that the enemy were about to evacuate the works in our front. To settle this question in the minds of the officers, the 100th Indiana was directed by the General to advance its line far enough to ascertain whether the enemy remained in his fortifications in force or not. This we did, the enemy showing a strong line in his works. We received the praise of the General, but lost three men in the attempt, and on the 30th we repeated the experiment and lost two more men. On the 31st we remained in camp.

On June 1st, at 4 A. M., the 100th abandoned its line and moved about seven miles to the left, to a point near New Hope Church, entered the front line and relieved a Regiment of the 20th Corps. We lost two men in doing this. The bullets flew thick and fast over this ground. From May 25th to June 4th, there was severe and constant fighting at New Hope Church, burned Hickory and on Pumpkin Vine Creek by the 4th, the 14th and 20th Corps and by the 23d, 15th and 17th Corps, some of which was very sanguinary. On the 2d we were in reserve. On the 3d we were ordered to advance on the main line sixty yards. This movement was neatly and successfully performed with the loss of one man, and resulted in forcing the Rebel army to evacuate all of the Altoona pass, without fighting them at that place.

On the 4th we remained in camp, in the works, and as the Rebel army was very strongly fortified at New Hope Church—too strongly for us to assault—we just marched away and left them in their works, and moved around to their right, and during the night the Confederates, being forced to do so, abandoned their position and retreated further south. At midnight on the 5th the army moved rapidly to the left again and rested until daylight on the 6th, when we again moved six miles and went into camp near Acworth, Georgia, where we remained during the 7th, 8th and 9th of June. Altoona Pass was, on the 6th, adopted as a base of supplies.

On the 10th of June we marched six miles to Big Shanty, a station on the railroad northwest of Kenesaw. The 100th took a position fronting Kenesaw and fortified during the entire night. On the morning of the 11th our lines were close up to the enemy, and during the 12th,

13th and 14th we remained quiet, except continual skirmishing. A severe engagement was fought at Pine Mountain during the day. There was sharp canonading in front of General Howard and Hooker's line, and a canon shot from Captain Simonson's Indiana Battery killed Lieutenant-General Polk of the Confederate army, then standing in an exposed place on Pine Mountain. Johnson, Hardee and Polk were standing together at the time. Loring succeeded to the command of Polk's Corps. Our Signal Corps had the key to the Rebel signals and it was known at once in our army that General Polk was killed.

During the night the Rebel army retreated from the mountain tops again to the southward, and on the morning of the 15th of June Pine Mountain was found abandoned by the enemy, and at 11 A. M. the 100th Indiana moved rapidly to the left and supported the 2d Brigade in an encounter with the rear of the fleeing Rebel army. We attacked them savagely and killed, wounded and captured a great many of them. General Logan says that on the 15th he moved General Harrow's command to the extreme left. Walcott, Williams and Oliver's Brigades charged gallantly against the enemy, killing and wounding many and capturing 350 prisoners, twenty-two of whom were commissioned officers. Our loss was forty-five killed and wounded. (Logan's Official Report.)

Early on the 16th the 14th and 23d Corps advanced and fought the Confederate army, which was again strongly entrenched along the rugged hills, between Kenesaw and Lost Mountain. At the same time we advanced and gained some good positions. The 20th Corps had a bloody engagement at Golgotha, and a portion of the 16th Corps defeated a Rebel force at Rome Cross Roads.

June 17th, 1864.

On the 17th, the enemy abandoned Lost Mountain and the long line of admirable breastworks connecting it with Kenesaw. We continued to press at all points, skirmishing in dense forests of timber and across deep ravines, until we found him again, strongly posted and intrenched, with Kenesaw as his salient, his right wing thrown back, so as to cover Marietta, and his left behind Noyes Creek, covering his railroad back to the Chattahoochee. This enabled him to contract his lines and strengthen them accordingly. From Kenesaw he could look down on our camps and observe every movement and his batteries thundered away, but did us but little harm, on account of their extreme height, the shot and shell passing harmlessly over our heads, as we lay up close against his mountain town. During our operations about Kenesaw, the weather was villainously bad, the rain fell almost continually for three weeks, rendering our narrow wooded roads mere mud gullies, so that a general movement was impossible, but our men daily worked closer and closer to our entrenched foe and kept up an incessant picket firing, galling to him. Every opportunity was taken to advance our general lines closer and closer to the enemy, General McPherson watching the enemy on Kenesaw and working his left forward, General Thomas swinging as it were on a grand left wheel, his left on Kenesaw, connecting with General McPherson and General Schofield all the while, working to the south and east along the Sandtown road." (Sherman's Report).

On the 19th, the Rebel Army abandoned their very strong line of works and took up a new line, about two miles to the rear. The right of Hood's Corps was on the Marietta and Canton road, Loring's Corps was on Kenesaw Mountain and Hardee's Corps on Lost Mountain, with its left across the Marietta and Lost Mountain road. We closed up on their lines rapidly and intrenched at the base of the mountain and kept up an incessant skirmish fire, by which a great many of the enemy were killed and wounded, while at Pine Knob the contest was a veritable battle.

On the 20th the enemy were sorely pressed by the constant firing of our men and at Powder Springs, by the 20th Corps and the Cavalry. From the 20th till the 25th we continued to push forward our skirmishers up the side of the mountain, driving those of the enemy before us who occupied rifle pits on the slope. On the 24th we attempted to gain the summit by a double line of skirmishers, but the enemy was found in very strong works and the effort failed.

On the 22d Hood's Corps attacked the lines of Generals Hooker and Schofield at a place now known as Kolb's House, but was repulsed with dreadful slaughter, leaving a vast number of dead and wounded on the field.

On the 24th General Sherman made an order to assault the enemy on Kenesaw Mountain.

On the 25th the 100th Indiana moved two

miles to the right, with the Brigade, and relieved a Division of the 14th Corps on the line of battle, and on the 26th the other two Divisions of the 15th (our Corps) moved over and took position with us. They began the movement at 8 P. M., and though it was only three miles, it was not completed until daylight on the 27th. This placed us all in line directly under the enemy's guns on Little Kenesaw.

The 100th Indiana in the Assault on Kenesaw, June 27, 1864.

The best account of this assault is given in the official report of General Logan, found on page 99, serial 74, a part of which is in the words following:

"In pursuance of special field orders No. 51, * * I organized the Division of Brigadier-General M. L. Smith, consisting of Brigadier-General Lightburn's and Brigadier-General Giles A. Smith's Brigades and Col. C. C. Walcott's Brigade of the 4th Division, General Harrow, commanding, into an assaulting column, under command of General M. L. Smith, with orders to be ready at 8 o'clock precisely on the morning of the 27th, to assault the enemy's works on the south and west slope of Little Kenesaw Mountain. The column for assault being formed, I directed it at 8 o'clock precisely to move forward. Immediately after uncovering themselves they became engaged. The advance was continued in two lines steadily, in the face of a destructive fire from three batteries of about twelve pieces, throwing shot and shell, and from a musketry fire, from the sharp-shooters of the enemy, situated below the first line of the enemy's rifle pits, and also from the rifle pits. After a most stubborn and destructive resistance, my attacking column succeeded in taking and holding two lines of the enemy's rifle pits, and advanced toward the succeeding works of the enemy, situated just below the crest of the mountain. It soon became evident that the (Rebel) works could not be taken * * on account of a steep declivity, from twenty to twenty-five feet in height, of perpendicular rocks. * * After vainly attempting to take the works, * * I ordered them to retire to the last line of works captured, * * and these were held and fortified. * * Seven commanding officers of Regiments were killed or disabled. Our loss was 80 killed, 506 wounded, 17 missing; aggregate, 603. We took 83 prisoners."

This assault was a great disaster to the Federal army, about 2,500 men were uselessly sacrificed. The enemy lost, about 800. Our men pressed the enemy closely around Kenesaw during the 28th, 29th and 30th of June. General Sherman determined to dislodge the enemy from Kenesaw, by other means than by direct assault; accordingly on the 1st of July, he ordered General McPherson to move the 15th Army Corps to the right and on the 2nd the movement was begun, in the night time, the 100th Indiana having the advance. We marched all night, over rocks and through thickets, that seemed impregnable, under the guidance of a staff officer, all the time in sight of the Rebel lights on the top and sides of Kenesaw.

We were followed by the whole of the 15th and 17th Corps, the Confederates were greatly surprised by this move and retreated hastily, from the highest mountain top in Georgia and the strongest military position in the South, halting at Smyrna Church about five miles southwest of Marrieta, where they were found strongly posted behind very formidable works. If this movement by the right flank had been made instead of the fatal mistake of assaulting the Mountain on the 27th a loss of 2,500 good soldiers would have been saved to us.

We followed the Rebel army on the 3rd and encamped near Marrieta.

On the 4th we made a forced march of 12 miles further to the right, on the 5th at 11 A. M. we overtook and engaged the enemy near the Chattahoochee River about 8 miles north of Atlanta. We had orders to press the enemy in our entire front, while the 14 Army Corps had orders to move to the right and cross the river at Sandtown west of Atlanta.

During the day the Union Army was engaged with the enemy at Nickajack Creek, Smyrna Camp ground and at Vinings, in all of which the Confederates were routed. On the 6th there was severe skirmishing along the Chattahoochee and on the 7th the 14th Corps crossed at Sandtown and captured a gun and some Rebels and took a strong position on the east side of the River. On the same day Garrard's Cavalry destroyed the factories at Rosswell, which had been making clothing for the Rebel Army. The man who pretended to be the owner of the factory, run up a French flag and asked protection as a Frenchman, but he had been making

lots of cloth for the Rebels and down came his flag and his factory. During the night of the 7th one-half of the 100th skirmished with the enemy, and the other half fortified all night and occupied the works as rapidly as they were built. During the 8th and 9th, the ford at Rosswell's was secured by the Cavalry and Power's Ferry two miles below Rosswell, was taken; so we had by the 9th secured three good fords on the Chattahoochee and the enemy had again retreated, this time across the Chattahoochee and the Union Army, was in possession of all the strong holds between Chattanooga and the Chattahoochee and was within eight miles of Atlanta and three Corps, were about all across the river.

On the 10th the 100th Indiana was temporarily relieved from active duty on the front, in which it had been engaged for about ninety days without intermission, having done more than its share of the hard fighting; it was ordered to report at Marietta, Georgia, where we arrived on the 11th and went into camp on the ground where is located the national cemetery, at that place, on the eastern edge of the town.

The Confederate Army on the 11th occupied the high ground on the south of Peach Tree Creek and along the southeast bank of the Chattahoochee, below the mouth of the former.

On the 13th the Brigade marched through Marietta. On the 14th it crossed over the Chattahoochee River and took a position about a mile out from the river and fortified, where it remained until the morning of the 17th, when it moved to the left, in the direction of Decatur, engaged the enemy formed in line of battle and fortified.

We first encountered Johnston's Army at or near Ringgold about the 5th of May, and for seventy-three days we had engaged it constantly—had driven it out of the mountain gaps and passes where it had fortified itself. We had driven it from the hill sides, the mountain tops and gorges for a distance of a hundred miles, always attacking it in front or flank, and only the impregnable character of its strongholds and the very excellent generalship of General Johnston prevented us from killing and capturing his whole army. These results so displeased Jefferson Davis that on the 17th day of July he sent a telegram as follows to General Johnston:

"Richmond, July 17, 1864.
"General J. E. Johnston: * * * I am directed by the Secretary of War to inform you that as you have failed to arrest the advance of the enemy to the vicinity of Atlanta, far in the interior of Georgia, and express no confidence that you can defeat or repel him, you are hereby relieved from the command of the Army, * * * which you will immediately turn over to General Hood.   "S. Cooper, A. and I. General."

General Johnston received this dispatch on the night of the 17th. The Confederate War Department telegraphed General Hood as follows:

"You are charged with a great trust * * * be wary, but no less bold. * * * God be with you."

General Johnston delivered a short, but very complimentary farewell address to his soldiers. General Hood expressed an opinion to Jefferson Davis that it was unwise to change commanders at that time. On the 18th he telegraphed Jefferson Davis that he had assumed command of the Army (Serial 76, pages 885 *et seq*).

On the same day at 10 A. M., one of our spies who had just come out of Atlanta informed General Sherman that General J. B. Hood had succeeded General Johnston, and General Sherman said that Hood was brave and rash and that the change in commanders meant a fight. (Sherman's Memoirs, 2, p. 72.)

On the 18th Major R. M. Johnson was detailed on General Harrow's staff and left the Regiment for the front. On the same day the 1st Brigade, to which the 100th belonged, moved to within one mile of Decatur, to the east of Atlanta and went into position and fortified. On the 19th the Brigade moved again, passed through Decatur, on the road towards Atlanta. About 2 o'clock the 1st Brigade, Col. Reub Williams, commanding, moved to the support of Morgan L. Smith's Division and was placed on his left. During this time the enemy shelled our line unmercifully. In the evening the other two Brigades came up and went into position on the left, when the whole Division moved forward and took position in front of the enemy and at once fortified.

On the 20th the Army of the Cumberland was assaulted by the Confederate army under the new commander, J. B. Hood, and a bloody battle was fought. The enemy made the attack just before 4 P. M. He was driven back into his entrenchments, leaving 500 dead and 1,000 wounded lying on the field. General Sherman estimates the entire loss of the enemy at 5,000. The Union loss was 1,500 all told. The heaviest loss was sustained by the 20th Corps. The engagement is known as the Battle of Peach Tree Creek. (From Sherman's official report.)

The 21st was spent in caring for the dead and wounded on both sides, and the Union army felt the enemy's lines, which he occupied in force, at an average of about four miles out of Atlanta.

Battle of Atlanta.

On the morning of the 22d it was found that the enemy had abandoned their line of works in our front and the 1st Brigade was ordered to advance and take a position in the line of works abandoned by the enemy.

At 7 A. M. this was done and the works were reversed so as to front toward the enemy. At noon very heavy firing began in front of the 17th Corps on our left, which soon became general and by night fall the Battle of Atlanta had been fought and won by the Union army.

This was General Hood's second attack within three days, and is usually denominated Hood's first sortie. The 15th Army Corps bore the brunt of the battle. The fighting in front of Harrow's Division was very severe. The brave and intrepid Major Johnson, of the 100th Indiana, had charge of the Division skirmish line, and was surrounded and taken prisoner while bravely doing his duty in the thickest of the battle. Major Johnson is favorably mentioned for gallantry in the official reports of Generals Harrow, Williams and Col. Heath. He was taken prisoner very near the spot where General McPherson was killed and under very similar circumstances.

In this battle General McPherson, commanding the Army of the Tennessee, was killed, to whose memory the highest tributes have been paid. General Logan at once assumed command. In his official report, speaking of this battle, he says:

"The fighting along the entire line of the Corps (15th) was of the most desperate character, often being hand to hand. The troops could not have acted more gallantly or behaved better. The losses were on that day 118 killed, 414 wounded, 535 missing; aggregate, 1,067. The Corps captured 481 prisoners and buried over 400 dead Confederates in front of their line."

Of the entire Confederate loss in this engagement, 3,240 were killed; 2,200 dead were actually counted. 800 dead bodies were delivered under a flag of truce, so that their entire loss was not less than 10,000. General Hood makes no mention in his official report of what his losses were, and blames General Hardee for the failure of the attack. The Union loss was 3,722 killed, wounded and missing. (See official report General Sherman; also Hood's official report, Serial 74, p. 631.)

On the 26th we placed some batteries in position and began to shell the enemy pretty lively. This was kept up all day and at midnight, the Army of the Tennessee left its works on the Decatur road and moved silently, behind the other Corps of the Army, to Proctor's Creek, the 16th Corps formed on the right of the Army, the 17th next and the 15th on the extreme right. The line of the latter Corps, facing almost east and being west and southwest of Atlanta.

On the night of the 27th, the First Brigade

was halted in the rear of the 16th Corps, which was then the left of the Army of the Tennessee, where it remained in line of battle throughout the night.

Battle of Ezra Church.

On the 28th at daylight, the First Brigade moved to the right about a mile and a half when it was halted and formed in line of battle, to support the Third Brigade, Col. Oliver commanding. This was quickly done, and the whole Division then moved forward, through a dense wood and halted at the edge of the timber, with several open fields in our front.

The First Brigade was then placed on the right of the Third and the whole line moved to the edge of the fields, at the crest of the hill in front. This was done under a severe fire of artillery from the enemy's batteries posted at the further side of the open fields before us. Col. Williams ordered the line to fortify at once. "Scarcely had these orders been given and the men had time to throw up a slight protection, before the enemy were reported advancing in force" across the fields in our front. "And very soon our skirmishers were driven in, closely followed by the enemy's main line, they were soon repulsed and driven back, but only to come again, with more determination and increased numbers" (Col. Reub. Williams Off. Report). The enemy made one assault after another and for six hours, an incessant roar of musketry was kept up and every assault or attempt to drive our men from their position was fruitless. During the battle the 90th Illinois was taken from its position, to support the Third Brigade which was hard pushed by the enemy at one time. Col. Gilmore of the Twenty-sixth says "his line was assaulted four times," the fourth assault being the most desperate of the day. The enemy were within ten steps of his lines. One hundred and twenty-nine dead Rebels, were buried in front of the Twenty-sixth Illinois, which had forty men killed and wounded.

This engagement took place about two and a half miles west of Atlanta, and is called by us the Battle of Ezra Church. The fight was essentially a 15th Army Corps battle, although Generals Blair and Dodge rendered valuable assistance at an opportune time, as the 15th Army Corps was fighting two Corps of the Rebel army. General Logan says, in his official report, that the enemy moved forward in good order, intending to break our lines. During the first hour's fighting, which was terrific, the enemy lost ten men to our one, but they reformed again and made a most desperate assault. Four assaults were made. The battle lasted from 11:30 until dark. The Rebels had one battery, we had none. The Union loss was 50 killed, 439 wounded and 73 missing; total loss, 562. Harrow's Division captured 5 battle flags, 2,000 muskets and 179 prisoners. 600 dead Rebels were buried in front of the 15th Corps the next day. The weather was so hot and the ground so hard that the interment of the bodies was very superficial and many hands and feet were left exposed.

General Logan also says in his official report, that the enemy's loss could not have been less than 6,000 or 7,000. The assault was made by Lee's and Hardee's entire Corps. This battle is denominated Hood's second sortie. His official report of this battle consists of twelve lines, and says nothing about his losses. (Serial 74-631-2.)

Notes of the Battle.

The enemy formed on the Lickskillet Road; that is, Johnson's, Sharp's, Brantley's and Manigault's Brigades of Hindman's old Division, and assaulted the 15th Army Corps at Ezra Church. These four Brigades lost 807 men. Manigault was in reserve. The Confederates fought with great desperation. They seemed determined to drive us off the field, but not an inch was yielded.

They did not know that we were there in force until they were almost upon our works. When the 15th Corps turned loose on them Manigault's Brigade stampeded, but it recovered and fought bravely through the battle.

Toulman's Confederate Brigade took 1,143 men into the action; 269 were lost. The 25th Alabama took in 173 men; loss 125. Manigault's Brigade, although in reserve part of the time, lost 170 men. The 44th Mississippi "had half their number shot down." The 24th and 29th Mississippi, consolidated, lost 180 out of 430. (Serial 74, official reports.)

General Harrow says, in his official report, that "If the soldiers of the 15th Corps had no other claim to consideration than their efforts on that day (July 28th) it would be enough to entitle them to the lasting gratitude of their country." (No. 74, p. 278.)

From the 29th of July to August 4th the Union lines were strengthened and in many places advanced. On the latter date Major Brown and sixty soldiers of the 70th Ohio fell in taking an advanced position from the enemy. On this date the 100th Indiana and 26th Illinois were transferred from the 1st to the 2d Brigade and the entire 3d added to the first. This gave us only two Brigades in Harrow's Division instead of three.

The 100th Indiana in the Siege of Atlanta.

By this battle, the investment of Atlanta was begun; from the 2nd to the 5th, the Union line was steadily extended to the right. On the 5th General Schofield lost about 400 men, in an effort to break the enemy's lines, on Utoy Creek.

On the 6th, General Hascall flanked the enemy out of the position, from which General Schofield had failed to dislodge him. At this time the enemy's lines were about fifteen miles long, reaching from Decatur around Atlanta and nearly to East Point and ours was still longer. The enemy had, before crossing the Chattahoochee a total of 86,475 men as follows, at Resaca he had 71,235. Then on May 17th he got Jackson's Cavalry 4,477 at Adairville. French's Division of 4,413 joined on the 18th at Cassville. May 24th the First Alabama (Canty), 650. On the same date Quarles Brigade of 2,400 at New

Hope Church, and the Georgia State Militia under General G. W. Smith at Kenesaw on June 20th, 3,300 total 86,475. This force, less the losses from Tunnel Hill to Atlanta, was the number Hood had in his army during the siege of Atlanta.

On the 10th four rifled cannon were put in position and put to work day and night causing frequent fires in the City of Atlanta.

On the 13th the 100th Indiana marched from Marietta, Georgia to Vinings Station, near the Chattahoochee River and on the 14th took a position, right on the Lickskillet Road, where the bullets were flying briskly from the Rebel lines around Atlanta.

On the field where we were encamped and along the Lickskillet Road, more than 500 bodies of dead Confederates were buried, as we were right in the middle of the field of July the 28th. The ground was very hard, and the bodies were buried in such haste, that it was poorly and very superficially done. One grave on this field contained 116 and another near by 125 bodies, besides there were a large number of other graves, containing a great many bodies each. A detail of the 100th reinterred all these bodies and covered them deeper.

Our supplies ran short at this time and five days' rations were ordered for seven days. Several soldiers were killed on the line daily in our front.

On the 18th, at 10 P. M., there was a picket fight all along the lines, each shot, at the flash of the guns on the opposite line. Capt. Percy, chief engineer on General Harrow's staff, was killed, Taylor of Co. "B" wounded. On the 19th the

100th went into the skirmish pits and again fired all night. Had a tremendous rain storm during the night. On the 20th we were relieved by the 103d Illinois. Company "G," while in the skirmish pits, had James H. Nelson killed and John C. Clark, Company "B" was shot through the head.

The 100th went into the skirmish pits again on the 23d, and on the 24th we pressed the Confederate line hard all day. The artillery aided us by firing into the enemy's pits. On the 25th we sent all of our baggage to the rear, and were very lightly equipped and prepared for rapid work. David Soule of Company "B" was killed. We received orders to move at a moment's notice. The 4th Corps moved from the extreme left to the extreme right. The 20th Corps went back to the Chattahoochee River.

The Siege of Atlanta Raised.

On Friday, the 26th, all surplus wagons and incumbrances of every kind, and all sick soldiers were ordered back to the Chattahoochee bridge, to our intrenched position. The 100th Indiana moved into the works and remained all day. At night the whole army moved away and left that Regiment in line in front of the whole Rebel Army. We were about six feet apart in the works, and kept up an incessant firing to mislead the enemy until 10 o'clock P. M., when we moved out of our works and away from Atlanta. We were the last Regiment on that part of the line to leave our works. We marched till 3 A. M.

The Confederates threw shot after us for at least three miles, killing one man. The night was extremely dark and the road was rough and in the woods.

We first moved westwardly, toward Sandtown, then by a circuit, we bore to the south, and crossed Camp Creek. On the 27th we marched from early morning until 2 P. M. through the woods when we halted and fortified. This move brought us close to Fairburn, southwest of Atlanta.

On the 28th, we bore to the southeast seven miles and camped on the West Point Railroad. On the 29th we were roused up at 2 A. M. to tear up railroad track, at a point only seventeen miles southwest of Atlanta. Some dead Rebels were lying in the road at a bridge, showing that other troops had passed before we did.

On the 30th, we moved forward at 8 A. M., marched till evening, crossed Flint River; the 100th was out as flankers all day. We halted about a half a mile west of Jonesboro and formed in line of battle, about half way from Flint River to Jonesboro, with an open field directly in front of the 100th. The Regiment just covered the field. At 9 P. M. we fell in and fortified all night, skirmishing all night in our front. The trains were run by the enemy all night, bringing troops from Atlanta to Jonesboro, and massing them in our front.

Condensed Rebel Despatches.

The Rebels did not know what had become of us after we left our works at Atlanta. Major

General Stevenson dispatched to General Hood at daybreak, that he occupied our picket line. General French dispatched General Sanders, asking him if he had any information as to where we were. General Stewart dispatched General French at 10 A. M. not to leave his trenches until it was known where we were. General Hood ordered the respective commanders to push their scouts carefully forward and at 10 A. M. he ordered General Walthall to hold his command under arms ready to move at a moment's notice. At 1.45 A. M. the same order was given to General Maney; and to Generals Smith and Ferguson at 8:15 A. M. At 9 A. M. he ordered General Jackson to "ascertain what is going on." (Serial 76, p. 991).

On the 27th Hood telegraphed Jefferson Davis that we had no forces within four miles of Atlanta. At daybreak Generals Lee and Stewart reported to Hood that we were gone, but Hardee said we were still in his front. (Serial 76, pp. 994-995.)

On the 28th, at noon, Hood ordered General Armstrong to keep his forces well in hand, so that when he found us he could fall on us with effect. (Serial 76, p. 997.)

On the 29th, at 2 P. M., he ordered General Hardee "to ascertain the position of the enemy." (76-499.)

On the 30th, at 12:40 P. M., he dispatched Hardee, that no troops need be sent to Jonesboro, but at 6 P. M. he ordered Hardee to keep us off the railroad at Jonesboro if possible. At 5:45 P. M. Lee's command was ordered under arms, and at 6:35 P. M. Hardee was ordered to Jonesboro, and at 8:45 P. M. the same orders were sent to General Lee. (No. 76, p. 1003.)

On the 30th, at 5:15 P. M., General Lewis was ordered by General Hood to prevent us from crossing the Flint River. He also gave General Armstrong the same order. The truth was our movements had completely mystified the Confederate generals. Having found out on the 30th where we were, General Hood, on the 31st, at 3 A. M., ordered Hardee's and Lee's Corps to be in position and that they "*Must attack and drive the enemy across the river*" (meaning the Flint, which was only a half a mile in our rear.) Ten minutes later he dispatched Hardee that he "Must not fail to attack the enemy so soon as he could get his troops up," and said, "I trust that God will give us victory." At 3:20 A. M. he dispatched Hardee, that he must say to his officers and men that the necessity is imperative; that the enemy *must* be driven into and across the river, and at 10 o'clock he again dispatched Hardee, that he "desired the men to go at the enemy with the bayonet fixed, determined to drive everything they may come against. (76, p. 1006–7.)

The 100th Indiana in the Battle of Jonesborough.

In obedience to the foregoing dispatches from General Hood, the Confederates undertook to drive us into Flint River, without flattering results. We were all in line at day break, in good works. The enemy was in plain sight in our front, where they had planted a battery during the night. Skirmishing went on briskly all day. About 2:30 P. M. the enemy shelled our line severely. Shortly afterward they charged upon us across the open field in our front, with great impetuousity. We repulsed them with severe loss. They reformed and moved to our left, then attacked us again in front and were again repulsed. The 100th captured Col. Bass, the major and a lieutenant of the 2d Rebel Kentucky, and 16 privates. The Colonel's arm was shot off. Sergt. M. L. Conkey and Lewis Kieth, of Company "B" and Sergeant Batts of Company "K" were killed. J. Prosser and J. Critchet, of Company "A," wounded. William Sharp, of Company "C," and John Hettinger, of Company "F," orderlies on General Harrow's staff, were both killed. General Harrow speaks very highly of them, in his official report of this battle.

The enemy were very neatly repulsed in

front of Harrow's Division. They fought bravely and faced our line in the open field with great determination. Their batteries threw both shell and canister into our line.

As the 100th covered the only open ground on the battlefield, that Regiment bore the brunt of the battle, and fought from behind good works and sustained a very small loss. Hazen's Division was on the left, Harrow's on the right and General Osterhaus in reserve. General Logan says: "The most terrible and destructive fire I ever witnessed was directed at the enemy and in less than an hour he was compelled to retire discomfited and in confusion." (His Official Report.)

The most determined part of the assault was maintained by General Hazen. * * It raged fiercely in front of Harrow and Osterhaus, the enemy approaching their line, at the average distance of 40 to 100 paces. * * In front of the Second Division, (Hazen's) 186 bodies of the enemy were buried, 99 prisoners captured, not including 79 wounded, also two stand of colors taken. The enemy's wounded General Hazen estimated at 1,000, afterward found to be greater. General Harrow buried 12 of the enemy's dead and took 56 prisoners, not including 60 wounded; the Confederate dead were removed by them. General Osterhaus estimates the enemy's loss in his front at 500. He discovered 131 graves in a secluded part of the field.

General Logan says that in front of the 15th Corps there were found 500 killed, left on the field, and 5,000 wounded and 241 prisoners. The 15th Corps had only 154 killed, wounded and missing. In front of General Corse's Division of the 17th Corps, the enemy lost 500 killed, wounded and missing, while that Corps suffered the insignificant loss of 18 killed and wounded. Col. Bryant, of General Blair's Corps, estimates the enemy's loss in his front at 262 killed, wounded and missing. The great difference in the number killed on each side respectively shows the folly of assaulting a well armed and well intrenched line of old soldiers by even greatly superior numbers.

The Army of the Ohio and Cumberland engaged the enemy in a severe and bloody battle, in which the Confederates were defeated with great loss. On the night of the 31st, fifty men of the 100th, under command of the writer, erected a fort in the rear of the right of that Regiment. On the 1st, skirmishing was kept up. One man of Company "E" was killed, and Sergeant Isaac Hockman and one man of Company "G" wounded. There was heavy firing on the left all night.

At about 2 o'clock A. M. the sounds of heavy explosions were heard, in the direction of Atlanta, about twenty miles to the north. At 4 A. M. there was another series of explosions, which it was then thought might be a night attack on the 20th Corps, but were in fact caused by the blowing up of the enemy's magazines when they retreated from Atlanta.

The 100th Indiana in the Battle of Lovejoy.

On the 2d, at daylight our skirmishers advanced to Jonesboro and found that the enemy had retreated toward Lovejoy. By order of General Walcutt, eight companies of the 100th took the advance of the 15th Army Corps and moved south toward Lovejoy. About half a mile south of Jonesboro they struck the enemy's cavalry. The 100th Indiana deployed on the right and the 6th Iowa on the left of the road to Lovejoy.

"Then commenced a brisk, running fight for the next four miles, the 100th Indiana driving the enemy so fast that he did not have time to take advantage of the rail works previously constructed." The enemy then formed a long line of infantry in the front and opened on the 100th with artillery to prevent the capture of a wagon train in plain sight. These two Regiments were so exhausted that, by order of General Walcutt, they were relieved by the 46th Ohio and 103d Illinois. These at once charged the Rebel lines with great impetuosity, causing them to burn some of their wagons and retreat rapidly toward Lovejoy.

"September 2d the Brigade, especially the 100th Indiana, the 103d Illinois and the 46th Ohio and the 6th Iowa in advance, in pursuit of Hardee, did splendidly, captured forty prisoners and punishing the enemy severely in killed and wounded." (Official Report General Walcutt, Sec. 74, p. 322.)

Lieutenant J. H. Moore, Co. "A," was mortally wounded by a shell. We took a commanding position close up to the Rebel main line. We heard here for the first, of the fall of Atlanta.

We strenghtened our works and kept firing on the enemy. On the 4th, Anthony Olinger, of

Company "A," was mortally wounded by a shot in the head. Sergeant Drake, Company "E," was also severely wounded. The bullets flew in close proximity to our heads all the time we were at that place.

On the 5th we got up at 1 A. M. and marched back to Jonesboro and encamped on the spot, where we fought on the 31st. We arrived there in the mud at 1 o'clock A. M., having marched only six miles and a half in 24 hours and went into camp tired, wet and hungry.

On the 6th we took a stroll over the battlefield of the 31st of August at Jonesboro. One house in the town contained 250 Confederate wounded. The effects of our shot, shell and minnie balls were to be seen everywhere. On the 8th we reached East Point, and went into camp, where we remained, drawing some supplies and going through the routine of camp life for two or three weeks.

In Camp at East Point.

On the same day we arrived from Lovejoy and went into camp at East Point, General Hood sent in a flag of truce to General Sherman's headquarters, to arrange for an exchange of prisoners, to which the latter acceded, with a specific understanding that Major R. M. Johnson of the 100th Indiana was to be brought from Charleston, South Carolina, where he was confined in a position which was exposed to the fire of our own batteries.

On the 19th, Col. Heath left for the North

and the command of the Regiment devolved upon Captain Headington, of Company "H," who performed that duty with credit to himself and to the entire satisfaction of the officers and soldiers of the Regiment.

September 21st our scouts reported great activity in Hood's army. On the 22d the truce for the exchange of prisoners expired and the details from the 100th to attend the exchange returned to camp.

September 24th scouts reported that Jefferson Davis was at Macon, Georgia, on his way to pay a visit to Hood's Army.

September 25th Jefferson Davis, accompanied by two of his aides-de-camp, arrived at General Hood's headquarters about 3 P. M. He made a speech to Hardee's soldiers, in which he detailed the plans of General Hood. Our scouts were present and heard the speech. They then stole through the Rebel lines and on the morning of the 26th were at General Sherman's headquarters and gave him the details of the speech. Davis was enthusiastically received by the Confederate soldiers. At 8 P. M. on the 26th, he made a short speech. He told the Kentucky and Tennessee troops in Hood's Army that they were going to march around Sherman's Army, and that they would soon be at their old homes in Tennessee and Kentucky.

September 27th, at 6 P. M., Davis and his attendants left Hood's camp for Montgomery, Alabama. On the 29th, Hood moved his headquarters from Palmetto to Pray's Church, and his Army crossed the Chattahoochee, moving to the northwest. (Vol. 77, page 803.)

On the 29th, Major R. M. Johnson, having

Major R. M. Johnson,
After his exchange as a prisoner.
(From an old war times picture.)

been exchanged by request of General Sherman, returned to the Regiment and assumed command, he having been under fire at Charleston, South Carolina, with other Union officers, who were placed in a certain position in that city, which was made known to the Union forces, so as to prevent them from throwing shot or shell into that part of the city. The Major related some terrible experiences which he had had while he was a prisoner in the hands of the enemy. His return was the occasion of a demonstration by the officers and men of the command, for we all liked Major Johnson. Under Confederate prison life and rations, his flesh had rapidly disappeared. He looked as if he had suffered greatly while in Rebel prisons, but reduced as he was in flesh, he was as haughty, brave and proud in spirit as before his capture.

Retrospective View of the 120 Days' Fighting.

Let us now review the ground we have passed over so hastily, for the purpose of obtaining a more comprehensive notion of the vastness of the work we had performed from the 5th of May until the 5th of September, 1864. At the latter date we had driven the Rebel Army out of its innumerable fortifications in Northern Georgia, and more than a hundred miles over and across a mountainous and hilly country, through gorges, gaps and passes in the mountains, deemed by the enemy to be impassable for any army, and over and across several large rivers and into the fastnesses beyond, assaulting their many almost impregnable positions at every opportunity. We had just taken Atlanta and had pressed the retreating army forty miles beyond that place.

Several sanguinary battles had been fought, in nearly all of which we were victorious, although our enemy occupied his earthworks in chosen strongholds. Prior to and at Resaca he fought us from the mountain tops; such as Rocky Face, Buzzard Roost, Tunnel Hill and Taylor's Ridge, and from such fortified places as Ships, Dug and Snake Gaps and other fastnesses. Yet his losses were as great as ours. At Resaca his losses were 2,800 and ours 2,600. On the 20th of July, at Peach Tree Creek, our loss was 1,710 killed, wounded and missing, while that of the enemy was 4,796. On the 22d of July General Hood, who had succeeded General Johnston, on the 17th made a sortie upon the Union army of the Tennessee, in which the total Union loss was 3,641, of which 1,000 were prisoners, making the total killed and wounded 2,641. The total loss of the enemy was 8,499, of which 3,220 were killed on the field. On the 28th of July General Hood made another sortie on the Army of the Tennessee at Ezra church, on the Union right, in which the total Union loss was 50 killed, 439 wounded and 73 missing, total 562; while the enemy's loss was "6,000 or 7,000" (Logan's Official Report, Serial 74, p. 105); or as taken from the enemy's own reports, their loss was 4,642. Thus in the three engagements of July 20th, 22d and 28th the total Union loss was 5,913, while the total loss of the enemy in the same engagements was 19,295, a difference of 13,382, or more than three to one in favor of the

Union soldiers, where the battles were fought, mainly without works, or very temporary works, as was the case with those three battles around Atlanta. In nearly all the others the enemy occupied the mountains, hills and gaps. The loss of the enemy cannot be known accurately, as in many cases official reports of their casualties were designedly never made. The following estimates are from the most reliable sources obtainable. From May 5th to May 9th the enemy lost 600 men, from May 9th to May 16th we have no complete official report but he lost at and about Resaca 2,800 killed, wounded and missing. At and about Dallas, Georgia, he lost 3,000 killed, wounded and missing, from May 25th to June 4th. From June 9th to June 30th, about Kenesaw, Pine Mountain, Pine Knob, Golgotha, McAfee's Cross Roads, Lattimore's Mills, Culp's House, Powder Springs, and the engagements at and about Kenesaw, 4,600 killed, wounded and missing, and from July 6th to July 10th he lost 600 at Vinings and the Chattahoochee River, and at Jonesboro he lost 2,000 killed, wounded and missing. These losses make a total of 30,937. But these do not include many small engagements, nor do they include the enemy's loss from the 28th of July to the 26th of August, during the siege of Atlanta, which if estimated inside of all reason was at least 5,000. During the month which the siege lasted the artillery and musketry firing was incessant, making the total loss within all reason 40,000, from Dalton to Lovejoy. During this time our cavalry had several engagements, where the losses were heavy. These estimates are from Sherman's and Logan's official reports and "Johnston's Narrative" and Hood's "Advance and Retreat." This loss of 40,000 deducted from the 86,000 which the Confederates had at Kenesaw, less their losses, would leave Hood about 45,000 after the evacuation of Atlanta, which is just about what he actually had. The losses in the Rebel army for August and to September 5th were 7,443 killed, wounded and missing. The Union loss during the same time was 5,139, and the total Union loss from Dalton to Lovejoy was 27,245 killed and wounded and 4,442 missing, total 31,687, being a difference of 8,313 in favor of the Union army. The Rebels took 4,442 prisoners, while the Union army took 12,983. Their names, rank and Regiments are on the official rolls (Sherman Memoirs, p. 132), so that the army under Sherman, during the 120 days fighting had destroyed several arsenals and depots, had taken one-half of the state of Georgia, 100 miles of the enemy's country, had consumed all that could be found in that territory, and had destroyed one-half of the whole Rebel army in its front, and was yet strong, defiant and eager for a battle. Courageous, well disciplined, proud of its achievements, flushed with victory and commanded by generals who, like the men in the ranks, were patriots and acted together harmoniously and for the good of their country; so that upon the whole the net results of the summer's fighting was greatly in favor of the Union army from every point of view.

The 100th Indiana in the Pursuit of Hood's Army—1864.

As soon as the Union Army had withdrawn from Lovejoy to the vicinity of Atlanta, General Hood began to recruit and increase his army from every available source. His encampment was at and about Lovejoy, Newman and Palmetto, only a few miles southwest of ours. He began to move his forces to his left gradually before Jefferson Davis visited his camp. After that event, however, increased activity was noticeable in his camp, and he moved to the west of Atlanta, so that by the 1st of October his army had all crossed the Chattahoochee River, about twenty miles southwest of that place, and his headquarters were at Dark Corners, about ten miles northwest of East Point. He had evidently begun the march around our left and to the north, as detailed by Jefferson Davis. There was no other proper course open to General Sherman than to follow him. We had spies in his camp every day, and our General knew every movement that he made. The 4th, 14th, 15th, 17th, 20th and 23d Corps of the Union Army lay quietly in camp. Girard's cavalry was at Decatur, six miles east of Atlanta, and Kilpatrick's near Sandtown, eight miles west. October 2d the 4th Corps was ordered to prepare to march. The Rebel Army was at Powder Springs. October 3d, the 17th Corps was ordered to march to Smyrna Church on the 4th, and the 4th Corps was ordered to be in line at that place on that date. Stewart's Rebel Corps arrived at Big Shanty, and tore up and destroyed several miles of railroad, working all night for that purpose.

(See also Serial 39 p. 783.) On the 4th the 15th Corps received marching orders, and on the morning of the 5th broke camp early and marched northward from East Point. We left Atlanta to our right crossed the Chattahoochee at Vinings, then marched in deep mud until 10 P. M., and went into line five miles southwest of Marietta. We made twenty-five miles.

While Stewart's Corps was yet at Big Shanty destroying the railroad, an order from General Hood was received by him, directing that French's Division of his Corps should "Move up the railroad and fill up the deep cut at Allatoona with brush, rails, dirt, etc." In obedience to this order, French moved his Division from Big Shanty at 3:30 P. M., and arrived at Acworth, six miles distant, before sunset, having with him Major Myrith and twelve (12) pieces of artillery. There he was detained until 11 P. M. waiting for rations. As soon as these were drawn, the march was resumed. Citizens reported to French that there were about three and one-half Regiments in the garrison and about 100 men at the bridge. French arrived before Allatoona at 3:30 A. M. on the 5th. (Serial 77, page 14.)

The Battle of Allatoona.

Allatoona is about 18 miles northwest of Kenesaw and about 8 miles south of the Etowah river, and is the place where the railroad passes through the Allatoona range of hills. The railroad cut is nearly 100 feet deep, and on each side of this cut the Union Army had erected a redoubt. This is the cut which General French was ordered, by General Hood, to fill up with brush, dirt and rails. The place was garrisoned by 890 men. General Corse, in obedience to the orders of General Sherman, arrived at Allatoona at 1 A. M. on the morning of the 5th, with a total of 1,054 re-enforcements, making with the garrison, 1,944 men. Soon after the re-enforcements were unloaded, the enemy fired on our picket line (3 A. M). The 18th Wisconsin was sent out to re-enforce the picket line, and just before break of day the enemy were pressing so hard on the pickets that a battalion of the 7th Illinois was sent out as an additional support.

As soon as it was light enough to see, General Corse withdrew the men from the outer lines to the inner line of works on the summit of the hills on either side of the cut. At 6 A. M. the cannonading and musketry was brisk. At 8 A. M. a flag of truce came in, on the Cartersville road, bearing a summons from General French to surrender in these words:

"Commanding Officer U. S. Forces,
      "Allatoona.

"Sir: I have placed the forces under my command in such a position that you are surrounded, and to avoid a needless effusion of blood, I call on you to surrender your forces at once and unconditionally. Five minutes will be allowed you to decide. Should you accede to this, you will be treated in the most honorable manner as prisoners of war. I have the honor to be,

  "Very respectfully yours,
      "S. G. French.
"Major General Commanding C. S. Forces."

To this demand for a surrender, General Corse answered as follows:

"Major General S. G. French,
"C. S. Army, etc.

"Your communication demanding surrender of my command I acknowledge receipt of, and would respectfully reply, that we are prepared for the 'needless effusion of blood' whenever it is agreeable to you.

"I am very respectfully
"Your Obedient Servant,
"Jno. M. Corse,
"Brigadier General Commanding U. S. Forces."

The men in the fort were notified by General Corse to prepare for a hard fight. In a very short time Young's Brigade of 900 Texans made a furious assault on the 39th Iowa and 7th Illinois. They moved along with great rapidity until they struck Rowitt's Brigade, and while the fighting was going on at that point, Sear's Rebel Brigade came in line of battle from the north and swept the Union line back until the 39th Iowa was flanked, but this also brought the enemy's flank within range of Tourtelotte's line, from which they suffered severely. The two Brigades of the enemy rallied and the fighting became sanguinary, and had it not been for the desperate resistance of the 39th Iowa, the battle might have been lost. The enemy recoiled, and what was left of the 7th and 93d Illinois and the 39th Iowa, fell back into the fort. These three Regiment's had fought Young's and a portion of Sears' and Cockrell's Brigades for two hours and a half. Col. Redfield of the 39th Iowa was killed—shot four times. The 12th Wisconsin battery did heroic work. The enemy kept closing in on the fort. General Corse was wounded at 1 P. M. At 2 P. M. the enemy massed behind a hill 150 yards northwest of the fort, but they were unable to do so successfully under the withering fire of the Union lines. Charge after charge was made by the Confederates, and the battle raged incessantly until about 4 P. M., when the enemy withdrew, leaving his dead and wounded on the field. Our loss during this engagement was as follows:

	ENG.	KLD.	WD.	MSG.	TOT
7th Ill., 9 Co's	267	35	67	39	141
12th Ills. Detached	155	9	49	..	58
50th Ills., 8 Co's	267	15	63	..	78
57th Ills. Co's "A" "B"	61	4	8	1	13
93rd Ills. Infantry	290	21	52	10	83
39th Iowa, 8 Co's	280	40	52	78	170
4th Minnesota,	450	11	33	..	44
18th Wisconsin	150	2	12	84	98
12th Wisconsin Bat.	24	5	16	..	21
Totals	1944	142	352	212	706

Of the 706 casualties, 212 were missing; those were mainly on picket and were taken prisoners at the Block House. This fixes our loss in killed and wounded at 494. (Official report General Corse, Serial 77, p. 766.)

The Confederate loss at Allatoona, will never be truly known, as their official reports are so notoriously unreliable that no credence can be given to them. In this instance, 231 Rebel dead were buried on the field at the time. We took 411 prisoners, three colors and 800 stand of arms.

Brigadier-General Young, who was captured, said that their loss was 2,000. The assaulting forces consisted of the 4th, 35th, 36th, 39th, 46th and 7th Regiments of Mississippi (Sear's), the 1st, 4th, 2d, 6th, 3rd, 5th Missouri Infantry, and the 1st and 2d Missouri Cavalry; the 32d, 10th, 14th and 9th Texas Regiments, and the 29th and 39th North Carolina, and 12 pieces of artillery, under Major Myrick. That is, 18 Regiments of Infantry, 2 of Cavalry and 12 cannon. During the week following the battle, the garrison found nearly a hundred dead bodies, in addition to those buried by General Corse. Those were men who had gone away from the line after being fatally wounded, and died. (Serial 77, page 718, et seq.)

For the purpose of creating an Iron Brigade, to be used for assaulting and routing the enemy, and driving him from selected positions quickly, General Sherman caused the 100th Indiana, 97th Indiana, 6th Iowa, 46th Ohio, 26th, 40th and 103d Illinois, to be armed in part with Spencer repeating rifles. (See Sherman's Memoirs 2, p. 187.)

The 100th Indiana camped in a field adjacent to the Allatoona battle ground. Some bodies were found in the brush by our men, which had not been found by the burying squad. The men of the 100th slept two hours, had reveille at 4 A. M., crossed the Etowah river and went into camp at 5 P. M. four miles south of Kingston. The men were very tired, having marched 16 miles. Total from East Point, 69 miles.

On the 10th the 100th Indiana marched 15 miles, to within four miles of Rome, a total of 84 miles, and bivouacked for the night.

On the 11th the Regiment reported early to department headquarters, and in obedience to orders, we were sent on a scouting expedition, directly towards the advance of the Confederate Army, to the north and west. our route was diagonally across the country. We marched 12 miles to Floyd, and halted at dark, prepared our meal without fire, then marched rapidly through a mountainous or hilly country 10 miles to get 2 miles, which, on account of the miserable roads we traveled, took nearly all night, making 25 miles, or a total of 109 miles. At daylight we lay down in a field to rest. We slept one hour, at a point 25 miles from Resaca. We then started on good roads and went into camp at Calhoun at sundown. We were all very tired, having marched 50 miles, with but one hour's sleep, and a total of 129 miles. The first place Hood's Army struck north of Allatoona was Resaca. The 17th Iowa, Colonel Clark R. Wever, garrisoned the place. General Hood disposed his Army in front of Resaca, intending, perhaps, to assault the place. He demanded the surrender of the post upon such terms as have never been considered in line with civilized warfare, in these words:

"Headquarters Army of the Tennessee.

"In the field, October 12, 1864.

"To the officer commanding United States forces,
"Resaca, Georgia.

"Sir: I demand the immediate and unconditional surrender of the post and garrison under your command, and should this be acceded to, all white officers and soldiers will be paroled in a few days. If the place is carried by assault, no prisoners will be taken.

"J. B. Hood, General."

At the time this unprecedented demand was made, Col. Clark R. Wever was in command of the garrison. His answer to the demand was as follows:

"Headquarters, 2d Brigade, 3d Division,
"15th Army Corps, Resaca, Georgia,
"October 12, 1864.
"To General J. B. Hood:

"Your communication of this day just received. In reply I have to state that I am somewhat surprised at the concluding paragraph, to the effect, that if the place is carried by assault, no prisoners will be taken. In my opinion I can hold this post. If you want it, come and take it.

"I am, General, very respectfully, your most obedient servant,

"Clark R. Wever, Com'dg Officer."

This stern refusal to surrender probably led General Hood to believe that if he assaulted Col. Wever's forces he would meet with a repetition of French's experience at Allatoona, and he withdrew his forces and moved on to Snake Gap. We had reveile at 3 A. M., reached Resaca at 8:30 A. M., halted a short time for rations, then moved rapidly toward Snake Gap, where firing could be plainly heard. We entered the Gap at 5 P. M. The Confederates retreated from Resaca through this gap and they felled a great many trees across the narrow gulch to impede our pursuit. We passed over the field before the dead had been collected for burial. On the 16th we had reveille 4:30, marched at 7. We passed through Villainow twelve hours behind the Rebel Army; we crossed Taylor's Ridge through Ship's Gap. The Rebels had an intrenched line of battle on the crest of the pass to resist our approach. Our Brigade had the advance. We formed in two lines and assaulted the enemy in position; the 100th Indiana was in the second line. The 29th Missouri engaged the enemy in front; our Brigade passed to their right and the 26th Iowa was moved around their left, and when the attack was made most of the Rebel force fell into our hands, including two whole companies of the 24th South Carolina Infantry (Serial 77, p. 742). Quite a number were killed and wounded. The prisoners had parched corn in their haversacks. We encamped shortly after passing through Ship's Gap, and the army passed to the front and encamped on the western slopes of Taylor's Ridge

The long lines of camp fires made a beautiful scene at night. On the morning of the 17th our skirmishers could be seen for miles gradually driving the Confederates before them. We moved down the mountain slope at 10:30 A. M. and marched to Lafayette about five miles distant and went into camp. On the 18th we marched at 8 A. M. from Lafayette almost directly south, crossed the Chatooga River at Island Town and went into camp three miles north of Summerville. The Chatooga valley was very rich and we supplied ourselves well with forage. We had now marched 179 miles since we left East Point. On the 19th we marched rapidly in pursuit of the enemy to a point near the Alabama state line, nine miles southwest of Summerville,

Georgia, and went into camp at 7 P. M. Robert M. Steele, of Captain Dalbey's Company "I," died there. Forage was plenty, fine water and a good country. The Confederate army retreated rapidly before us in the direction of Gadsden, Etowah county, Alabama.

The roads during this day's march (20th) were extremely hilly and mountainous. We pursued the enemy sixteen miles in zig-zag directions. We crossed a very rough mountain after dark and went into camp near Gaylesville, Alabama. The Rebel army was forty-eight hours ahead of us. They kept to the south of the mountains and went into camp at the town of Gadsden, Alabama. Our cavalry picked up a great many stragglers from their army. We had now marched 204 miles.

On the 21st we passed through Gaylesville and went into camp on Little River, Alabama, near its junction with the Chatooga. We marched nine miles. On the 22d and 23d we remained in camp at Little River. Our cavalry came in from the front and reported the enemy in force under General Wheeler in an intrenched position at Blount's place, near King's Hill. General Howard ordered the strength of the Rebel position to be tested and our Division (Wood's) and Hazen's and Batteries "B," First Michigan and First Iowa were directed to perform this service.

The 100th Indiana Pursues Hood's Army to Gadsden, Alabama.

At 2 P. M. on the 24th we marched westwardly nine miles and went into camp at sundown near Leesburg, and on the 25th we had reveille at 3:30 and marched at 5 A. M. We soon struck the enemy's cavalry pickets and skirmishing began. They fell back to their main line at Blount's place, where the cavalry had reported the Rebels in force. Our skirmish line drove the enemy away while our lines of battle were being formed. General Osterhaus having ascertained from citizens that there was a force of 2,000 Rebels at Turkeytown valley, on the Gadsden road, about five miles further on, we moved against them, and when our forces had got almost through the valley, the Rebels opened on them with artillery. Wood's Division formed in line on the left and two Brigades of Hazen's Division on the right. The Rebels were on high ground in our front, with about 2,000 men and two pieces of artillery. They were intrenched so as to sweep the whole valley. We engaged their attention in front with our skirmishers and battery "B," 1st Michigan, so closely that they never observed Hazen's two Brigades, which, as well as Jones' Cavalry Regiment, were ordered forward. The latter delivered his volleys right into the Rebel ranks, which threw them into the wildest confusion and they fled precipitately. Cornelius Coleman, of Company "D," was the only man of the 100th wounded. This was the parting salute to Hood's Army, the 100th being the last to deliver the parting blow. General Sherman had determined to march to the sea and to let Hood go to Tennessee. At this moment an order was received from General Howard not to pursue the fleeing Rebels, so we marched back four miles and went into camp, and on the 26th we marched at 7 A. M. and reached our camp on Little River at 2:45 P. M., having marched exactly 48 miles in 48 hours. This engagement took place nine miles northeast of Gadsden, Alabama.

The 100th Indiana Faced Toward the Sea.

We remained in camp on the 27th and 28th. On the 29th we had reveille at 3:30 A. M., and marched to Cedar Bluffs, on the road leading back to Rome, Georgia, we crossed the Coosa on the 17 A. C. Pontoons; marched 11 miles, total 261 miles, and encamped in a miserable place on the south side of the river. This was the first day's march back toward Atlanta and the sea.

On the 30th we went into camp at 2:30, within four miles of Cave Springs, southwest of Rome, Georgia. The Rebel guerrillas fired on some of our men. On the 31st we only marched four miles to Cave Springs and went into camp. On the 1st of November we marched nine miles to Cedartown, almost directly south of Rome about twenty miles. The guerrillas slipped up and fired on some of our men during the day.

On the 1st of November we marched all day in the rain. On the 2d we marched at daybreak 12 miles and encamped in the pine woods on the Yellow Stone road; total, 302 miles. On the 3rd we marched 15 miles in the mud and rain and encamped on the Burnt Hickory road, in the woods. On the 4th we took the Powder Springs road and marched 15 miles, mainly in the direction of Vinings, or Smyrna. We moved out early on the 5th to the southeast, struck our old works at Smyrna at dark, and encamped five miles southwest of Marietta, Georgia. Marched 15 miles; total, 347 miles. Here we halted to prepare ourselves for continuing our march toward the sea.

On the 6th we made estimates for clothing and shoes, both of which the men needed very badly. On the 9th we were paid. On the 12th we destroyed railroad iron and ties—burned the ties and bent and twisted the rails after being heated in the middle by the burning ties. On the 13th we drew clothing and then marched through the city of Atlanta and encamped at Whitehall, near our old works during the siege—marched 15 miles; total since we left East Point, in pursuit of Hood, 362 miles, a considerable part of which was in zigzag directions, on account of the roads, being very crooked or occupied by other columns.

The 100th Indiana on the March to the Sea.

MEMORABILIA BY E. J. SHERLOCK.

The march through Georgia to the sea was first thought of by General Sherman. Prior to the fall of Atlanta such a campaign was unheard of. But Sherman had such a movement in contemplation and was maturing his plans for its execution prior to Jefferson Davis' visit to Hood's army on the 25th of September, for on the 20th, before we started to follow Hood, he wrote Gen. Grant that "If you will fix a day I will be in Savannah. I will insure our possession of Macon and a point on the river below Augusta. The possession of the Savannah River is more than fatal to the possibility of Southern independence. They may stand the fall of Richmond, but not all of Georgia."

Numerous dispatches which passed between Grant, Sherman, Lincoln and Secretary Stanton, contained in Serial No. 79, all go to show that the most that the authorities did at Washington was to acquiesce in Sherman's plans to march to the sea.

On the 13th Grant wrote the Secretary of War that he believed that Sherman's proposition to march through Georgia was the best that could be adopted, and that "such an army as Sherman had, with such a commander, would be hard to corner or capture," and at 11 o'clock that day, General Grant made an order for the same supplies for us which we received at Savannah after the fall of Fort McAllister, and at 8:30 P. M., on the 13th of October, 1864, E. M. Stanton wired General Sherman that his plans had been approved and that supplies would be sent down to Hilton Head and would be sent to him on transports (Serial 79, pp. 239-240).

Sherman notified Grant on the 7th that the movement to the sea would begin on the 10th or the day after, to which Grant answered on the same day, "Great good attend you." (Serial 79, p. 679.)

On the 7th the engineer's department was ordered to "take special charge of the destruction of Atlanta; of all depots, car houses, shops, factories, foundries, being careful to knock down all furnace chimneys and break down the arches." (Serial 79, p. 680.)

At that date the 15th Army Corps was bivouacked at Camp Smyrna. The men were being paid, clothed and equipped. On the 9th special field orders No. 120 were issued from Kingston by General Sherman for the government of the army during the contemplated movement through Georgia. A brief synopsis of which was:

First: That the right wing, the 15th and 17th Corps, was to be commanded by General Howard and the left wing, the 14th and 20th by General Slocum.

Second: The order of march was provided for—the cavalry under Kilpatrick was to receive special orders from General Sherman.

Third: Provided for the movement and the kind and number of trains.

Fourth: Provided that the "Army will forage liberally on the country, etc., etc." The manner in which it must be done, and that no soldier should enter a private dwelling.

Fifth: Provided for the destruction of such property, as was regarded contraband of war, by orders of army commanders only.

Sixth: Provided for the confiscation of horses, mules, and such other property, as might be needed by the infantry and cavalry, distinguishing between the rich and the poor, in the seizure thereof.

Seventh: Provided for taking such negroes, as would be serviceable in the army, as teamsters or pioneers.

Eighth: Related to the organization of a good pioneer corps for each Army Corps. (Serial 79, pp. 713-14.)

On the 10th General Corse was ordered to destroy, during the night, "All public property not needed by his command, in Rome, Georgia, such as foundries, bridges, mills, workshops, warehouses, etc. The 14th Corps was ordered to destroy the railroad from the Etowah to Big Shanty. The 15th and 17th from Kenesaw to Chattahoochee, and the 20th Corps from that river into and including the city of Atlanta." (No. 79, pp. 627 and 729.)

The destruction of Atlanta began on the morning of the 11th of November, 1864. General Sherman left Kingston for the front on the morning of the 12th. By evening of the latter date the 14th, 15th, 17th and 20th Army Corps were all concentrated at Atlanta, with the cavalry on the front and right of the 15th Corps, the latter being commanded by General P. J. Osterhaus, the 17th by General Frank P. Blair.

The 15th Corps was composed of four Divisions: the 1st, General C. R. Woods; 2nd, General W. B. Hazen; 3rd; General John E. Smith; 4th, General John M. Corse.

The 17th had three Divisions: the 1st, General Joseph A. Mower; the 2nd, General M. D. Leggett, and the 3rd, General Giles A. Smith.

The 14th Army Corps had three Divisions: the 1st, General W. P. Carlin; the 2nd, General James D. Morgan, and the 3rd, General Absalom Baird.

The 20th Corps had three Divisions: the 1st, General Nathaniel J. Jackson; the 2nd, General John W. Geary, and the 3rd, General

William T. Ward; making thirteen Divisions in all.

The Cavalry Division was commanded by Brigadier General Judson Kilpatrick. One Brigade was commanded by Col. Eli H. Murray and the other by Col. Smith D. Adkins.

November 14th our forces consisted of 55,329 infantry, 5,063 cavalry, and 1,812 artillery; total, 62,204, as good fighting men as the world ever produced. Skilled in the art of war, inured to hardship, well disciplined, of excellent morals, and as brave and fearless as lions in their native jungle. The picture of health, flushed with victory after victory, on many bloody and well-won fields; they fairly bounded, as they marched out into the enemy's country, with all the confidence and self-reliance, which an army can feel, which is deeply conscious of its own invincibility and superior prowess.

Such was the character of the army which, on Tuesday morning, November 15, 1864, marched out of Atlanta, feeling that it was unconquerable before any army which could be brought to oppose it. On the latter date we had reveille at 3 A. M., and the 15th and 17th Corps and the cavalry moved out. We left East Point to our left, passed Rough and Ready Station; the 97th Indiana in advance, drove the Rebel Cavalry from our front after a lively skirmish. We went into camp at 2 P. M., having marched 8 miles southeast of Jonesboro and 36 miles from Camp Smyrna, which was 14 miles north of Atlanta. We found some Rebel pickets at Rough and Ready, who fled percipitately on the approach of our advance. A force of Rebels made some show of resistance at Jonesboro, but it was quickly driven away; but at Stockbridge, near our camp, the Rebel General Lewis with about 1,000 men and a section of artillery, made some resistance, but was soon routed by the 29th Missouri, which was our advance. There was some cannonading in the evening; the day closed with the four skirmishes of East Point, Rough and Ready, Jonesboro and Stockbridge. (92–81)

Stockbridge Village, November 16, 1864; marched at 9 A. M. We were in the rear, having had the advance yesterday. Forage was plenty and water good; passed through McDonough and five miles to the south; marched 14 miles; total 50 miles. The cavalry found a force of Wheeler's army in the old Rebel works at Lovejoy. They showed fight; Col. Murray charged their line, captured two three inch rifled cannon and killed and wounded a large number. Wheeler, after the engagement, made a stand at Bear Creek, but was again charged by the 10th Ohio, when his lines broke and his forces fled to Griffin, 14 miles distant, with a loss of killed, wounded and prisoners of 500. 100,000 rounds of ammunition, three caisons, four boxes of fixed ammunition and 175 stand of small arms were destroyed. The advance of the 15th Corps met a Rebel force at Cotton River Bridge, which was quickly dispersed, and the day closed with the action at Lovejoy and the two skirmishes of Bear Creek and Cotton River Bridge (92–362).

On the 17th we started from camp, five miles south of McDonough, at 1:30 P. M. One mile below Locust Grove, the 3d and 4th Divisions of the 15th Corps took the (left) Jackson road. We camped at 10:30 P. M. on the main Macon road, between Griffin and Jackson, having marched 15 miles; total, 65 miles. Lewis' Rebel Brigade was reported at the bridge on the Towaligo River. The 5th Kentucky, Col. Baldwin, charged their position and found only a weak line, which was quickly routed, the main body having retreated, and the day closed with the skirmish at Towaligo Creek (92-1).

On the 18th the 100th Indiana took the advance, directly east to Indian Springs, a summer resort, and encamped; got plenty of Rebel newspapers, printed on all kinds of paper; marched five miles; total, 70 miles.

The Confederate officials promulgated some highly inflammatory addresses to the people of Georgia, exhorting them to rise up in their might and crush out the invaders. But the Union Army moved along from day to day, the same as if they had never been delivered. The following are specimen appeals by those who kept out of danger:

"Richmond, Va., Nov. 18, 1864.
"To the people of Georgia:
"You have now the best opportunity ever yet presented to destroy the enemy. Put everything at the disposal of our Generals, remove all provisions from the path of the invader and put all obstructions in his path. Every citizen with his gun and every negro with his spade and axe can do the work of a soldier. You can destroy the enemy by retarding his march. Georgians, be firm! Act promptly and fear not.

B. H. Hill, Senator."
"I most cordially approve the above.
"James A. Seddon,
"Secretary of War."

And the following is another address of about the same tenor:

"Corinth, Nov. 18, 1864.
"To the People of Georgia:

"Arise for the defense of your native soil! Rally round your patriotic Governor and gallant soldiers! Obstruct and destroy all roads in Sherman's front, flank and rear, and his army will soon starve in your midst! Be confident and resolute! Trust in an overruling Providence and success will crown your efforts! I hasten to join you in defense of your home and friends.

"G. T. Beauregard." (92-867)

These appeals did not cause the Georgians to *arise*, nor did General Beauregard ever join them where there was any danger. He sent the following advice, however, to General Wheeler:

"Major General Wheeler:

"Employ your cavalry to best advantage, retarding advance of Sherman's Army and destroying supplies in his front.

"G. T. Beauregard." (92-867)

Gen. Wheeler obeyed the order far enough to get in our front, but he was not able to retard our advance. Gen. Lee dispatched Jefferson Davis as follows:

"Petersburg, Nov. 19, 1864.
"His Excellency Jefferson Davis,
"Richmond, Va.

"All roads, bridges, provisions, etc., within Sherman's reach should be destroyed. The population must turn out. * * * Savannah will probably be Sherman's object. Troops that can be spared from Charleston, Savannah, etc., should take the field under Hardee.

"R. E. Lee." (92-869)

And some Rebel Congressmen at Richmond contributed their advice to the people of Georgia, as follows:

"Richmond, November 19, 1864.

"To the People of Georgia:

"We have had a special conference with President Davis and the Secretary of War. Let every man fly to arms! Remove your negroes, cattle, horses, and provisions from Sherman's army and burn what you cannot carry. Burn all bridges and block up the roads in his route, assail the invader, in front, flank and rear, by night and by day; let him have no rest.

"Julian Hartridge and

"Six other members of Congress." (92-869).

Jefferson Davis also told the people of Georgia how to defeat and destroy us in the following dispatch:

"Richmond, Va., November 22, 1864.

"Col. William Browne, Aid de Camp, Augusta Yards: Convey to all Generals my instructions, that every effort will be made by destroying bridges, felling trees, planting subterra shells and otherwise to obstruct the advance of the enemy. All supplies * * * will be destroyed * * * to impede the march of Sherman's army and prevent it from foraging on the country.

"Jefferson Davis." (92-880)

So it appears by the record, that Jefferson Davis, Robert E. Lee, Beauregard, and the members of the Confederate Congress all advised the South to destroy all that was in Sherman's front. In some instances the citizens of Georgia were ably assisted in carrying out some portions of these orders by the soldiers of the Union army; and the following dispatch shows that Davis was in favor of filling the roadways with bombs to retard our advance.

"Richmond, Nov. 18, 1864.
"General H. Cobb, Macon, Ga.:
"Get out every man. * * * Employ negroes in obstructing roads by every practicable means. Col. Rains, at Augusta, can furnish you with shells prepared to explode by pressure, and these will be effective to check an advance.
"Jeff Davis." (92-Davis-865.)

On the 19th we marched at 7 A. M. Company "A," 100th Indiana, was advance guards of the Division. Moved 7 miles to Planter's Factory on the Ocmulgee River, said to be owned by White & Scott of Macon, had dinner of biscuit, butter and burnt wheat coffee. Company "A" guarded the factory, crossed on the pontoons, marched in mud and rain, over a rough country, in a zigzag course until 2 A. M. Roads were simply impassable for anything but Yankees. Marched 14 miles; total 84 (92-1).

The rear of the 15th Corps did not get across the Ocmulgee until the 20th. We marched at 5 A. M., again in the advance. We sent out large forage parties, got plenty of corn meal, meat and flour. The 17th Corps took the Milledgeville road at Hillsboro. We marched all night, halted on the field where Stoneman was defeated, marched 17 miles; total 101 miles. The First Brigade of Hazen's Division, 15th Army Corps, routed the Rebel cavalry at Clinton, a town which lay in our line of march. Kilpatrick met the enemy's cavalry under Wheeler four miles out of Macon; he drove them across Walnut Creek and charged into their works at Macon, but could not hold them. A train of cars were burned and a mile of track torn up near Griswoldville, and the day closed with these four skirmishes with Wheeler's cavalry (92-363).

Thirteen cars, loaded with car wheels, were burned at Griswoldville on the 21st by the 9th Michigan, as well as the soap and candle factory and an arsenal engaged in manufacturing pistols and sabres for the Confederate Army, embracing in all 44 houses. There was considerable skirmishing done at that place during the time, in which the Rebels were worsted and driven back toward Macon (92-363).

We marched eight miles in the rain, encamped about twelve miles northeast of Macon. We had some skirmishing with Rebel cavalry in the evening, near Griswoldville, before we went into camp. (My Memo.)

The following property was destroyed at Griswoldville on the 21st: Four miles of railroad track, one water tank, thirteen railroad cars, three sets engine drivers, twelve car wheels, twenty tons of wrought iron, one pistol factory, one soap factory, one candle factory, one foundry in the employ of the Rebel Government, 400 boxes of soap, twelve wagons, one wagon load of tools and one blacking factory; also the railroad station house (92-368).

The cavalry engaged the enemy near Macon during the day. The 9th Pennsylvania cavalry covered the rear to Gordon, where another encounter took place, in both of which the Rebels were routed. The day's operations closed with four skirmishes (92-1 and 363). (92-369).

The 100th Indiana in the Battle of Griswoldville.

On the 22d the weather was cool. Walcutt's Brigade covered the rear. We fell in line, marched half a mile in the rear of the train, then halted. We could see the 9th Pennsylvania fighting the Rebels off to our right. Quite a number on each side were killed and wounded. Our Brigade was ordered forward.

The 97th Indiana deployed as skirmishers and drove the Rebel cavalry from the field. Gen. Woods, commanding the Division, was ordered to make a demonstration toward Griswoldville, and he selected Walcutt's Brigade for that purpose; which was composed of the following Regiments: The 40th Illinois, Lt. Col. Hall, 206 enlisted men; 46th Ohio, Col. Alexander, 218 enlisted men; 103d Illinois, Major Willison, 219 enlisted men; the 6th Iowa, Major W. H. Clune, 177 enlisted men; 97th Indiana; Col. Catterson, 366 enlisted men, and the 100th Indiana, Col. R. M. Johnson commanding, 327 enlisted men, and one section of Battery "B," 1st Michigan, Capt. Arndt. Total present for duty; 1,513 men. (No. 92, p. 97.)

Our skirmish line drove the enemy to a point west of and beyond Griswoldville, when by direction of Gen. Osterhaus, the Brigade was drawn back to a position on some high ground on the Duncan farm, near the edge of the woods, with

Brevet Major General Charles C. Walcutt.

Captain 46th Ohio, April 18th, 1861. Major June, 1861, and assigned to staff of Gen'l C. W. Hill, Major 46th Ohio, October 1st, 1861; Lieut. Colonel, January 30th, 1862, Colonel 46th O. V. I., October 16th, 1862; Brigadier General of Volunteers July 30th, 1864; Brevet Major General of Volunteers March 13th, 1865, for special gallantry at the battle of Griswoldville, Georgia, November 22nd, 1864 when he was severely wounded.

a large expanse of open ground in front, the flanks being refused so as to cause each to rest very nearly on Sand Creek, a swampy, miry stream, which lay in our rear, from wing to wing. Some temporary works were thrown up by the Regiments in the field, of rails, logs and dirt. This being done the soldiers proceeded to get their dinner. (92-105)

Now, it so happened that the Rebel Army, consisting of seven Brigades and Capt. Anderson's Battery, in all about 6,600 men, exclusive of Wheeler's cavalry, had been ordered to march from Macon to Augusta, as the Confederate Generals believed that we were movng on that place. The 1st Brigade of the Georgia troops moved in advance of the other Brigades along the railroad and missed our column. When the other six Brigades came along by Griswoldville, they encountered our pickets, and seeing Walcutt's Brigade from the road they were marching on toward Augusta, their Commander, Brigadier General P. J. Phillips, supposing that we were a small force, determined to assault us. He disposed his forces as follows: Two Brigades, the Athens and Augusta, formed his right, a Brigade of the State Line was placed on the left of the Athens and Augusta Brigades, and on the left of this line was formed McCoy's Brigade, the left of the latter Brigade "resting near and south of the railroad," and General Anderson's Brigade was formed all on the north side of the railroad, "his left resting parallel with the railroad," and Col. Mann's second Brigade was formed in line of battle in the rear of the State Line and McCoy's Brigade, in a secure place to act as reserves, and Anderson's Battery was put in position on the highest ground on the north side of the railroad. (Jones' Siege of Savannah, page 29.) (Rebel Dispatches, 92-877.)

In this position an advance was ordered by the Confederate General. There were two Brigades of Wheeler's Cavalry in reserve.

We were eating dinner at the time. We saw the long lines of battle advancing upon us, whereupon every man of the Regiment prepared himself for battle, and every officer and man did his duty nobly.

The following is the official report of the battle by Col. R. M. Johnson of the 100th Indiana:

"Having arrived at the point designated upon Duncan's farm, we formed line of battle, covering the Macon road, with our flanks resting in the timber, while in front and center was the open field; the Regiments composing the command were assigned positions on the line as follows: On the right of the road were placed the 6th Iowa Infantry, 103d Illinois Infantry, and 97th Indiana Infantry. On the left of the road were posted the 40th Illinois Infantry, 100th Regiment Indiana Volunteer Infantry and 46th Ohio Infantry, while in the center of the road, the section of Artillery, which had accompanied the Brigade, took up a position. In less than one hour after getting into position as above stated, our skirmishers became engaged with the advance of the enemy, who was moving upon us, and it soon became apparent that a heavy battle must ensue, as it was evident the enemy intended to endeavor to drive us from our position, and with that view had formed in heavy force upon our front, and opened upon our barricades with four pieces of artillery. Brigadier General Charles C. Walcutt, Commanding 2nd Brigade First Division 15th Army Corps, perceiving this, ordered me to take the three right Companies of my Regiment and support the section of the 1st Michigan Battery, occupying the center of the line, which order I immediately obeyed. I had no sooner done this, than from the manuevering of the enemy, it became apparent that he would endeavor to turn our extreme right flank, and to checkmate him there, General Walcutt ordered me to withdraw three more Companies of my Regiment from the left flank and putting them in position on the extreme right flank, take charge of that end of the line, and at all hazards to hold the enemy at bay at that point. I accordingly moved Company "A," "B" and "C" of my Regiment to the extreme right of the Brigade line, and placing Company "A" and "C" on the line deployed Company "B" as skirmishers to extend the line to the right, instructing the men to shelter themselves behind trees, and to hold their positions at all hazards. Companies "I," "K" and "H" having been placed in the center of the Brigade line and the 46th Ohio Volunteer Infantry, having by order of General Walcutt, previously moved to the right, I had only Companies "D," "E," "F" and "G" of my Regiment with which to hold what had been the line occupied by the 100th Regiment Indiana Volunteer Infantry and the 46th Ohio Volunteer Infantry. These Companies I deployed along the works so as to cover the two Regimental fronts. The three Companies in the center I placed under the immediate command of Captain John W. Headington, and he continued to manage them during the remainder of the fight with skill and sound discretion. On the right flank my men were much exposed, having no works to shelter themselves, but the ground being rather favorable, I succeeded in checking the enemy so suddenly in his effort to turn our line that he did not afterwards attempt seriously to get around our flank, nor did he even have time to discover the strength of our line or number of our forces at that point. In this engagement, which lasted from one o'clock until dark, the enemy made some seven distinct assaults upon our lines, which we handsomely repulsed, with heavy loss on his part each time. Toward evening I received an order from Colonel R. F. Catterson, 97th Indiana Infantry, who in the meantime had assumed command of the Brigade, owing to Brigadier General Walcutt's having been wounded, to be ready, with a heavy skirmish line in my front, to charge the enemy at the sound of the bugle and to bring in such of the enemy as had remained behind in the last repulse and taken shelter under the cover of a ravine which ran along our front. This movement was accordingly executed and resulted in the capture of several prisoners, most of whom were wounded. We found a considerable number of small arms, which I had brought in and turned over to the Brigade Commander and the wounded men were sent back to the hospital for care and treatment. After the close of the fight and the gathering up of all the prisoners obtainable and the property left by the enemy on the field, in obedience to orders received, we withdrew from the works and rejoined the column. In this engagement, I lost 2 men killed and 18 wounded, a list of which is hereto attached, as follows:

Captain Eli J. Sherlock, "A," wounded right foot by an exploding shell.
George Buchanan, "A," wounded left shoulder; shrapnell.
Levi B. Powell, "A," wounded left hand and knee; minnie ball; severe.
Aaron Wolford, Corporal, "C," killed.
Joseph Harris, Corporal, "E," wounded left arm.
Henry Fairchild, Corporal, "C," wounded right thigh; severe.
Thomas N. Holloway, Private, "G," wounded in jaw; severe; minnie ball.
Jacob Baumgarten, Private, "I," killed.
William Kelley, "I," wounded thigh and shoulder; severe.
Elias H. Jones, "I," wounded hip; died.
Daniel Trout, "I," wounded head; severe.
Robert Ostler, "I," wounded head.
John M. Cook, "I," wounded head and shoulder.
James Bolinger, First Lieutenant, "K," wounded right hip.
Bart. F. Smith. "K," wounded face; severe.
J. N. Norwood, "K," wounded leg; severe.
George Borntrager, "K," wounded leg; severe.
Moses N. Pugh, "K," wounded in breast.
Michael Grumen, "K," wounded in abdomen.
William Pollard, "K," wounded right hand; severe.
Francis E. Gillett, "C," killed.

Total killed, 3; total wounded, 18; missing, none.

Total number of casualties, 21.

Prisoners captured represent that the enemy attacked us with 15 Regiments of Infantry and 7 Regiments of Cavalry, and yet the gallantry of our men was such that we successfully held him at bay, and drove him from the field.

In justice to my men, I should state that at one time, the ammunition being scarce, they voluntarily fixed bayonets and expressed their determination to hold their line as long as there was a man of them left. My officers all behaved with conspicuous gallantry and at all times during the engagement kept cheering their men and telling them to hold their ground and beat back the enemy. My Regiment occupying and holding the left flank center and right flank of the Brigade line, I could not well be present at each point but a part of the time, but I am assured that every man and officer did his full duty and behaved gallantly. The strength of my Regiment in this engagement was 330 effective men, armed as follows:

Springfield rifled muskets, cal....... 58   305
Spencer rifles, cal................. 52   25

Total number of guns................   330
(Official Report R. M. Johnson.)

Col. Catterson's report of the battle (Extract):

"It was at this moment that Gen. Walcutt received a severe wound and was compelled to leave the field. I immediately assumed command and discovered the enemy moving to the right. I suppose he contemplated turning my right flank. As I had already disposed of every available man in the Brigade, and my left being so strongly pressed, that not a man could be spared from it. I sent to the General commanding the Division for two Regiments. The 12th Indiana Infantry was sent and immediately placed in position to the extreme right, also a squadron of cavalry to watch the right and left flanks; but the day was already ours, as the enemy had been repulsed and driven from the field. I immediately sent forward a line of skirmishers, who succeeded in capturing about 42 prisoners and 150 small arms. The battle commenced at 2:30 P. M. and lasted until sunset. During the engagement the enemy made three separate charges, and were as often repulsed, with terrible slaughter. I would gladly notice the many deeds of daring during the action, but to do so of every man who distinguished himself would be to mention each man by name in the Brigade; but suffice it to say, the conduct of both officers and men was most superb. The loss of the Brigade in killed was 14; in wounded, 42— this number includes only those sent to the hospital. The loss of the enemy in killed and wounded could not have been less than 1,500, about 300 of whom were killed." (Catterson's Official Report, 92-105.)

General Woods' report:

"I cannot speak in too high terms of the coolness and gallantry of Brig. Gen. C. C. Walcutt and Col. R. F. Catterson, 97th Indiana Infantry. The skill with which they handled the troops and the result's obtained, show them to be men of marked ability. The Rebel loss, as near as could be ascertained without actual count, was 300 killed and from 700 to 1,200 wounded. Major General Phillips, Col. Mann, 5th Georgia, and Col. George are reported by the prisoners taken to have been killed, and Brig. Gen. Anderson to have been wounded. Twenty-eight prisoners were captured and turned over to the Provost Marshal of the 15th Army Corps. Fifteen wounded were brought in and left in a house, not having transportation for them. Our loss was 13 killed, 79 wounded and 2 missing." (Official Report Gen. Woods, 92-98.)

The following is Gen. Osterhaus' report of the battle:

"In the afternoon the Rebel commander

brought forward four Bigades* of Infantry and a battery of artillery, supported by a strong cavalry force, to dislodge Gen. Walcutt from his position. For several hours their attempts were repeated, with the greatest impetuosity. Their artillery threw a terrific fire into the frail works of Walcutt, while their columns of infantry marched in heroic style to within fifty yards of our line. It was all in vain. Walcutt and his brave Brigade proved that superior skill, coolness and valor made up for the great disparity in numbers. When night came on the enemy retired, leaving over 300 dead on the battlefield and a number of wounded, who were taken care of by our medical corps; also a number of prisoners were taken. Our loss was comparatively light. The brave Gen. Walcutt was wounded by a piece of shell during the fight and Col. Catterson assumed the command of the Brigade." (Official Report General Osterhaus, 92-83.)

The following congratulatory order was issued to our Brigade by General Howard:

Headquarters Department and Army of the Tennessee.

Gordon, Ga., November 23, 1864.

'Major-General Osterhaus,

"Commanding Fifteenth Army Corps:

"General: I take sincere pleasure in congratulating the Brigade of General Walcutt, of General Woods Division, of the Fifteenth Corps, on its complete success in the action of yesterday. Officers from other commands, who were looking on, say that there never was a better Brigade

*This report should read six Brigades.

of soldiers. I am exceedingly sorry that any of our brave men should fall, and for the suffering of those that are wounded. The thanks of the army are doubly due to them. I tender my sympathy through you to the brave and excellent commander of the Brigade, Brigadier-General Walcutt. It is hoped that his wound may not disable him.

"Very respectfully, your obedient servant,

"O. O. Howard, Major-General.

"P. S. The loss of the enemy is estimated from 1,500 to 2,000 killed, wounded and prisoners.   "O. O. Howard, Major-General."

(Rebellion Records, Serial 92, page 96.)

The following is General Sherman's notice of the battle:

"During the 20th, General Kilpatrick made a good feint on Macon, driving the enemy within his intrenchments, and then drew back to Griswoldville, where Walcutt's Brigade of infantry joined him to cover that flank, whilst Howard's trains were closing up, and his men scattered, breaking up railroads. The enemy came out of Macon (22) and attacked Walcutt in position, but was so roughly handled that he never repeated the experiment." (Official report General Sherman, 92-788.)

A portion of the troops we fought at Griswoldville were the same state line troops who, under General G. W. Smith, fought us at Kenesaw and Atlanta.

The following is an extract from General G. W. Smith's Confederate report of the battle:

"Notwithstanding my order to avoid an engagement at that time and place, a collision occured, we being the attacking party. Several of the best field officers of the command were killed or wounded. On this occasion the State and Confedetate forces were confronted by Wood's Division of the 15th Army Corps, General Walcutt's Brigade, with two pieces of artillery, being in advance. The battle of Griswoldville will be remembered as an unfortunate accident, whose occurence might have been avoided by the exercise of proper caution and circumspection. It in no wise crippled the movements of the enemy and entailed upon the Confederates a loss, which under the circumstances could be illy sustained." (Jones Siege of Savannah, 26-7.) (From official report General G. W. Smith, serial 92, 414).

The following is from the official report of Brigadier-General Phillips, who commanded the Confederates at the Battle of Griswoldville:

"The officers and men deported themselves well during the entire action, which lasted from 3 P. M. until dark, held their positions and retired in good order to Griswoldville, where I had intended to encamp, and bring off those of our wounded and dead that had not been removed from the battle field; but, on my reaching Griswoldville, I received an order from the Major-General commanding ordering me to fall back to the trenches at Macon, where I arrived about 2 o'clock A. M.

"I can but believe if the flank movement had been carried out with all the forces assigned to that duty that it would have resulted in dislodging and probably routing the enemy, notwithstanding that he was I am satisfied fully equal if not superior to our forces. Whilst we have to regret the loss of many gallant officers and men, yet we cannot but hope that they died not in vain." (Jones' Siege of Savannah, p. 31. Official report General Phillips.)

It will be observed that General Phillips makes no statement concerning the number killed and wounded. The writer has been three times over the field since the war and men are living there now (1896) who helped to bury the dead, and it is firmly stated that the Confederate loss was 1,600, or more men than we had engaged, of whom 312 were killed.

The 100th Indiana picketed the battlefield that night, and aided all the Confederate wounded left on the field. The enemy had removed the most of their wounded and dead during the last assault.

On the 23rd our Brigade moved out at 9 A. M. five miles to Gordon and encamped; a total of 128 miles.

On the 24th we marched at 7 A. M., 13 miles without a halt, to Irwinton, Wilkinson county, and went into camp. The Cavalry Corps crossed from the right wing over to the left wing at Milledgeville, and crossed the Oconee river at that place.

Friday, November 25th, at 6:30 A. M., we marched 12 miles to Lightwood Natural Bridge and went into camp; total, 153 miles. We opened on the enemy at the Oconee river with Artillery, the 12th Wisconsin Battery. Our men set one end of the bridge on fire, while the Rebel forces were firing on them from the other. See following Rebel dispatches:

"Oconee, November 24, 1864, 8:55 P. M.
"Major-General McLaws:
"I have held the bridge to the last extremity. The enemy have succeeded in setting fire to the trestlework on the other end of the bridge; it is burning slowly. We still hold this side, and shall continue to hold it, until driven back. The enemy are in heavy force on the other side. I believe I have more than Kilpatrick's Division in front of me. Wheeler has not yet come up.
"H. C. Wayne,
"Major-General."
(92-892.)

The Confederate Cavalry in our front on the march to the sea were more than twice the number General Kilpatrick had, as shown by the following dispatch:
"Oconee, November 24, 1864.
"Captain Elliott,
"Assistant Adjutant-General:
"General Wheeler with 10,000 men is crossing Blackshear Ferry, twenty miles below here, and he is coming to our assistance. We still hold our position at the bridge. The enemy have burned the long trestle on the other side. Our loss this morning, 2 killed and 5 wounded.
"A. L. Hartridge,
"Major, Commanding."

The strength of Wheeler's Cavalry is also shown by the following dispatch, dated Augusta, November 24, 1864:
"Dr. W. S. Morris:
"General Wheeler with 10,000 men is now

crossing Oconee river twenty miles below bridge at Blackshear Ferry, and coming to assistance of General Wayne. Enemy have burned long trestle work on other side of bridge.

"J. A. Brenner."
(92-894.)

On the 26th, we marched to the Oconee River. The 15th and 17th Corps marched side by side. We crossed the river at Ball's Ferry and encamped at Irwin's Cross Roads, having marched 15 miles and a total of 168 miles. Quite a Rebel force was stationed at this ferry and opposed the advance for a short time, when they were shelled out by the 12th Wisconsin Battery.

On the 27th we marched east from Irwin's Cross Roads, on the main Savannah road. The 100th Indiana covered the train. We went into camp at 8 P. M. near the village of Drummond, having marched 15 miles; total, 183 miles. The cavalry had another brush with Wheeler's at Sylvan Grove. It then struck the railroad at Waynesborough, burned the station and a train of cars, and also the bridge over Briar Creek. It was the intention to surprise the garrison at Millen and liberate our prisoners, but it was here ascertained that they had been removed two days before. Wheeler again attacked our cavalry with the usual result. The cavalry crossed the Ogeechee at the Shoals and struck the railroad at Waynesborough. (92-363.)

On the 28th, we moved out from Drummond at an early hour and marched to the southeast, through Johnson county, Georgia, and encamped near the eastern edge of that county, having marched 13 miles. The Cavalry Division was near

Waynesborough. It crossed Rocky Creek and waited for the Rebel cavalry to come up, which it did, the entire Rebel force charging as it came on, but it was repulsed again and again, and was forced to retire after losing not less than 600 men killed and wounded. (92-55.)

On the 29th, the 100th Indiana marched in rear of the 15th Army Corps train, on the headwaters of the Cannouchee River, with scarcely a halt all day. The soldiers captured a great many horses and mules, which were hidden in the timber by citizens on our approach. Marched ten miles; total 206 miles. About 9 P. M. we waded across a deep creek. The cavalry was on the left and was drawn up on the Louisville and Millen Road, and at about 2 P. M. the enemy charged upon the cavalry and was repulsed with great disaster.

On the 30th, we marched through Pine Barrens toward the Cannouchee River, we passed through Summerville, Georgia, and went into camp at noon, having marched 12 miles; total 218. The country was very poor. Very few farms or plantations; we marched in the pine woods all day. Saw very few citizens.

On the 30th, Wheeler with about 12,000 Cavalry attacked Morgan's Division of the 14th Army Corps, and was repulsed at Louisville by the 10th Michigan. On the same day the Cavalry on the Louisville and Millen Road were attacked several times from the rear by the Confederate Cavalry. (92-183.)

On December 1st, the 100th marched early in the advance from the vicinity of Battle Ground to within three-fourths of a mile of the Ogeechee River, here we found a better country;

forage was plenty. We marched 10 miles: total 228. The 17th Corps moved down the east side of the Ogeechee, destroying the depots and railroads.

December 2nd we marched early in a very swampy country on the west side of the Ogeechee and very close to that stream. We only marched 5 miles: total 233. The whole army made a kind of left wheel upon Savannah, and we occupied the right. This gave us the shortest distance to travel.

December 3d we remained in camp all day.

December 4th we marched before daylight down the west side of the Ogeechee River, through a low swampy country. We got some rice straw for the animals—the first we had seen. Marched 15 miles, total 248 miles.

The 14th Corps moved at 6:30 A. M. ten miles across the country toward the Savannah River, took dinner at Hargroves Plantation and encamped near Habersham (92-184). The 20th A. C. crossed the Little Ogeechee at 5 P. M., having in charge the ammunition train, pontoon train and the Corps supply train, and had a skirmish with the enemy at that place (92-19). The cavalry had an engagement with the enemy, which was a hand to hand encounter. There were left on the field more than two hundred Rebels who were all wounded by sabre cuts only. The fight took place right in the town of Waynesborough. There was also an engagement at Lumpkins station, one at Station number 5 on the railroad, and one at Statesborough by General Hazen's Division of the 15th Corps. The enemy was routed after thirty minutes fighting. (92-62)

On the 5th we marched early and hard,

down the Ogeechee and crossed Belcher's Mill Creek. The Rebels had burned the bridge. This was the first signs of an enemy we had seen for several days. They were reported to be in force across the Ogeechee. Forage was plenty. We traveled on the main Savannah road twenty miles, total 268 miles (92-33).

The 100th Indiana and the 40th Illinois were put in the rear of the Pontoon train. We marched at 3 P. M. down the river fourteen miles, total 282 miles. We got possession of the ford, but had some skirmishing with the enemy to do so. Some of the 15th Corps crossed the Ogeechee. The 17th Corps destroyed railroad all day (92-32).

The 100th Indiana and 46th Ohio were ordered to cross the Ogeechee above Wright's toll bridge and to feel forward some distance and then fortify strongly. This we did and remained in our works until 11:15 P. M., at which time we were recalled. We re-crossed the river and rejoined the Brigade. The trains, troops and the cattle for the army had all passed before our recall. The river bottom was very bad, the stream being divided into six channels at that point. The 17th Corps marched all night in quick-sand bottoms and bad roads. (92-33.)

A Brigade of Rebels behind some rail piles at Jenck's bridge, were very handsomely routed by a Regiment of Hazen's Division, the 53rd Ohio. (92-649.)

December 8th, the 100th marched at 6:30 A. M. We forded several small streams during the day, all running into the Ogeechee. We obtained some Rebel newspapers containing an account of Hood's defeat at Franklin on the 30th of November. We marched 23 miles; total, 305. Firing toward the Cannouchee could be plainly heard. The Rebels opposed the crossing of that stream by Hazen's and John E. Smith's Divisions, with two pieces of Artillery and with Infantry, but they retired quickly before these forces. (92, Hazen, 110.)

On Friday, the 9th, the night was cold and the 100th remained in camp. The country was swampy; heavy firing was heard toward Savannah. Hazen's Division crossed the Cannouchee river in the morning and struck the Gulf railroad near Eden, and destroyed about ten miles of track. One Brigade of John E. Smith's Division moved forward to the Ogeechee canal and skirmished with the enemy until dark and went into bivouac 14 miles from Savannah. (92 Itin., 29.)

The 17th Corps skirmished with the Rebels during the day. Several torpedoes, which had been planted by the Rebels in the road, exploded, killing and wounding several men. The Corps encamped at Pooler's Station. (92 Itin., 32.)

On the 10th, the 100th marched at 8 A. M. down the west side of the Ogeechee River, over a very swampy country, crossed the river on pontoons at noon; the approach was very bad, and a great many horses, mules and cattle were lost in the quagmire by getting off the corduroy. We followed the Ogeechee Canal nine miles in the direction of Savannah, then turned to the right two miles and built works, having marched 18 miles; total 323.

The 20th Corps "reached the main line of the enemy's works in front of Savannah and took position on the left, with its left resting on the Savannah River, the 14th on the right of the

20th and joining the left of the 17th Corps beyond the canal near Lawson's Plantation. The line was as close as possible to the enemy, and preparations were made for an assault. Batteries were established on the Savannah River, so as to prevent any boats from passing. The steamer 'Ida,' while attempting to pass up the river, was captured on the 10th and burned." (92–Slocum–158.)

December 11th the entire four Corps were in line all night, just out of range of the Artillery. We got up at 4:30 A. M., when the picket lines were engaged briskly; at day break there was heavy cannonading on both sides, a wide, deep creek was between our lines and a Rebel Fort, which was right in our front. Corse's Division was shifted to the right, and at noon we left our works to fill up the gap thus made in the line. We left the main road, moved two miles to the right and rested till night, when we covered our train, which passed all night within short range of the Rebel Batteries. (92–Osterhaus–88.)

We formed in line on Corse's left, with our left on the main Savannah Road. The roads were nothing but quagmires. We had 400 negroes, who constructed of pine logs and poles a double corduroy from our front to the rear. These dispositions put the Union Army in line around Savannah and completely invested the city, leaving only the causeway leading to the east as a means of escape for the Confederate Army, which, including Wheeler's Cavalry and Ferguson's command, numbered about thirty thousand (30,000) or just about half as many men as were in the Union forces. General Hardee had about 18,000 inside of the city's defences, about 300 pieces of artillery; the Rebels had cut the Ogeechee Canal and had overflowed the rice fields and all the low lands between their outer defenses and our lines, so that there were but few places where an assaulting column would not have to charge through water several feet deep and in many places a quarter of a mile wide, before the enemy's works could be reached, which of itself would, in December, have been sufficient to kill a man. Had such not have been the conditions and situation, the Union Army would have moved right into Savannah, immediately on its arrival in front of the city. The position of the Union Army around Savannah was: the 15th Corps on the right; the 20th Corps on the left; the 17th Corps, the right centre, and the 14th Corps the left centre. (Serial 92, pp. 88, 440.)

I will now give the position of the Confederate forces as they confronted our line during the the siege. The Confederates began to fortify Savannah as soon as the Union Army left Atlanta, under the direction of John McCrady, McLaws chief engineer. The first guns were put in position on the 20th of November, and the first troops entered the works on the 7th of December.

Beginning with the Confederate right, that is, the troops in front of the 20th Corps, was the Georgia state troops, reaching from the Savannah River almost to the Georgia Central Road; Gen. G.W. Smith, a front of about two miles, his right under Gen. Anderson, his left under Gen. Carswell. About 2,000 men of the Georgia state troops were intrenched near the Louisville road, and the 1st Brigade of the Georgia militia on the Augusta road; the space between was occupied by the Cadets. The 2d and 3d Brigades of the Georgia militia held the line from the Augusta road to the bank of the Savannah River (making two lines at this point). Col. Hill with the 3d Georgia Brigade occupied the advance works. On Col. Williamson's rice canals he had a detachment of Cadets and Pruden's Battery, supported by Anderson's Light Battery and Hamilton's Battalion of Light Artillery. (Jones' Siege of Savannah.")

General McLaw's Division formed the center of the Confederate line; it began just to the right of the Georgia Central Railroad and extended along in front of the 14th and 17th Corps to the Daly Farm. His left was commanded by General Baker and his right by General Lewis. This Division was made up in part of North Carolina Troops, 4th Tennessee, 12th South Carolina Cavalry, the 2d, 4th and 9th Kentucky, the 3d Georgia Reserves, the Athens, Georgia, Brigade, the 5th Georgia Reserves and the 1st Georgia Regulars, Daniel's and Abell's Batteries, supported by Barnwell and Wagner's Batteries. The Confederate left was commanded by General A. R. Wright, extending from the Daly Farm or Telfair Swamp to the railroad bridge over the Little Ogeechee. His subordinates were General Hugh W. Mercer, who had the line from Telfair Swamp to Lawton's house, and General Jackson, from Lawton's house to the bridge. Along this line was the Augusta and Athens Battalions, Nesbit's Regiment, Brook's Battalion, the 55th Georgia, the Augusta Artillerists, Clemen's Battalion, Richardson and Barnwell Batteries,

Wheeler and Simpkins, Jackson's Local Infantry and Battery, Barnes, Von Zinken's Local troops, Ferguson's Brigade Savannah Local Reserves, Brook's Light Battery, Jones and Gerard Batteries, Moxville's, Hamilton's and Barnwell's Artillery. (See "The Siege of Savannah," by Charles C. Jones, Jr., Lt. Col. and Hardee's Chief of Artillery.) These organizations foot up nearly 20,000; sixty-four organizations were in our front. Mr. Jones says there were only 16,745 inside the fortifications. (See *ib.* 91.)

Fort McAllister.

December 13th. The following is from General Hazen's official report of the assault on Fort McAllister:

"At daybreak on the 13th of December, the troops were put in motion, reaching the vicinity of McAllister at about 11 A. M. About one mile from the Fort a picket was captured, revealing the whereabouts of a line of torpedoes across the road. Some time was lost in safely removing them, when leaving eight Regiments at that point, nine were carried forward to about 600 yards from the Fort, and deployed with a line of skirmishers sufficiently near the Fort to keep the gunners from working their guns with any effect, those firing in the rear being in Barbette. The grounds to the right of the Fort being mostly cut through by deep streams, rendered the deployment of that part of the line slow and difficult, and was not completely effected till 4:45 P. M., at which time every officer and man of the nine

Regiments being instructed what to do, the bugle sounded the forward, and at precisely 5 o'clock the Fort was carried. The troops were deployed in one line as thin as possible, the result being that no man was struck in the assault till they came to close quarters. Here the fighting became desperate and deadly. Just outside the works a line of torpedoes had been placed, many of which were exploded by the head of the troops, blowing many men to atoms, but the line moved on without checking, over under and through abatis, ditches, palisading and parapet, fighting the garrison through the Fort to their bomb proofs, from which they still fought, and only succumbed as each man was overpowered, individually." (92-Hazen, 110.)

Notes of the Battle.

The Union loss was 24 killed and 110 wounded. Captain John H. Grace, of the 30th Ohio, who led the first assault on Vicksburg, was killed. Colonel Wells S. Jones, 53rd Ohio, Commanding Brigade, was severely wounded. The Regiments most conspicuous for gallantry were the 70th, 47th and 30th Ohio Infantry. The captures were, including killed, 250 officers and men, 24 pieces of Artillery, 40 tons of ammunition and a large amount of public and private property. (92-Hazen, 111.)

The capture of McAllister was announced to to the army in Field Order No. 131.

The garrison of Fort McAllister was commanded by Major George W. Anderson. It consisted of the Emmett Rifles, Clinch's Light Battery, Companies "D" and "E," and the 1st Regiment of Georgia Reserves. The following are the Confederate casualties: Captain N. B. Clinch, of Clinch's Light Battery, 11 wounds; Captain Morrison, shot through both legs; the total of killed and wounded 48, 16 of whom were killed. (See Jones' Siege of Savannah, 127.)

The fall of this fort put us in communication with our fleet. We had had no communication with the outer world since November 15th. There was great anxiety for our safety in the North. But little had been heard of us for thirty days and we were denominated "The Lost Army." General Sherman, at 11:30 P. M., on the 13th, dispatched the Secretary of War that we had reached the coast in safety and had established ourselves on salt water as a basis, and that the whole army was in excellent condition. (92 Sherman, 101.)

The Union troops all along our lines tightened their grip on Savannah. Only one road around the city was not in our possession. On the night of the 16th a sergeant and fifteen men of Brooks' Rebel Battalion, being part of Mercer's command, forced their pickets on the causeway and deserted in a body to the Union side, with their arms and accoutrements. (Jones' Siege of Savannah, 137.)

By the 17th we had drawn our lines so tightly around the city that the General felt as if a demand for its surrender should be made. He therefore sent a flag of truce in on the Augusta Road, demanding of General Hardee the surrender of the city.

After due consideration, General Hardee

sent his answer to General Sherman's demand for a surrender, in which the demand was refused.

As soon as Hardee's refusal to surrender was received, orders were issued to all commanders and the lines were tightened, and the Union soldiers increased their fire on the Confederate lines of works, and preparations for an assault were begun. These facts being observed by General Hardee, preparations for an evacuation of the city by the Rebel army was begun, and General Beauregard dispatched General Hardee that:

" * * Whenever you shall have to select between the safety of your forces and that of Savannah, sacrifice the latter and form a junction with General Jones." And on the 9th the order was repeated in substance. (Jones' Siege of Savannah, 109.) And on the 15th Beauregard had dispatched Hardee that: "Under no circumstances must he be cut off from joining with General Jones." (Serial 92-967.)

On the 18th Jefferson Davis dispatched General R. E. Lee to send two Divisions from his army to Hardee in Savannah, to resist our approach. General Lee answered Mr. Davis that he could not do it without imperiling Richmond. (92 Davis, 966.) Hardee seeing therefore that Lee could give him no assistance, on the 19th sent out to his Generals a "*confidential circular*," giving all the details of and instructions for, the evacuation of the city, in substance as follows:

The light batteries were to cross the Savannah River first, then the troops at Whitemarsh, Fort Jackson and Bartow, next the troops at Rosedew, Beaulieu, etc., then at 8 P. M. Wright's was to begin crossing on the pontoons. McLaw's

Division to follow at 11 P. M., General Smith's Division at 12 midnight. Wright's skirmish line to leave their works at 10:30 and Smith's at 2 A. M. Pontoons to be destroyed, heavy artillery spiked, Ammunition thrown into the river and all guns on inner defenses to be spiked. (Jones' Siege of Savannah, 155.) (Serial 92-967.)

Before the time for General Hardee's army to evacuate a fog arose, which became so dense that no movements of any kind could be made. The pontoons were laid across the river at the foot of Broad street. On account of this delay Hardee issued a second confidential circular on the morning of the 20th, ordering that the evacuation take place on the night of that date and the pontoons were thickly covered with rice straw to deaden all sounds. The evacuation took place, so that by 3 o'clock A. M. on the 21st his army was safely on the east side of the Savannah River. (Serial 92-972.)

On the 22nd, General Sherman moved his headquarters into the city of Savannah, and the different Corps of the Army were located in and about the city. Thirty-one thousand bales of cotton and 350 cannon fell into our hands; also railroad cars, engines, steamboats and immense quantities of rice and public and private property. Everything was quiet in the city, a good provost guard was placed on duty, and quiet and order reigned everywhere. General Sherman sent the following message to President Lincoln:

"Savannah, December 22, 1864.
"To His Excellency, President Lincoln.
"Washington, D. C.

"I beg to present you, as a Christmas gift, the city of Savannah, with one hundred and fifty heavy guns and plenty of ammunition; also, about twenty-five thousand bales of cotton.

"W. T. Sherman,
"Major-General."
(92-783)

This message was received by the President the evening before Christmas, and was published throughout the North, in the morning papers of that day, and is said to have greatly added to the joy and festivities of the occasion throughout the country.

Hardee's Army was moved to Charleston and other points. The General on the morning of the 19th, sent two Divisions from Savannah to destroy the Gulf railroad as far Southwest as the Altamaha river. The 100th Indiana, with 150 wagons, went in the same direction for forage The first day 20 miles were made, the second the expedition passed through Hinesville and encamped at Walthourville; on the 21st passed on toward the Altamaha bridge, loaded 150 wagons of the 15 A. C. train with corn and other forage, gathered up 100 head of beef cattle, and returned to Savannah on the 23rd, and encamped on the Ogeechee road, near to and on the west side of the city.

The following is a correct list of casualties

since we left Atlanta the 12th day of November, 1864:

	Killed. Off. Men.	Wounded. Off. Men.	Missing. Off. Men.	Aggregate Off. Men
15th and 17th	5 35	11 172	00 19	16 226
14th and 20th	2 23	6 112	1 258	9 393
Cav. Div	3 35	17 120	00 000	10 155
	10 93	24 404	1 277	35 774

Confederate prisoners captured:

	Off.	Men.	Total
15th and 17th A. C's	34	632	666
14th and 20th A. C's	30	409	439
Cav. Div.	13	220	233
	77	1,261	1,338

The total loss in making the march was 10 officers killed, 24 wounded and 1 missing; total, 35 officers, 93 men killed, 404 wounded, 277 missing; total 774 men; total, men and officers, 809. The prisoners captured numbered 77 officers and 1,261 men; total, 1,338. The loss of the enemy in killed and wounded will probably never be known, but must have been 4,000, as nearly or quite one-half of that number were killed and wounded at Griswoldville alone. (Serial 92-15.)

The 100th Indiana sustained the severest loss of any Regiment on the march to the sea. At Griswoldville it had temporary works. The enemy were in the open field in its front, but the fire of the Regiment was so withering and terribly destructive that the Confederates were not able to deliver their fire with any effect. Had it not been for these three conditions, the 100th Indiana would certainly have been almost annihilated. More than one-half of the Confederate dead and wounded at Griswoldville were in its front. In that engagement the 327 enlisted men of the 100th Indiana, killed and wounded, upon a fair estimate, a thousand men, or more than three to the man.

So that in truth, and without egotism, it may be said that the 100th Indiana occupies, with respect to the march to the sea, the highest place of honor.

The Union Cavalry, on the march to the Sea, numbered 5,000. The Confederates had more than twice that number. General Wheeler alone having ten or twelve thousand, besides there were other smaller commands. In every encounter the Union Cavalry were the victors on the march to the Sea. It had 38 killed, 127 wounded, and 233 captured; total loss 398. (Serial 92, p. 15.)

On receipt of General Kilpatrick's Official Report of the operations of the Cavalry on the march to the Sea, General Sherman sent that officer a very flattering letter in acknowledgment of the very efficient manner in which his command was handled on the march to the sea. (92-368.)

General Lee issued the following general orders to the Confederate Generals, after which no reliable reports of their losses were ever made:

Headquarters Army of Northern Virginia.
General Orders No. 63.   May 14th, 1863.

The practice which prevails in the army, of including in the list of casualties, those cases of slight injuries, is calculated to mislead our friends and encourage our enemies, by giving false impressions as to the extent of our losses.

It is therefore ordered, that in the future, the reports of the wounded shall only include those whose injuries in the opinion of the medical officers render them unfit for duty. It has also been observed, that the published reports of casualties are in some instances accompanied by a statement of the number of men taken into action. The commanding General deems it unnecessary to do more than to direct the attention of the officers to the impropriety of thus furnishing the enemy with the means of computing our strength. In order to insure the immediate suppression of this pernicious and useless custom.

By command of General Lee.

W. H. Taylor,
Assistant Adjutant General.

(Cox Regimental losses, 559.)

Beginning with the engagement at Five Points, Virginia, January 1, and ending with the engagement at Point Spring, Alabama, on December 29, 1864, there were fought during that year, seven hundred and seventy-nine battles and skirmishes. The most important of these engagements and such as the losses on one side or the other amounted to five hundred or more, together with the losses on each side respectively, are given below, to wit:

Date.	Engagement.	Federal Loss.	Confed. Loss.
February 20	Olustee, Fla................	1,828	965
April 8	Sabine Cross Roads, La................	2,900	1,500
April 9	Pleasant Hill, La......................	1,100	2,000
April 12	Fort Pillow, Tenn.....................	574	80
April 17-20	Plymouth, N. C................	1,600	500
April 30	Jenkins' Ferry, Ark................	1,155	1,100
May 5-7	Wilderness, Va....................	37,737	11,409
May 5-9	Rocky Face to Dalton................	837	600
May 8-18	Spottsylvania to the Nye.............	26,461	9,000
May 9-10	Swift Creek, Va.....................	490	500
May 9-10	New River and Cloyd's Mountain....	745	900
May 12-16	Drury's Bluff, Va....................	3,012	2,500
May 13-16	Resaca, Georgia...................	2,600	2,800
May 15	Newmarket, Va.......................	920	405
May 16-30	Bermuda Hundred................	1,200	3,000
May 23-27	Battle on North Anna River........	1,973	2,000
May 25 to June 4	Dallas, Georgia.............	2,400	3,000
June 12	Cold Harbor, Va......................	14,931	1,700
June 5	Piedmont, Va........................	780	2,970
June 9-30	Battles about Kenesaw, Georgia......	8,670	4,600
June 10	Guntown, Mississippi...............	2,240	606
June 11-12	Trevillian Station, Va..............	735	370
July 6-10	Chattahoochee River, Georgia.......	730	600
July 9	Monocacy, Md.......................	1,959	405
July 13-15	Tupelo, Mississippi................	648	700
July 20	Peach Tree Creek....................	1,710	4,796
July 22	Atlanta, First Sortie................	3,641	8,499
July 28	Ezra Chapel, Ga., 15th Army Corps....	584	4,645
July 30	Petersburg Mine Explosion...........	4,008	1,205
August 14-18	Strawberry Plains, Va...........	3,550	1,109
August 18-21	Six Mile House.................	4,543	4,000
August 25	Ream's Station....................	2,442	1,500
August 31	Jonesboro, Georgia................	1,149	2,000
Sept. 1 to Oct. 30	Trenches before Petersburg...	1,804	1,000
September 28-30	New Market Heights, Va......	2,429	2,060
October 5	Allatoona, Georgia.................	700	1,942
October 19	Cedar Creek, Va.................	5,905	4,200
October 27	Hatcher's Run...................	1,902	1,000
November 22	Griswoldville, Ga., March to Sea..	84	1,600
November 30	Franklin, Tennessee.............	2,320	6,252
December 15	Nashville, Tennessee............	2,140	15,000

At Savannah and Beaufort, January, 1865.

ITINERARY

Of the march of the Federal army under General Sherman through the Carolinas in the year 1865, written at the time the events occurred, by Captain Eli J. Sherlock, of the 100th Regiment of Indiana Infantry, to which is added excerpts and extracts from the official reports and correspondence, Federal and Confederate, of that campaign, published by the Government in 1895-6, in Serials 98, 99 and 100. The events recorded relate principally to such operations as were participated in by the 100th Indiana.

On the 2nd of January an "extremely confidential" order was issued by General Sherman, directing that the right wing should move to Beaufort by transports, and that the left wing and Cavalry should work across the causeway to Hardeeville, and by a rapid movement secure Sister's Ferry and the Augusta Railroad to Robertsville, and the troops, guns, shot, shell, provisions and wagons to be ready about Pocotaligo "for another swath," all to move in the direction of Columbia about the 15th, and all necessary preparations for this purpose were at once begun, although the weather was very unfavorable. (99-8.)

January 7, 1865, preparations for the movement into the Carolinas progressed rapidly. The landing of the 17th Corps at Beaufort threatened Charleston, while the left wing passed up the river to Sister's Ferry, so as to threaten Augusta. (99-2.)

On the 8th, the 15th Army Corps received orders to march, and on the 9th it began to move to Thunderbolt Bay under General Woods' Special Orders No. 6 at 7 A. M.

On the 18th, at 8 A. M., we embarked on a transport at Thunderbolt and landed at Beaufort, South Carolina, and went into camp before night, near the old city, which had a dilapidated appearance and was very full of negroes.

On the 19th, we had reveille at 5, marched at 8 A. M. about 4 miles out on the Pocotaligo road and went into camp. On the 20th, rain fell all day. We spent the night without shelter. During the day our tents and baggage arrived from Savannah. A detachment of the 17th Corps made a reconnoisance from Pocotaligo to the Salkehatchie river, and had an encounter with a Confederate force of General Wright's Division. (99-70.)

On the 26th, we were located about 50 miles from Savannah in the direction of Charleston. The left wing occupied the country about 40 miles above Savannah. The distance between the two being about 30 miles, the former threatening Charleston and the latter Augusta. The Confederate Generals were in a quandary as to which place we would go. A military commission composed of Hardee, G. W. Smith, and Beauregard was held, to consider what it was best to do. This body announced officially that it was impossible for an army to move through North and South Carolina in mid-winter. It was not the plan to move against either of those

The 100th Indiana embarking on a transport for Beaufort, South Carolina, January 18, 1864. This cut shows the exact spot (Thunderbolt Inlet) where Sherman's army reached the sea, the 100th being the last regiment of the army to embark. [From photo by Sherlock.]

places, but to do just what this commission decided we could not do.

On the 27th, we had heavy and continuous rains, making the roads simply impassable. We took up our line of march on this date in the direction of Gardner's Corners, marched out about 4 miles without a halt, and found some ground high enough to keep us out of the water. (99–137.) The Confederate Generals were at sea as to what our intentions were and did little else than to exchange dispatches informing each other where they were and communicating such facts as they observed in regard to our movements. (See these dispatches in 99–1011, *et seq.*)

We waited all day in the rain on the 28th, and until 8 A. M. on the 29th, expecting every hour to move. We marched 21 miles out from Gardner's Corners over a low wet country which was the picture of desolation; not an animal or citizen was to be seen. We encamped 25 miles out from Beaufort the way the road leads.

On the 30th, we marched at 7 A. M., through mud, water, sand and pine woods. The sun shone very warm that day. We marched about ten miles, to McPhersonville, South Carolina, and encamped among the tall pines; there were no houses to be seen in the part of the town embraced in our camp. The 17th Corps was on our right and had been firing on the enemy all day. A skirmish also took place at Lawtonville (98–2) between Wheeler's Cavalry and a detachment of the 20th Corps. We came to several places where the Confederates had felled a great many large trees across the road wherever it crossed a swamp or stream.

On the 31st, we remained in camp all day,

in the timber; other troops were moving to the front, the wind blew fiercely all day; the noise created by moving of the trains was drowned by the noise of the wind in the timber. We were now out about thirty-five or forty miles from Beaufort.

The March Through the Carolinas.

MEMORABILIA BY CAPTAIN ELI J. SHERLOCK.

The movements of the Army in the vicinity of Beaufort and Savannah, after the surrender of the latter place, were all preliminary to a campaign through South and North Carolina. On the first of February, the initial movements were complete and the army was in position and prepared for an aggressive forward movement, and on that date, at 7 A. M., we marched out to Hickory Hill, South Carolina, about 25 miles from Pocotaligo and about 104 miles from Savannah, by one route, and 65 miles west of Charleston, where we bivouacked with the 17th Corps between us (the 15th) and the west bank of the Salkehatchie river. The whole army moved forward simultaneously, on different roads, leading in the same general direction.

On the 2nd, we marched at 7 A. M.; the roads were fair. We got some forage for the animals; we saw a great many carcasses of cattle, which the enemy had killed on the plantations and rendered unfit for use by our army. We made twelve miles and encamped at Loper's Cross Roads, about 62 miles from Beaufort. During that day we had six encounters with the

Rebels: One at Lawtonville; one at Barker's Mill; one at Duck Creek, near Loper's Cross Roads; one at River's Bridge, Broxton's Bridge, and one at the Salkehatchie river; the enemy retired in each of these skirmishes. (98-2)

On the next day we advanced to within a mile of Buford's Bridge on the Salkehatchie. The enemy were intrenched on the north side of the river. The approach to the bridge was along a narrow causeway, across a swamp about 80 rods wide. We were within plain sight of the enemy. We left our baggage in our camp and moved up the river, and formed in line of battle in front of the enemy as if we were preparing to assault him in position. It was already late. We remained in line until dark and then quietly returned to our camp; the object being to attract the enemy's attention in front while a force was being thrown across the river above and below his position. We only marched two miles. Total, 64 miles from Beaufort. We had two skirmishes with the enemy. (98-194.)

On the 4th, we moved our camp half a mile up the river to some higher ground; our brigade then formed again, in front of the bridge. The weather was foggy and the forces sent above and below effected a crossing and skirmished with the enemy. A detachment of the 100th Indiana was sent forward on the causeway, which soon discovered that the enemy had destroyed the bridge and evacuated his works, which were quite formidable. We repaired the bridge, crossed the river and encamped in the enemy's works. We had two encounters with the enemy. (98-194.)

On Sunday, February 5, 1865, we encamped

about 8 miles north of Buford's Bridge. Most of the 15th Corps crossed over during that day. We saw some Confederates; they said that the Confederate Army had gone beyond the Edisto river. Had very high winds all day. We marched about 10 miles. Citizens said that we were about ten miles from the South Carolina railroad. Total miles marched, 74.

We had two encounters with the enemy. The advance of the 15th Corps found him in some force at Duncansville, but soon dislodged him and then rebuilt a bridge over the Little Salkehatchie 100 feet long, which he had destroyed. (98-195.)

Camp on Little Salkehatchie river February 6, 1865. On Buford's Bridge road we moved cautiously as if expecting an attack. We had flankers out on both sides. The Confederates had cut down a great many trees in the swamps to impede our march. There was no forage. Marched six miles—total about 80 miles. We had four little fights during the day. (98-89-83.)

On the 7th we moved early. We were expecting to fight. Hardee believed that we were moving on Charleston, by our threatening along the line of the Combahee on our right and the demonstrations of the left wing and the cavalry towards Augusta led the enemy to believe that the latter place might be our objective. We struck the line of the South Carolina railroad at Bamberg, where we encamped, having marched five miles, total 85 miles.

We had three encounters with the enemy's cavalry. The 3rd Cavalry Division met and drove them out of Blackville toward Augusta,

The 11th Iowa encountered the enemy at the bridge over the Edisto and drove them out of a strong position there. (98 Belknap, 417.)

Bamberg, South Carolina, on the South Carolina railroad, Feb. 8, 1865: We destroyed railroad all day from Bamberg to Graham's Turn Out, mostly in the rain and in the usual manner of destroying, by burning the ties and heating, bending and twisting the rails. The men were all wet, mad and tired.

On the 8th the army met the enemy in four encounters. The 3rd Cavalry Brigade, Colonel Spencer, the 1st Alabama in advance, encountered the enemy five miles from Blackville and drove them through the town into a strong position near White Pond, where our cavalry attacked them with great impetuosity. General Spencer says that there "commenced one of the most thorough and complete routs I ever witnessed. The ground was strewn with guns, haversacks, etc. Five battle flags were taken, also the brigade and four regimental flags and a large number of horses and prisoners." (98 Spencer, 892.)

Bamberg, South Carolina, Feb. 9th: We had orders to move towards Graham's Turn Out. Bad, foggy and damp weather rendered the roads almost impassable, yet we obeyed the order promptly.

On the 9th our forces had two encounters with the enemy, one of which was at Binnaker's bridge across the South Edisto river. The 1st Brigade, 1st Division 17th Corps, engaged the enemy in front while they crossed a force below, which waded through the water for nearly a mile waist deep, in the night time; the water was freezing cold. The men held their guns and ammunition above their heads. The Rebels attacked them just as they reached high ground, but the Union soldiers dispersed them after a spirited engagement. (98 Mower, 390.) The 55th Illinois and 57th Ohio skirmished with the enemy a greater part of the afternoon, at Holman's bridge on the South Edisto. The enemy evacuated during the night. (98 Jones, 287.)

Graham's Turn Out, South Carolina, February 10. We destroyed more railroad track in the usual way. The men came in wet and tired. We destroyed everything pertaining to the railroad, except the earth of which the road-bed was made and even that was rendered useless to the enemy. So much rain had fallen that military operations were greatly impeded. The enemy showed himself in only two places. Lee's Rebel Corps was in position on the south fork of the Edisto, and Stevenson's Rebel Corps was pressed back to the line of the North Edisto. (Rebel Dispatches.) (98-1047.)

Camp 100th Indiana, near Holman's Bridge, February 11th, 1865: Marched at 7 A. M. to Holman's Bridge on the Edisto River. Marched westwardly about six miles, then north about four miles. We found a bridge destroyed, as usual, by Confederate Cavalry. Some firing on our right. Our men repaired the bridge. We encamped at the edge of the swamp, near the bridge, on the south side of the South Edisto. Saw a few women and children, but not a man. The women said that the men had crossed the river. We marched about six miles; total, 91 miles from Beaufort.

Camp 100th Indiana, near Shilling's Bridge,

on the North Edisto River, February 12, 1865: Reveille at 4:30. General 6, marched 7. The 2d Brigade crossed the South Edisto River at Holman's Bridge this morning and marched in a zig-zag way, though mainly north, through pine woods and swamps, until we reached the south side of the North Edisto River at Shilling's Bridge, where we encamped. We found some forage. Marched about 18 miles; total, 99 miles. Some firing on the right. When we arrived at Shilling's Bridge we found the enemy strongly posted behind works across the river and swamp. General Logan sent Hazen's Division above and John E. Smith's below, with orders for both to cross, while the 100th Indiana was deployed on a high ridge, half a mile in front of the enemy, to attract their attention, while the other troops crossed above and below, which was so effectually done that the enemy's retreat was nearly cut off. Eighty prisoners were taken, quite a number were killed and wounded and 200 stand of arms were gathered up, which were thrown away by the enemy in his flight. (98 Howard, 196.)

Camp 100th Indiana, 20 miles north of Shilling's Bridge, February 13. Reveille 4:30. General 6. Marched at 7, crossed the North Edisto and took a blind road on the left; marched nearly all day in the woods, through swampy lands. The roads were very bad and the men were muddy, wet and tired. Our camps were so wet that there was scarcely enough dry ground to sleep on. General Sherman and staff were camped in the woods near us. The soldiers thought we had marched 25 miles, but my estimate was 22 miles; total, 121 miles. We marched in two colums all day. We encamped on Rucker's plantation.

Wolf's Plantation, S. C., February 14, 1865: We marched early as far as Sandy Run, on the same blind road, or plantation road. Here we struck the main state road, crossed Sandy Run at 2 P. M., and marched four miles further in the direction of Columbia, and went into camp at this place at 4 P. M. We found the Rebel cavalry here, but General Wood threw out four companies as skirmishers, and they were driven away, but during the night they captured a picket post of the 31st Iowa. They made several dashes at our picket line before daylight. (98 Woods, 242.)

February 15th: Camp a half a mile north Congaree Creek, S. C.: We moved out of camp at daylight, on the main road leading to Columbia, the 100th Indiana having the advance. We immediately encountered the enemy and met with a stubborn resistance all day, driving them from one barricade to another, and being obliged to march with a heavy skirmish line, constantly covering our advance. Our progress was necessarily slow. In the afternoon we reached the open fields which lay to the south of the Little Congaree river or Congaree creek, having made five miles. Here the enemy was found on the river bank in considerable force, with three pieces of artillery protecting his position. Colonel Catterson, by direction of General Wood, deployed the 2nd Brigade in the fields on the right of the road, with orders to press the Rebel left flank. Colonel Stone deployed his 3rd Brigade on the left with orders to press the right flank of the enemy. Colonel Woods' 1st Brigade was held in reserve. The 4th Iowa deployed as skirmishers in front of Stone's Brigade and two companies of the 100th Indiana, by direction of Colonel R. M. Johnson, were placed under command of the writer and thrown out as skirmishers in the open field south of the bridge and in front of the Confederate battery, and an advance was ordered. The 4th Iowa doubled the enemy up and effected a crossing beyond his right, at the same time the detachment of the 100th Indiana poured a galling fire into the fort in their front, and the enemy hastily withdrew his battery. At this moment the high bridge was discovered to be on fire and the men of the 100th Indiana rushed forward to save the bridge, and while one portion poured a a rapid fire into the fleeing enemy, the other, with boards, shoved the large piles of burning resin which the enemy had placed there, off of the bridge, which was 30 or 40 feet high, and it was saved. The 100th Indiana men advanced rapidly and formed a line beyond the bridge and was immediately followed by Generals Wood, Logan and Sherman and their staffs and the army, which was quickly formed in line of battle. The enemy were right in our front drawn up in line of battle, in plain view and almost within gun shot. This move brought us within plain view of the houses in Columbia, the capital of the Mother of Secession, and we were of the opinion that if there ever was an opportune time and place for the secession forces to make a stand it was then and there. General Sherman sent Captain Audenreid, of his staff, to inquire of the writer if he could not advance his skirmish line far enough toward the enemy's line of battle to fire several buildings which obstructed the range of our batteries. This was quickly and successfully done, and the 12th Wisconsin battery was placed in position. During this time, about one company of Rebel cavalry made a charge on our skirmish line but our Spencer rifles were too much for them and they broke before they reached our line. Sergeant Cherry of Captain Brouse's Company "K" was killed by a Rebel cannon shot. Night came on and we went into camp and fortified. As Captain Audenreid was returning to the group of generals he saw this company of Rebel cavalry coming on the charge, and urging his horse to a gallop, the latter fell headlong and by the time the horse and rider had picked themselves up the Rebel cavalry was repulsed. On this occasion there was nothing between the several generals and their staffs but the line of 100th Indiana skirmishers. During the night the Rebels opened on us with a battery from the hills on the east side on the Congaree river. This necessitated the building of traverses, which the men did with a will. The writer was placed by Colonel R. M. Johnson on the top of our breastworks, and when the Rebel cannon flashed, gave the alarm instantaneously, at which every man dropped into the ditch until the cannon shot had passed over, and until our traverses had progressed far enough to protect us. The manner in which the soldiers of the 100th drove the enemy out of the fort and saved the bridge was referred to in very complimentary terms by the Generals who witnessed the feat (98 Woods, 242.) During the day we had five encounters with the Rebels, as follows: Congaree creek, Savannah creek, Bates' ferry on the Congaree river, Red Bank creek, and a cavalry fight at Two League cross roads near Lexington, S. C. (98-3.)

Our casualties at the crossing of the little Congaree were 5 men killed and 10 wounded. (98 Woods, 244.)

During the engagement Battery "H" 1st Illinois, Battery "B" 1st Michigan, and the 12th Wisconsin Battery fired 39 rounds into the enemy's ranks. (98-89.)

February 16th, camp between Broad and Saluda Rivers, above Columbia: We moved northward past Columbia, on the west side of the Congaree River, up to the factory on the Saluda River, and crossed over that stream and encamped between the Saluda and Broad Rivers. Saw a good many women and girls at the factory, who presented a strange appearance as they leaned on the fences, all dressed in coarse brown cotton cloth. The ludicrous appearance of these poor people provoked the most amusing remarks from the soldiers. We marched about six miles. Total, 137. The Rebel Cavalry made some opposition to our movement about Columbia, but we were delayed very little on that account. Battery "H" 1st Illinois, the 12th Wisconsin Battery and Company "H" 1st Missouri Light Artillery shelled the city of Columbia, firing 215 rounds into the city. (98-89.)

Columbia, South Carolina, February 17th: As soon as the bridge was finished over Broad River we crossed and marched down into the city of Columbia. I saw a good many stores and warehouses with the glass fronts broken in. We met a great many negroes, of all shades of color, age, and sex, who were drunk. They had clothing, tobacco, chinaware and other articles. They gave our soldiers considerable tobacco as we marched by them. We marched through the city and encamped on the side of a hill half a mile southeast. A very large pile of cotton bales were on fire in the street when we entered. I saw many stores broken open, the negroes said by Rebels. It was a very windy day. Some houses caught fire from burning cotton flying in the air. At 11 P. M. the whole city was on fire. The command was ordered out. The soldiers helped men and women to save clothing and other effects. Marched about 4 miles. Total, 141 miles from Beaufort.

The Third Brigade, Col. Stone, entered the city first, then came the second; the 100th Indiana being in advance. The city was surrendered to Col. Stone by M. Goodwin, the Mayor, and the Aldermen, who came out in a carriage to meet our forces. (98 Stone, 264.)

The Confederate forces evacuated Charleston on that day, so the two twin secession cities of the South, the home of traitors, fell on the same day.

Columbia, February 18th, 1865.

I took a walk over the stricken city. Nothing but destruction was to be seen. The citizens were taking care of such property as they had saved. The soldiers were assisting them. The railroads and warehouses, foundries and arsenal were being destroyed. Some refugees were with us. I was at the arsenal and saw some old cannons which were used in the war of the Revolution. The command remained in camp. Our position at Columbia forced the evacuation of Charleston as much as if we had been within the range of its guns, and by order of our army commander, the 100th Indiana was directed to inscribe on its regimental flag the names of Charleston and Columbia. The Rebels blew up their commissary depot at the former place and with it 200 human beings were blown to atoms. (98-1019.)

We captured at Columbia a large number of printing presses and material for printing confederate money and also several hundred thousand dollars of the new bills printed ready for circulation. Our men used this money in playing poker for recreation on the march.

Columbia, February 19th.

The work of destruction went on, several wagon-loads of shells exploded between the water-works and the Congaree river and killed several men engaged in destroying ammunition. The citizens took shelter in the houses, wherever they could get it, regardless of ownership. We remained in camp all day. We destroyed 550 bales of cotton which were stored about the city. (98 Woods 243.) The railroad depots, arsenals, machine shops, the armory with a large quantity of machinery, a powder mill which was well equipped for operations, and three large store houses full of ammuintion were destroyed. (98 Howard, 199.)

Camp on Peay's Ferry Road.

February 20th, 1865.

Reveille, 5, General 6; marched at 7 A. M., northward on the east side of the railroad 20 miles. Total, 161 miles. Having made a detour by way of Robert's Cross Roads and Muddy Spring to Rice Creek, on the Peay's Ferry Road, where we went into camp about 10 p. m. (98 Howard, 199.) (98 Catterson, 259.) Camp near Longstown, on Winnsboro Road.

February 21st, 1865.

We marched at 8 a. m. over a hilly country and encamped about 40 miles north of Columbia, at Longstown, on the main road leading from Winnsboro to Camden. The country was barren and we got but little forage for men or animals. Marched 20 miles. Total, 181. (98 Logan, 228.)

Camp near Peay's Ferry, on Catawba River, February 22, 1865: We marched north yesterday and east today. It rained all day, we were very wet and the roads very bad; sandy country, some pine. We put down our pontoons. Marched 15 miles; total, 196. (98 Adams 353.)

Patterson's store, near Flat Rock, South Carolina, February 23rd, 1865: The day was dark and misty. We crossed the Catawba River on the pontoons; marched over bad roads. The train and column was strung out. Marched about 6 miles; total, 202.

Near Pine Tree Church, Feb. 24.

Marched at 8 a. m. amidst rain, mud, sand hills, pine smoke, profanity and bad roads. This place is near the Flat Rock of Revolutionary fame. Marched 9 miles; total 211. The 2nd and 4th Divisions of the 15th Corps entered Camden and destroyed all the stores and public buildings in the place. (98 Logan, 229.)

The 100th Indiana crossing the swollen Catawba river, near Flat Rock, in South Carolina, February 23d, 1865.

Camp 100th Indiana,
Tiller's Ferry Road, Feb. 25, 1865.

Marched at 7 A. M. eastwardly. Got some forage. The land was swampy in many places. We were on the road from Peay's Ferry, on the Catawba River, to Tiller's Ferry, on Lynch's Creek. Marched about 10 miles over miserable roads. Rained so hard we could make no fires. Total marched, 221 miles.

Tiller's Ferry, Feb. 26, 1865.

Marched at 8 A. M.; reached Lynch's Creek at evening; rained all day, the river was very high and over the bottoms; we put down our pontoons, then the river fell at once, leaving half the pontoons on the ground; we thought the Rebels dammed the river below with timber and that the dam gave way. We marched about 9 miles; total 230 from Beaufort. (98–5.)

Tiller's Ferry, Monday, Feb. 27, 1865.

The rain ceased; we remained in camp. The men were all engaged in drying their clothes and blankets. We crossed some men over the river on horses. About noon the river was very high, we had to build a bridge here about three hundred feet long before we could cross. (98 Woods, 246.) (98 miles, 473.)

Tiller's Ferry, South Carolina,
Feb. 28, 1865.

We made muster rolls all day; remained in camp. The engineers were busy completing the bridge; the men crossed the pack mules and horses over by swimming them alongside a raft of planks and logs. The weather was very unfavorable for military operations, and had been for many days. (98 Woods, 246.)

Camp 15 miles northeast of Tiller's Ferry, March 1, 1865: We crossed Lynch's Creek and marched hard till night and went into camp in the woods. Rained very hard all day; put out all our fires and we had nothing to eat. Lynches Creek is about 280 feet wide at a high stage of water at Tiller's Ferry and from 5 to 6 feet deep. We marched northeast all day, 16 miles; total 246.

Camp 15 miles southwest of Cheraw, South Carolina, March 2, 1865: Reveille 5. General 6. Marched at 8 A. M.; bad roads, sandy country and pine timber; some hills. We encamped on a stream running about northeast, about 25 miles northeast of Tiller's Ferry and about 15 miles southeast of Cheraw, South Carolina. We saw but few farms, no forage. We marched 10 miles; total 256.

Cheraw, South Carolina, March 3, 1865: We marched at 8 A. M. to Cheraw, 15 miles or more, over a sandy country; this town is on the Great Pedee River. The 17th Army Corps train blocked our way till 1 A. M. We captured 25 cannons and a large amount of ammunition here. The Rebels burned a bridge across the Great Pedee, and also destroyed some stores and munitions of war.

Cheraw, South Carolina, March 4, 1865: We remained in camp, saw a large quantity of powder and many rifles, cannon, harness, caissons, siege guns and tents destroyed. The men were all in good health. The pioneers made a road beyond the river; a portion of the army crossed over on pontoons. The river was high. There was some firing on the hills about a mile or two east of the river-crossing. Our captures at Cheraw were 25 cannons, 16 limbers, 16 caissons, 5,000 rounds artillery ammunition, 20,000 rounds of infantry, 2,000 stand of arms, 1,000 cavalry sabres, locomotives, cars and several thousand bales of cotton. Mower's Division crossed on the pontoons at 3 P. M., and at once engaged the enemy on the high hills east of the Pedee River. (98 Blair, 381.)

March 5, 1865: Reveille 5. General 6. Marched at 8 A. M.

Camp on Fills Creek, about five miles east of Cheraw, March 6, 1865: It was muddy, foggy and rainy. We marched about east. We only moved our camp about three miles out on the Fayetteville road and encamped in the woods.

On this date General Joseph E. Johnston again took command of the Confederate army in our front. (99 Jefferson Davis, 1304.)

Camp near Goodwin's Mills, north of Cheraw, March 7, 1865: We had plenty of forage. Lieutenant Meeker, of the 100th Indiana, in command of the regimental forage detail, took possession of two mills and put several negroes to shelling corn. They shelled and ground enough to supply the Brigade, and brought it a long distance. We had also plenty of chickens and sweet potatoes. The country here was much better than heretofore.

March 8, 1865, Laurel Hill, North Carolina: Marched at 7 A. M. We crossed the state line between North and South Carolina at noon.

Camp Bethel, North Carolina, March 9, 1865: We marched at 8 A. M. about 15 miles in the rain and wet sand. We crossed the Little Pedee at Gilchrist's Bridge and went into camp on the east side of the river. Forage plenty for the whole army; saw no enemy; total, 308 miles. The streams were all flooded and the swamps were full of water, and every soldier's clothing perfectly saturated. The weather was cold and chilly, and many of the men had but little clothing and their shoes were worn out and their ponchos and blankets likewise.

Camp five miles east of Bethel Chapel near Little Rock Fish, March 10, 1865: Marched at 8 A. M., crossed the Lumber River and continued eastwardly on the Fayetteville road in the mud and rain. The men were all wet and the wagons mired down. Forage was plenty. The country was comparatively level. Marched five miles; total, 313 miles. We were also 20 miles from Fayetteville, N. C. The men had been soaking wet for about sixty hours, with nothing to eat but cold rations. The weather continued very cold; no fires could be built except of pine knots, while a rubber poncho was held over them to keep the rain off. The sufferings of the officers and men, as well as the animals, was very great.

Fayetteville, North Carolina, March 11, 1865: Marched at 7 A. M., 21 miles to Fayetteville. Rained most of the day. We took a large arsenal here. The city is on high ground, on the west bank of Cape Fear river.

A steamer came in from Wilmington.

Fayetteville, March 13, 1865: We buried O. S. Davis, of Company "A," 100th Indiana, in the cemetery. I made some measurements to determine his grave hereafter. The army was very orderly—not a citizen complained. Another steamer came in. I got a New York Tribune and read it aloud to a large crowd of soldiers, who wanted to hear the news. After I read it, a soldier of the 17th Corps offered me a one-thousand dollar bill, Confederate money, for it, which I refused.

March 14, Fayetteville: We remained in camp. More boats landed at our camp from Wilmington; they returned loaded.

March 15, 1865: Wednesday morning we heard some firing on the left. We marched at 10 a. m. about five miles east and encamped on the west bank of the South branch near the crossing. Marched five miles, total 346. (92–234.)

March 16, 1865, Camp near Beaman's Cross Roads: Reveille 5, General 6. Marched at 8 a. m.: crossed the South branch; marched slowly about ten miles and went into camp in the woods. Sandy and quite level. Heavy firing on the left. We halted north of Troublefields. We were moving directly on Goldsboro. More firing on the left. Marched ten miles, total 356. We had three encounters with the enemy. The firing we heard on the left was the battle of Averasborough. Our loss was 12 officers and 83 men killed, and 34 officers and 499 men wounded, and 54 missing, total 682. The Rebels lost a battery of three pieces and one caisson, their ambulance train and 175 prisoners. We buried 128 on the field; their wounded numbered 576; total 879. (98 Slocum, 423.)

Camp near Troublefield's store, March 17, 1865: We marched about ten miles through mud and pine woods, part of the time as flankers along the train. The men and animals were all much worn and tired out. Marched 366 miles.

Camp two miles from Lee's store, March 18, 1865: Marched about ten a. m. about eight miles and encamped in the pine woods about two miles from Lee's store. It was raining and muddy. We had to leave the roads and march in the timber. Total 374 miles.

Camp on Falling Creek, March 19, 1865: Twenty-three miles west of Goldsboro. We marched in rain and mud all day, and in the sand and pine woods. There was some firing on the left. We made about eight miles; total 382 miles.

The 100th Indiana in the Battle of Bentonville.

In line of Battle about two miles southeast of Bentonville, March 20th.

On the morning of the 20th of March the Second Brigade had the advance, the 100th Indiana in front. We moved on Falling Creek soon after daylight, and met the enemy at once, on the road leading from Cox's bridge to Bentonville. Posted behind a line of barricades. Six companies of the 97th Indiana were deployed on the right of the road and companies "A," "C," "I" and "H" of the 100th Indiana, under Major John W. Headington, on the left; and a charge was made on the Rebel line, which broke and fled towards Bentonville, closely pursued by our line. The country on the road, covered by the 97th, was all open fields, while that covered by the four companies of the 100th was mostly timber. The Rebels fled from the open fields to the timber in front of the 100th, which brought the entire Rebel force in their front. In this position a running fight of about three miles was made. The enemy were driven away from one barricade after another. At this juncture the 97th Indiana was relieved by the 6th Iowa. The 100 Indiana, with all the Rebels in its front, which had been doubled up during the running fight, was not relieved, but with the 6th Iowa continued to press the enemy back. Part of the time on the double-quick to a point three miles from Bentonville, where the enemy made a determined stand, in a line of works, with open fields in front of our entire line. Generals Logan, Wood and others, had followed the skirmish line closely, and Col. Johnson followed the Generals closely, with the other six companies of the 100th Indiana, his command being the head of the column. The ammunition of the 6th Iowa became exhausted just as we drew up in front of the enemy's line of battle, and that Regiment was relieved by the 46th Ohio. But Major Headington's four companies of the 100th Indiana, having pressed forward right up to the edge of the open fields, in front of the enemy's works, were not relieved. At this time the Confederate commander either discovered the group of Generals or that Major Headington's line was far in advance of its support and intending either to capture the Generals or to get in the rear of Headington's line he despatched a large body of Wade Hampton's

Rebel Cavalry to our rear, around our left, for that purpose, not being able on account of the timber, to see Col. Johnson's column, which he had judiciously kept well closed up on our skirmish line. The Rebels struck the right of his column and instantly the roar of battle began, right in the rear of Headington's line, which then had an entrenched Rebel line of battle in its front and a battle going on closely in its rear. In this situation some of the officers suggested to Major Headington that we were surrounded and had better cut our way out towards the right. In response to an inquiry by Major Headington to the writer as to what he had better do, the answer given by me was to hold our position as long as we had a man left, and this Col. Headington decided to do. In the meantime Col. Johnson instantly brought his line to face the cavalry, which had encountered the 100th, by one of those difficult movements, the necessity for which rarely happens in a lifetime, and his men delivered a withering fire into the Rebel Cavalry, from which they quickly recoiled, and the 46th Ohio, which had relieved the 6th Iowa, and was armed with Spencer rifles, charged the Rebel works in our front, and as the line of that Regiment came in line with Major Headington's line, the men of the 100th Indiana charged with it, and all went together over the Rebel earthworks, and the Rebel line, being Hagood's entire Brigade of Hoke's Division, was routed and fled from their position. It is, without doubt, true, that if Col. Johnson had not been well closed up on Major Headington's line, and had not so skillfully interposed the 100th Indiana between the Rebel Cavalry and the group of Generals, the latter would have been either killed or captured. The Generals were emphatic in their praises of the manner in which Major Headington's line had fought the enemy for several miles, and the skillful manner in which, and the opportune time, when the 100th was thrown between them and the gravest danger, by Col. Johnson. By direction of General Logan, the 100th was relieved from any further active duty during that day, and we were placed on the left to guard the road upon which the Rebel Cavalry retreated. Col. Catterson says in his official report that, "During its deployment (the 46th Ohio) the enemy was discovered turning the left of his skirmishers, having already gained their rear. The 100th Indiana was hurried forward to check this movement, and they accomplished their work with dispatch and marked gallantry." (98 Catterson, 259.)

General Woods referred officially to the gallantry of the 100th Indiana on this occasion. (92-246.)

In the trenches, near Bentonville, North Carolina, March 21, 1865: It rained all night and all day. The enemy were fortified in our front, with a small creek between us. We advanced our lines and captured some prisoners under some plantation houses. Skirmishing continued all night in the rain by the flash of the guns. During the night we put two brass cannon out in front of our lines in an open place in front of our Brigade, and left them there as an invitation to the enemy to come and get them, but they did not come to do so. A staff officer asked Col. Johnson for an officer to go on duty. The Colonel detailed the writer, and he reported to the officer and he placed me in front of our line, down close to the Rebel line, with orders to listen for sounds, such as firing or cheering on the right, where General Mower was to make a night attack. The skirmishing and cannonading went on nearly all night; this I reported to the officer, who returned to me quite often. Although raining, a fire was burning the pine leaves between the lines, and near my station it burned over the bodies of several dead bodies of Confederates, which in the fog made a terrible stench; the nose, ears, hair and hands of all the bodies being badly burned. General Mower on the right did heavy cannonading, the cannon shot went crashing through the pine timber. I was relieved at daylight. The 103d Illinois was thrown forward as skirmishers and drove the enemy from a strong line of rifle pits, covering the ground occupied by their medical corps as a field hospital the day before, where was strewn around their amputating tables, which in their flight was left, many legs and arms which had been amputated, and a large number of bodies of men who had died from wounds while waiting attention. Mower's Division charged right up to the Rebel works, when the enemy in great force pressed his lines back to their works. The ground was strewn with the dead and wounded. General Hardee's son was killed in this assault.

On picket, Bentonville, March 22, 1865: This was a fine morning; the enemy retreated during the night. The 100th Indiana advanced on the skirmish line early in the morning; we passed many dead bodies lying on the roadside. We came into Bentonville, where we found many of our wounded in a house. They had fallen into the enemy's hands in the battle of the 19th.

The enemy had placed barrels of resin on the bridge across Mill creek and fired it. The men of the 100th rushed on the bridge and saved it by pushing the resin off. Pugh of Co. "K" got shot on the line. Marched 3 miles; total 393 miles.

By order of General Logan our Brigade took the advance in the morning. The 100th Indiana lay across the Bentonville road, and we started out first and held the advance to the bridge over Mill creek. We pushed on beyond as far as Hannah's creek, skirmishing with the Rebels. We were recalled by order of General Wood at 6 P. M. The 100th Indiana formed a picket line from Mill creek to the Bentonville road. There were a great many bodies of dead Rebels in the timber between our posts. We built fires on the battlefield along our picket line, so that we could move about without stumbling over graves or dead bodies. (Off. Rept. Gen. Wood, 98-247.)

Camp between Bentonville and Goldsborough, March 23, 1865: We had reveille at 5, General at 6, marched at 8 back from Bentonville over the same road we went in on. Passed our old works and encamped on a sandy field. The wind was high all day and night; the sand drifted in camp so that none of us could sleep. We had had no sleep for three nights; it was clear and cold. We marched on the Goldsborough road nine miles; total 402 miles. The wounded all went forward towards Goldsborough in the ambulances.

Rouse's Plantation, Goldsborough, North Carolina, March 24, 1865: Reveille at 5 A. M.; marched at 8, crossed the Neuse river and passed part of the 10th Army Corps; got in here at 3

P. M. All troops were here; the road was open to Morehead, North Carolina. Marched 15 miles; total 417 miles from Beaufort. The army met the 10th and 23d Corps here, where we were all concentrated.

The army desolated a swath about 450 miles long, and on an average about 40 miles wide. This injury was done in the territory which furnished the sinews of war, in the way of subsistance, transportation, supplies, arms, ammunition and men to the Confederate Army, and contributed more to its downfall than any other campaign of the war.

On the march through the Carolinas, one hundred and twelve encounters with the enemy took place; fourteen or more of which were more than mere skirmishes, and some of which were battles. The exact losses of the enemy can never be known, as they had long prior neglected to make truthful, or in fact, any reports at all, of the losses sustained by their commands.

At Goldsborough, N. C.: The 15th Corps encamped on Rouse's Plantation, east of and near the city of Goldsborough.

In 48 hours after our arrival at that place the army had settled down to camp life. On the 27th a car load of mail came in for the 15th Corps, and our men all received letters from the loved ones at home, the first since we left McPhersonville, South Carolina.

On the 5th, S. F. O. No. 48 was issued by General Sherman to the army commanders, detailing the plan for the movement of this army with its entire equipment, north of Roanoke river facing west, with a base for supplies at Norfolk, with full communication with the Army of the Potomac to be begun on the 10th. (100–102.)

For some days reports had reached the army that Grant was pressing Lee's Army very hard, and on the 6th a message from Grant to Sherman said:

"We have Lee's Army pressed very hard, his men scattering and going to their homes by the thousands. He is endeavoring to reach Danville where Davis and his Cabinet have gone. I shall press the pursuit to the end; push Johnston at the same time, and let us finish up this job all at once." (100–109.)

On the 9th, the whole army was eager to move, they seemed to long for the excitement of battle and of the march. General Sherman's orders on the 5th were, that the 14th and 20th Corps should form the left and the 10th and 23rd the centre, the 15th and 17th Corps the right, with the Cavalry on the right of the 15th and 17th Corps. The news of the evacuation of Petersburg and Richmond and the retreat of the Confederate army toward Danville rendered a modification in the order of march necessary.

Goldsborough to Raleigh.

MEMORABILIA BY CAPTAIN E. J. SHERLOCK.

April 10th, 1865.

We moved soon after daylight. The 14th and 20th Corps took the two direct roads from Goldsborough to Smithfield. The 10th Corps, under General Terry, composed of three Divisions, in all twelve thousand and ninety-nine black men, (negroes) moved up from Faison's Depot and the Cavalry under Kilpatrick from Mount Olive, to the west side of the Neuse river, with orders to move rapidly up that side of the river, with the intention of placing themselves behind the enemy, between Smithfield and Raleigh. General Schofield, with General Cox's 23rd Corps, followed the 14th and 20th Corps in supporting distance. The 15th and 17th Corps made a detour to the right in leaving Goldsborough, going almost north to Pikeville, about fifteen miles, threatening Welden. The other portions of the army threatened Raleigh. We had gone but a short distance before we met the enemy's Cavalry, posted at every swamp and creek-crossing, to oppose us as long as they could and then run away.

April 11th. The 15th and 17th Corps crossed Little river at Pikeville and marched about half way from that place to Stantonsburg. These two Corps then filed to the left, at right angles to the road they had been marching upon, and moved northwest until they struck the Smithfield road, about 12 miles northeast of Smithfield.

Camp at Grelley's, April 12th, 1865:
A message reached General Sherman at Smithfield from General Grant, conveying to him the information that General R. E. Lee's army, of Northern Virginia, had been surrendered by its commander to General Grant,—many of our soldiers were too skeptical to give the report credence, but presently the information was announced to the troops in a special field order in the following words:

SPECIAL FIELD ORDER, NUMBER 54.

"Headquarters Military Division of the Mississippi:

"In the field, Smithfield, North Carolina, April 12th, 1865: The general commanding announces to the army that he has official notice from General Grant that General Lee has surrendered to him his entire army on the 9th inst., at Appomattox Court House, Virginia. Glory to God and our country and all honor to our comrades in arms, toward whom we are marching. A little more labor, a little more toil on our part and the great race is won and our government stands regenerated after four long years of war.

"W. T. SHERMAN,
"Major-General Commanding."

Raleigh, North Carolina, April 13th.

We reached Raleigh at 7:30. The enemy retreated to the north and west. As soon as General Sherman ascertained the direction the enemy had taken in his retreat, he at once made the following orders: The Cavalry was ordered to follow the fleeing enemy toward Hillsboro, to the northwest of Raleigh, thus forming the extreme right. The 15th and 17th Corps were ordered to turn their head of column upon Pittsboro, in Chatham, and Ashboro, in Randolph counties.

Camp near Morrisville, April 14th:

We moved from Raleigh to Morrisville, on the Chappel Hill road, fifteen miles west and a little north of Raleigh. The Cavalry pushed on to Durham, about twenty-five miles west of Raleigh on the North Carolina railroad. A deputation of citizens was sent down by Governor Vance to meet General Sherman respecting the surrender of Raleigh. As the head of Kilpatrick's column entered Raleigh a fanatical Rebel fired upon General Kilpatrick. The city had been previously evacuated by their forces and surrendered by a delegation of citizens to General Sherman. That was the last gun he ever fired-- the soldiers hung him at once.

Surrender of Johnston's Army.

At this stage of the war the Confederates were so sorely pressed at almost every point that on the 14th a request from Gen. J. E. Johnston to Gen. Sherman for a suspension of hostilities in the words following was received:

"Headquarters Confederate States Army, near Greensboro, North Carolina,

"April 13, 1865.
"Major General W. T. Sherman,
"Commanding United States Army:
"The results of the recent campaign in Virginia have changed the military condition of the Belligerents. I am, therefore, induced to address you in this form, the inquiry, whether we stop the further effusion of blood and desolation of property you are willing to make a temporary suspension of active operations and to communicate to Lieutenant General Grant, commanding the armies of the United States, the request that he will take like action in regard to

other armies. The object being to permit the civil authorities to enter into the needful arrangements to terminate the existing war.

"J. E. Johnston,
"Commanding Confederate States Army in North
"Carolina."

Gen. Sherman at once answered the forego-going from General Johnston, in the following words:

"Headquarters Military Division of the Mississippi, in the field,

"Raleigh, N. C., April 14, 1865.
"Gen. J. E. Johnston,
"Commanding Confederate Army:

"General: I have this moment received your communication of "this date." I am fully empowered to arrange with you any terms for the suspension of further hostilities between the armies commanded by you and those commanded by myself, and will be willing to confer with you to that end. I will limit the advance of my main column to-morrow to Morrisville and the cavalry to the University, and expect that you will also maintain the present position of your forces until each has notice of a failure to agree; that a basis of action may be had I undertake to abide by the same terms and conditions as were made by Generals Grant and Lee at Appomattox Court House on the 9th instant relative to our two armies, and, furthermore, to obtain from Gen. Grant an order to suspend the movements of any troops from the direction of Virginia. Gen. Stoneman is under my command, and my order will suspend any devastation or destruction contemplated by him. I will add that I really desire to save the people of North Carolina the damage they would sustain by the march of this army through the central or western part of the state.

"I am, with respect, your obedient servant,

"W. T. Sherman, Maj. Gen."

The foregoing reply to Gen. Johnston was at once forwarded to Kilpatrick at Durhams by a staff officer.

The following explanatory letter was forwarded to the latter:

"Headquarters Military Division of the Mississippi, in the field.

"Raleigh, N. C., April 14th, 1865.

"General: The letter by flag of truce is from General Johnston, which is the beginning of the end. Send my answer at once and to-morrow do not advance your cavalry beyond the University or to a point abreast of it on the railroad. I will be up to Morrisville to-morrow to receive the answer and it may be to confer with General Johnston. The Infantry will come to Morrisville.   Yours truly,

"W. T. Sherman, Maj. Gen."
"General Kirkpatrick, Comd'g Cavalry."

On the 17th General Sherman left Raleigh for Durham Station, near which place he was to meet General Johnston at noon. He arrived at the station in ample time. General Kilpatrick had horses ready for the General and his staff to ride out to the appointed place, followed by a detachment of Cavalry as an escort. The General and escort were preceded by a non-commissioned officer carrying a flag of truce. About five miles west of Durham the soldier carrying the flag of truce was met by one sent forward by General Johnston. General Sherman rode forward and was met and cordially greeted by General Johnston, the two Generals having never before met each other. They repaired to a small one-story hewed log house near, belonging to a man by the name of Bennett, and requested of the man the privilege of using his house for a short time. The man consented and withdrew his family and the two Generals entered the house and quite a lengthy conference ensued, each representing his side of the case. The meeting terminated without results but with an agreement to meet at the same place on the next day at the same hour to continue the negotiations and General Sherman and escort rode back to Durham and thence to Raleigh on the cars.

On the 18th General Sherman, accompanied by Generals Howard, Barry, Blair, Kilpatrick and others, left General Kilpatrick's headquarters at Durham and were soon at Bennett's house awaiting the arrival of General Johnston, who was delayed about two hours by an accident to his train. General Sherman wrote out a memoranda of terms of surrender, himself keeping in mind he said "The conversation of Mr. Lincoln at City Point" when he was visiting him on the 28th of the previous month, March.

A memoranda of the terms of surrender were written out and several copies of the "memoranda" were made and signed. By this time it was dark and each General and his attendants returned to their respective camps.

April 19th, Raleigh, North Carolina: General Sherman issued the following order to the troops respecting the suspension of hostilies:

"Headquarters Military Division of the Mississippi.

In the field, Raleigh, North Carolina, April 19th, 1865.

(Special Field Order No. 58):

The General commanding announces to the army a suspension of hostilities and an agreement with General Johnston and high officials, which, when formally ratified, will make peace from the Potomac to the Rio Grande."

April 24th, Raleigh, North Carolina:

General Grant and two staff officers arrived at Raleigh this morning. On the same train at 6 a. m. came Major Hitchcock bearing letters to General Sherman, notifying him that the president and cabinet had unanimously rejected the terms of surrender contained in his memorandum. The enclosures from Washington contained, first, a letter from the Secretary of War to General Grant in these words:

"War Department.

Washington City, April 24th, 1865.
"Lieutenant General Grant:

General: The memorandum or basis agreed upon between General Sherman and General Johnston having been submitted to the president, are disapproved. You will give notice of the disapproval to General Sherman and direct him to resume hostilities at the earliest moment. The instructions given to you by the late president, Abraham Lincoln, on the 3rd of March, by my telegraph of that date addressed to you, expressed substantially the views of President Andrew Johnston and will be observed by General Sherman. A copy is herewith appended. The president desires that you proceed immediately to the headquarters of Major-General Sherman and direct operations against the enemy.

"EDWIN M. STANTON,

"Secretary of War."

The next enclosure was a letter from General Grant in these words to General Sherman:

"Headquarters Armies of the United States.

"Washington, D. C., April 21, '65.

"Major-General W. T. Sherman, Commanding Military Division of the Mississippi.

"General:—The basis of agreement entered into between yourself and General J. E. Johnston for the disbandment of the Southern army and the extension of the authority of the General Government over all the territory belonging to it sent for the approval of the President is received. I read it carefully myself before submitting it to the President and Secretary of War and felt satisfied that it could not possibly be approved. My reason for these views I will give you at another time in a more extended letter.

"Your agreement touches upon questions of such vital importance, that as soon as read, I addressed a note to the Secretary of War notifying him of their receipt and the importance of immediate action by the President, and suggested that in view of their importance that the entire Cabinot be called together that all might give an expression of their opinions upon the matter. The result was a disapproval by the President of the plans laid down. A disapproval of the negotiations altogether except for the surrender of the army commanded by General Johnston, and directions to me to notify you of this decision. I cannot do so better than by sending you the enclosed copy of a dispatch (penned by the late President though signed by the Secretary of War) in answer to me on sending a letter received from General Lee proposing to meet me for the purpose of submitting the question of peace to a convention of officers.

"Please notify General Johnston immediately on receipt of this of the termination of the truce, and resume hostilities against his army at the earliest moment you can, acting in good faith.

"Very respectfully, your obedient servant,

"U. S. Grant, Lieutenant-General."

On receipt of the foregoing correspondence, General Sherman dispatched to General Johnston the following notice of suspension of the truce between them:

"Headquarters Military Division of the Mississippi. In the field, Raleigh, N. C., April 24, 1865, 6. A. M.

"General Johnston, Commanding the Confederate Army, Greensboro:

"You will take notice that the truce or suspension of hostilities, agreed to between us, will cease in forty-eight hours after this is received at your lines, under first of the articles of our agreement.

"W. T. Sherman, Major General."

And at the same time made the following further demand upon Johnston for the surrender of his army upon the same terms accorded to Lee at Appomattox.

"Headquarters Military Division of the Mississippi. In the field, Raleigh, April 24, 1865.

"General Johnston, Commanding the Confederate Armies:

"I have replies from Washington to my communication of April 18th. I am instructed to limit my operations to your immediate command and not to attempt civil negotiations. I therefore demand the surrender of your army on the same terms as were given General Lee at Appomattox, of April 9th instant, purely and simply.

"W. T. Sherman,
"Major General, Commanding."

And that he might have written evidence of the delivery of the foregoing notice and demand he forwarded the following to Kilpatrick at Durham Station:

"Headquarters Military Division of the Mississippi. In the field, April 24, 1865.

"General Kilpatrick:

"Send the enclosed notice to General Johnston immediately by an officer, who will obtain a receipt for it, and send the same to me, it is a notice that the truce will end in forty-eight hours after the notice reaches the Rebel lines.

"W. T. Sherman,
"Major General, Commanding."

Goldsboro, N. C., April 25th: General Grant was at General Sherman's headquarters yesterday afternoon. General Johnston, at Greensboro, received a dispatch from Jeff. Davis, at Charlotte, approving the terms of surrender contained in the "Memorandum" or basis made with General Sherman on the 18th, and within an hour afterward Johnston received from General Sherman a notice of the disapproval by President Andrew Johnson and Cabinet, at Washington, and the notice terminating the truce.

At 6 o'clock in the evening Johnston telegraphed the substance of the papers from Sherman to Jeff. Davis at Charlotte, and demanded instructions what to do, at the same time General Johnston suggested to Davis the disbanding of the Confederate Army as a means of preventing further devastation of the country, and advised the flight of Davis and Cabinet. At 11 P. M. Jeff. Davis forwarded to Johnston instructions suggesting that the infantry might be disbanded, with orders to meet at some designated place at a future fixed time. General Johnston disobeyed Jeff. Davis' order not to surrender, and at once sent another proposal to General Sherman requesting a further suspension of hostilities, to arrange a basis of surrender—the time being April 26th, at the same place and hour. This request from General Johnston reached General Sherman at Raleigh the 25th. General Grant was present when Johnston's request was received and he advised Sherman to afford Johnston another opportunity to surrender if he desired it and Johnston was notified that Gen. Sherman would meet him on the 26th at noon.

Grant had orders from President Johnson to "direct operations against the enemy," but he quietly and unostentatiously remained at Sherman's headquarters and permitted Sherman to conduct the further negotiations looking to a surrender of Johnston's Army. When Johnston decided to disobey Davis' order to report to him with the Confederate cavalry and mounted men, and to arrange another meeting with Sherman, he at once notified Jefferson Davis by telegraph, and when he received Sherman's assent to meet him again, he at once notified Davis of this also, and that he had set out so to do. Johnston says that this order, which he disobeyed, was the last order he ever received from the Confederate government.

April 26, Raleigh, N. C.

Just after sunrise, General Johnston, near Hillsboro, received General Sherman's consent to another meeting, and he at once started forward to meet General Sherman, who, after breakfasting with General Grant, went from Raleigh to Durham's Station by rail and from Kilpatrick's headquarters, near by, he went forward to Bennett's house, where the former meetings were held, accompanied by the usual escort. The two Generals met and General J. E Johnston immediately agreed to surrender his own army on the terms indicated in Sherman's demand of yesterday, and an agreement embracing the terms of surrender was drawn up and signed by the two Generals. The agreement was in the words following:

"Terms of a military convention entered into this 26th day of April, 1865, at Bennett's house, near Durham Station, North Carolina, between General Joseph E. Johnston, commanding the Confederate Army, and Major General W. T. Sherman, commanding the United States Army in North Carolina.

"1. All acts of war on the part of the troops under General Johnston's command to cease from this date.

"2. All arms and public property to be deposited at Greensboro and delivered to an ordnance officer of the United States Army.

"3. Rolls of all the officers and men to be made in duplicate, one copy to be retained by the commander of the troops and the other to be given to an officer to be designated by General Sherman, each officer and man to give his individual obligation in writing not to take up arms against the government of the United States until properly relieved from this obligation.

"4. The side arms of officers and their private horses and baggage to be retained by them.

"5. This being done, all the officers and men will be permitted to return to their homes, not to be disturbed by the United States authorities so long as they observe their obligation and the laws in force where they may reside.

"W. T. Sherman, General,
"Commanding the United States forces in North
"Carolina.

"J. E. Johnston, General,
"Commanding Confederate troops in North
"Carolina.

"Approved: U. S. Grant, Lieut. General."

General Sherman returned to Raleigh the same evening, presented the "Terms" to General Grant and requested him to approve them, which he did.

April 27th, 1865: General Joseph E. Johnston issued the following order to the Confederate troops under his immediate command at Greensboro, North Carolina, consisting of Hardee, Stewart and Lee's Corps of Infantry and Butler and Wheeler's Divisions of Cavalry, informing them fully of the terms of their surrender.

"Headquarters Confederate Army in North "Carolina.

"(General Orders No. 18.)

"Greensboro, April 27th, 1865.

"By the terms of a military convention made on the 26th inst. by Major General W. T. Sherman, United States Army, and General Joseph E. Johnston, Confederate States Army, the officers and men of this army are to bind themselves not to take up arms against the United States until properly relieved from that obligation, and shall receive guarantees from the United States officers against molestation by the United States Authorities so long as they observe that obligation.

"For these objects duplicate muster rolls will be made immediately after the distribution of the necessary papers, the troops will march under their officers to their respective states and there be disbanded; all retaining personal property.

"The object of the convention is pacification to the extent of the authority of the commanders who made it.

"Events in Virginia, which broke every hope of success by war, imposed on its General the duty of sparing the blood of this gallant army and of saving our country from further devastation and our people from ruin.

"Joseph E. Johnston, General.
"Commanding Confederate Forces in North
"Carolina."

The 100th Regiment Homeward Bound From Raleigh to Washington City.

On the 30th of April, 1865, the war was practically at an end. There was nothing more to conquer; the work of receiving the paroles of the Confederates and such public property as was to be turned over to the Federal authorities was being quietly conducted at Greensboro and other points and Sherman's army was now ordered to march to Washington City. The orders were issued, all were in readiness, and on the morning of April 30th the four Army Corps took up their line of march for that place. We crossed the Neuse river, north and east of the center of Raleigh four or five miles and encamped on the Cotenau, about midway between the Neuse and the Tar rivers.

On the 1st day of May we crossed the Tar river at Andrew's bridge and encamped on Stony creek.

On the 2d we crossed Swift's creek and encamped at evening on Fishing creek, just above the forks of that stream.

On the 3d we marched very hard.

On the 4th we encamped at a cemetery on the south bank of the Roanoke river.

On the 5th we crossed the Roanoke river and moved northward a few miles into old Virginia, and went into camp.

On the 6th we marched early and hard, almost directly north. We crossed the Meherrin river at Peniton's bridge and encamped.

On the 7th we moved to a point on the south side of the Nottaway river, ten miles northwest of Jarrett's Station and encamped.

On the 8th we made a hard march of not less than 35 miles. We marched through Petersburg across the Appomattox river and encamped on a small stream marked "Old Town" creek. Marched 40 miles.

On the 9th we encamped at Manchester on the James river, opposite Richmond, Virginia.

On the night of the 10th there was a thunder storm and three soldiers were killed by lightning. A great many of our men visited Richmond, the Libby prison, Castle Thunder and other places of interest about the city.

On the 12th, the 15th and 17th Corps marched in review by General Logan through the city of Richmond and encamped ten miles north of that place, near the Chickahominy river.

On the 14th, we crossed the Pamunkey about three miles below the junction of the North Anna and South Anna rivers and encamped about thirty miles north of Richmond.

On the 15th, we marched to a point about six miles south of Fredericksburg and went into camp.

On the 16th, we moved about six miles northward to Fredericksburg, crossed the Rapahannock river, thence to Acquia creek where we encamped.

On the 17th, we marched early as far as Dumfries on Quantico creek, and encamped at Ocoquan.

On the 18th, we marched from Ocoquan to a point near Mount Vernon, where we halted, and after having rested fell into line and marched down to Mount Vernon and passed in front of the tomb of Washington.

May 20th, 1865, an order was issued for a grand review of the armies on the 23rd and 24th instant.

Alexandria, Va., May 22nd: A good many of our men who were mostly in need of shoes and clothing and some other articles were supplied.

May 23: Preparations for review were going on all day. During the afternoon we fell into line and marched across the Potomac river on the long bridge and up into the city of Washington.

Camp at Crystal Springs, D. C. May 24th, 1865: On this day Washington city saw the grandest military spectacle ever witnessed in the United States or any other country. At 9 o'clock we moved toward the vast multitude. First, General Sherman commanding the army and his staff, then General Howard commanding the right wing and his staff, then came General John A. Logan commanding the 15th Army Corps and his staff, then General Woods and staff, then perhaps 200 musicians or more, then came the head of column, each column reaching just from curb to curb on Pennsylvania avenue. Every man kept the exact step to the music. The line was perfectly straight from curb to curb. Every leg and foot in the line came forward so exactly in time that the whole line seemed to be one solid leg. The marching was faultless and indescribable, simply superb. There is neither egotism nor exaggeration in the statement that few, if any, equalled and certainly none excelled the magnificent marching of the 100th Indiana on that great occasion, as its absolutely perfect movements were observed by the highest officials of our own nation and the diplomatic corps and representatives of other nations, as well as the vast concourse of spectators present. Cheer after cheer arose from the multitude, and as its old and tattered battle-flag, containing seventy-three bullet holes, came by, flags, bunting and wreaths were waved and lowered as a token of respect and admiration, and half of the officials on the great grand stand arose to their feet and uncovered their heads; the demonstration was so touching that we all felt deeply affected by it, and felt as if the character of that reception was almost enough to compensate us for the hardships we had endured for our country.

Camp at Crystal Springs, D. C., May 25, 1865: When the newsboy piped his presence in the early morning there was a great rush for papers to see what the people of Washington and the newspapers thought of us as soldiers. Nothing could have surprised or gratified us more than the unexampled praise bestowed upon Sherman's army; almost the entire space in the papers was taken up by the many descriptions given of decimated Regiments and tattered battleflags, together with incidents of the parade.

On the 26th, orders were issued to muster out and send home a very large portion of the army. The Company officers were busy making muster-out rolls for their respective Companies.

We were soon on board the cars on our way back to Camp Morton at Indianapolis, where we arrived in due time, receiving on our way through Virginia, Ohio and Indiana an ovation at every station. At Indianapolis we were met in the State House Yard by Governor O. P. Morton, who welcomed the survivors of the Old One Hundredth back to Indiana, and paid an eloquent tribute to the Regiment. In a few days we were mustered out of the service, and those of us who were so fortunate as to be one of the survivors returned to our homes and friends, and resolved ourselves at once into that class of citizenship which has had no equal in the history of any of the nations of the earth.

The Field and Staff of the 100th Indiana.

Colonel Sanford J. Stoughton entered the service from Ligonier, Noble county, Indiana. He was commissioned Colonel of the 100th Indiana Infantry October 19th, 1862, and mustered as such on the 29th. He resigned January 7, 1864.

Colonel Albert Heath entered the service from Elkhart, Indiana. He was commissioned Lieutenant Colonel on the 18th and mustered on the 20th of October, 1862, and commanded the Regiment during the pursuit of Price in Northern Mississippi and the sieges of Vicksburg and Jackson· He was severely wounded during the

Oliver P. Morton.
Indiana's War Governor.

Colonel Albert Heath.
100th Indiana Infantry.
(From an old war times photograph.)

assault on Missionary Ridge, November 25, 1863. He was commissioned Colonel, January 8, 1864, and discharged for disability May 10, 1865.

Colonel Ruel M. Johnson entered the service from Goshen, Indiana. He recruited Company "D" of the 100th Indiana in Elkhart county and was commissioned as its Captain August 22, 1862, and mustered on September 10th following. On the 18th of August he was promoted and commissioned Major, *vice* Robert Parrott killed. He was mustered September 5, 1863. On January 9, 1864, he was promoted and commissioned Lieut. Colonel, and on May 2, 1865, he was again promoted and commissioned Colonel of the Regiment. Colonel Johnson was fitted by nature to command men. He first attracted the favorable notice of his superior officers by his conduct at the siege of Jackson, Mississippi, for which he was recommended for promotion, (Loomis' Off. Report, 37-631). He again came into general notice on the battlefield of Missionary Ridge where he deported himself in a manner without a parallel. Col. John Mason Loomis, who commanded our Brigade, has said of the 100th Regiment and of the conduct of Col. Johnson on that day, that "they (the 100th) were suffering severely from the fire of Cleburne's Division, even after they had laid down. But he (Major Johnson) was still on his feet and had perfect control of his men. He could have led them forward with enthusiasm if it had been required. I remained mounted except when my horse was shot, * * * and was frequently on the line of Col. Johnson's Regiment, so that I had them in full view; and I had so much confidence in Col. Johnson, that I did not doubt his Regiment would stay with him if he lived. I only watched them to see if he did still live in that storm of lead and iron, often concealed in the smoke of bursting shell. The quiet temper of his men told me that he did still live." The same statement almost verbatim has been made by Col. John W. Headington and others, who saw the conduct of Col. Johnson on that day.

The foregoing statements by Col. John Mason Loomis and Lieut. Col. Headington are attested by the following named officers and soldiers of the Regiment, who were present and actively participated in the battle. Capt. Sherlock, Co. "A," Capt. Sabin, Co. "B," Capt. John K. Morrow, Co. "C," Sergt. John W. Miller, Co. "E," Capt. Leonard Akers, Co. "F," C. W. Rarick, Abram Geiger, T. N. Fowler, J. A. Nason and E. A. Rines of Co. "H," A. J. Snyder, John Zimmerman, Geo. W. Powers, D. S. Gillispie, Saml. Parker, J. Emerick, William Davis and Silas Goodrich of Co. "B," James Collins, Co. "E," D. E. Newman, Eli Lusher, Silas Mott, Jacob Crull, C. N. Coleman and Charles R. Kingsley of Co. "D," and many others.

The conduct of the 100th Regiment on that day and that of its brave commander became well known throughout the country and finally reached the dull ears of the war department, which was bound to take notice of the bravery of Col. Johnson, and in recognition of his services a medal of honor was duly awarded to him. The Secretary of War, in notifying the Colonel of

Colonel Ruel M. Johnson.
100th Indiana Volunteer Infantry.

The 100th Indiana firing on the Confederate lines while lying behind the railroad embankment; Walcutt charging on the hill to the left; Bushbeck's Brigade of the 11th Corps is seen over the tunnel charging the enemy, who had flanked us on the left; Col. Headington and Jo. Hawkins are holding the colors up on the right, while Col. R. M. Johnson is seen in the open field marching up and down the line with sword in hand cheering the men which he continued to do for four hours.

its issue uses the following language in his letter of transmittal.

"Colonel Ruel M. Johnson,
"Late of the 100th Indiana Volunteers,
"Elkhart, Ind.

"SIR: I have the honor to inform you that by direction of the President, and 'in accordance with the Act of Congress approved March 3, 1863, providing for the presentation of medals of honor to such officers, non-commissioned officers and privates as have most distinguished themselves in action, the Acting Secretary of War has awarded you a medal of honor for most distinguished gallantry in action at Chattanooga, Tennessee, Nov 25, 1863."

"In making the award the Acting Secretary used the following language:

"At that time, this officer was Major of the "Regiment, and after the Lieutenant-Colonel "commanding was wounded and left the field, he "took command of the Regiment, pushing for- "ward to the railroad in front of Tunnel hill, "through the most destructive fire of the enemy, "where the whole Brigade was ordered to lay "down, hold the ground gained and protect them- "selves as much as possible under cover of the "embankment. This was done by the men but "Colonel Johnson remained on his feet marching "for four hours from right to left and from left to "right along the battle line, cheering his men and "urging them to stand fast to their duty, being all "the time exposed to a most dangerous and gall- "ing fire of the enemy, only a few hundred feet "away, four bullets passing through his coat and "he receiving a wound in his right cheek by a "fragment of a shell."

"The medal has been forwarded to you today by registered mail. Upon the receipt of it please advise this office thereof.

"Very Respectfully,
"F. L. Ainsworth, Col. U. S. Army.
"Chief, Record and Pension Office."

During the winter of 1863-4, he made the 100th Indiana the best drilled Regiment, in the performance of field evolutions in the United States. No Regiment in the Federal service could go through the evolutions in daylight which that Regiment could perform on the double quick in the darkness—the drilling hours being from 3:30 to 5:30 A. M. each morning.

He came into general notice again on the battlefield in front of Resaca, May 13, 1864, when with a skirmish line composed of men from the 100th Regiment deployed in front of the Division, he drove a whole Confederate Brigade from the field in the presence of Generals McPherson, Logan and Harrow. (Official Rept. Gen. Harrow, 74-278.)

He was again brought to the notice of Gen. Logan by the shrewd and clever manner in which he brought off the Division skirmish line at Dallas, which he was placed in charge of by Gen. Logan, without the loss of a man, although the Rebel Army was confronting his line. After these successes he was detailed on Gen. Harrow's staff as skirmish officer of the Divison. At the battle of Atlanta he was taken prisoner on the front line by a force which had gained our rear during the many bloody assaults which took place

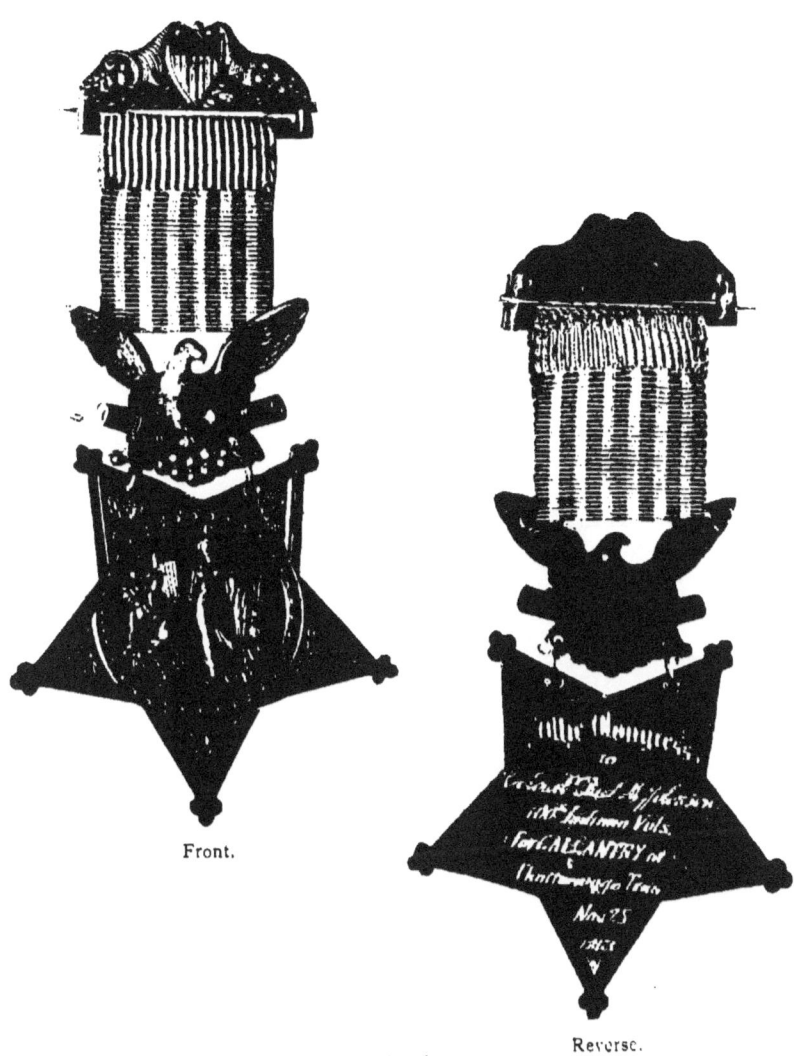

Front.   Reverse.
Medals
Awarded to Colonel R. M. Johnson for bravery in the battle of Chattanooga by the war department F.

Lieutenant Colonel John W. Headington.
100th Indiana Infantry.

on that eventful day. He is specially mentioned in the official report of Gen. Harrow and Col. Reub Williams for gallantry in that battle. (Official Rept. Gen. Harrow, 74-281.) (Official Report Col. Williams, 74-289).

The Colonel was started towards Macon, Georgia, as a prisoner, along with 1,700 men and 75 other officers. On the third day he escaped and had almost reached our lines, when he was recaptured and sent to Charleston, South Carolina, and placed under fire of our batteries. In September, 1864, a limited exchange of prisoners took place, and by special request of Gen. Sherman he was included therein.

He distinguished himself in the pursuit of Hood. On the march to the sea, the battle of Griswoldville, the campaign through the Carolinas, and specially at the battle of Bentonville, and his entire term of service was interspersed with brilliant achievements.

Lieutenant Colonel Headington entered the service from Portland, Jay County Indiana. He recruited Company "H," of the 100th Indiana, in that county, and was commissioned as its Captain on the 11th and mustered on the 23d of September, 1862. He was promoted to Major of the Regiment June 1, 1864, and to Lieutenant Colonel May 21, 1865. Col. Headington commanded the Regiment from the battle of Lovejoy until the return of Col. Johnson, after the latter was exchanged. He enjoys the remarkable distinction of having taken an active part in every campaign and every encounter in which the Regiment took any part, during the entire period of its enlistment. He was not an impetuous, hasty, or rash man, but was in possession of a cool head and good judgment at all times and in every emergency. The men all had implicit confidence in him. He was certainly the George H. Thomas of the Regiment; a good disciplinarian and withal, a genial, companionable officer, and when occasion required him to expose himself or his men he was perfectly oblivious to his personal safety.

He first came into special notice on the battlefield of Missionary Ridge, when, after seven out of ten color bearers and guards had been shot down, he accompanied Uncle Joe Hawkins of Company "H," in bearing aloft the Regimental flag. He received personal mention for efficiency and gallantry in the battle of Griswoldville, in which he took an honorable and conspicuous part.

Majors.

Major Robert Parrot entered the service from Lagrange, Indiana. He was commissioned Major on the 18th and was mustered on the 28th of October, 1862. He was one of those good men whom everybody loved —even an enemy would be ashamed to hate such a man. He was killed by the falling of a tree during a storm at Oak Ridge in the rear of Vicksburg on July 6th, 1863.

Major Venamon entered the service from Goshen, Indiana. He was commissioned First Lieutenant of Company "D," 100th Indiana, August 22d, 1862, and mustered on the 10th of September. On the 18th of August, 1863, he

Major W. H. Venamon.
(From an old war times photograph.)

Ed. Goldsmith,
Lieutenant and Adjutant 100th Indiana Infantry.

was promoted to the Captaincy of Company "D," and on May 1st, 1865, he was promoted Major of the Regiment. He was a quiet, unostentatious officer. He enjoyed the respect and confidence of his superior officers as well as that of the officers and men generally. Whenever duty required Major Venamon to perform any service, no matter how difficult or dangerous, he was always promptly there and performed that duty.

Adjutants.

Adjutant Edward P. Williams entered the service from Fort Wayne. He was commissioned August 27th and mustered August 28th, 1862. He was afterward promoted to A. C. S. and left the Regiment.

Adjutant William H. Ghere enlisted in Captain Thomas C. Dalbey's Company "I" as a private soldier. He was commissioned Adjutant June 15th, 1863, and resigned May 29th, 1864.

Adjutant Edwin Goldsmith entered the service from Orland, Stuben County, Indiana, was commissioned Second Lieutenant in Company "B" August 15th, 1862, was promoted to First Lieutenant January 30th, 1864, and to Adjutant, April 20th, 1864, and served as such until the end of the war and was mustered out with the Regiment. Adjutant Goldsmith received a flattering personal notice in Col. Heath's official report of the Atlanta campaign in the following words:

"I also make special mention of Lieut. E. Goldsmith, my Adjutant—cool and self possessed in time of danger. No one possesses the confidence of the men more than he does. I also recommend him for promotion." (See serial 74 p. 311).

Adjutant Goldsmith received favorable personal notice by Col. R. M. Johnson in his official report of the battle of Griswoldville. (See Johnson's official report.)

Regimental Surgeons.

Samuel France, Regimental Surgeon, entered the service from Syracuse, Indiana. He was commissioned December 2nd, 1862, and mustered January 6th, 1863. Dr. France served efficiently in the field with the regiment until after the surrender of Vicksburg and Jackson. He tendered his resignation August 11th, 1863, while we lay at Camp Sherman, on the Big Black River.

By his cheery words of badinage, or some well-told dry joke of professional or camp life, he says that he often did more than his pills or potions to restore the physical health or mental brightness to the depressed in spirits.

At Camp Sherman, on Big Black river, after the siege of Vicksburg, and the return of the Regiment from Jackson, Dr. France's health became undermined. He then conferred with Dr. Lomax and Dr. Shaw—the Brigade and Division Surgeons, who gave it as their opinion that his only hope of prolonging or saving his

Samuel France, M. D.
Surgeon 100th Indiana Infantry.

D. J. Swarts,
First Assistant Surgeon 100th Indiana Infantry.

life, was to resign and return to civil life, where he could have home comforts. He returned to his Indiana home at Goshen, much broken in health. Surgeon France was a skilled physician, and scientific surgeon, a whole-souled comrade and a warm-hearted friend of all the boys, whether he had the epaulette of office on his shoulders, or the badge of the patriot soldier, the knapsack, strapped to his back. Self-sacrificing free-hearted and generous, was Dr. France.

Assistant Surgeons.

First Assistant Surgeon 100th Indiana, David J. Swarts entered the army from Auburn, DeKalb county, Indiana. He was commissioned First Lieutenant of Company "A" August 13th and mustered Sept 10th, 1862. He was promoted to be First Assistant Surgeon October 3rd, 1862. Dr. Swarts served with the Regiment until the end of the war in the field and was an honest, faithful and very competent officer and had the respect and confidence of all the officers and men of the command. He was several times detailed on detached service at the Corps hospitals after a heavy engagement, in which a great many had been wounded. He enjoyed the distinction of being one of the best surgeons in the 15th Corps. Seventy-five surgeons were killed and wounded in battle during the war.

Dr. Leavitt enlisted as a private soldier in Captain Brouse's Company "K" 100th Indiana

Infantry. On the 12th of May, 1863, he was promoted to be assistant surgeon vice Richard Magee, dismissed May the 8th, 1863. On August 12th, 1863, he was promoted to be surgeon of the Regiment.

Assistant Surgeon Henry H. Hand entered the army as a private soldier in Company "C," 100th Indiana. His qualities soon attracted the attention of his superior officers, and as he possessed some knowledge of medicine and an aptitude and special capacity and qualifications for its practice and administration, he was promoted to be hospital steward of the Regiment January 1, 1864. He performed his duties in that capacity so faithfully that he was commissioned Assistant Surgeon of the Regiment. On the 22d of February, 1865, on the march through the Carolinas on the Peay's Ferry road, Dr. Hand and Henry Stebbins of Company "G" were ambushed by Rebels. Stebbins and his horse and Dr. Hand's horse fell dead. Dr. Hand was taken prisoner and sent to the Rebel prison in Florence, South Carolina, and confined within the dead line until he was exchanged at the close of the war.

Hospital Steward A. Devilbiss entered the service in Company "A," 100th Indiana, August 10, 1862. He possessed at that time some knowledge of medicine which recommended him to his superior officers as an excellent man for that service to which he was soon assigned. He served faithfully and efficiently until he was compelled to leave the service to save his life. He carried with him on his departure the gratitude of many a poor soldier whose sufferings he had alleviated.

Dr. Philander C. Leavitt.
100th Indiana Infantry.
(From a war times photograph.)

H. H. Hand, M. D.
Assistant Surgeon 100th Indiana Infantry.
(From a war times photograph.)

Chaplains.

Rev. Charles A. Munn entered the service as Chaplain of the 100th Indiana, from DeKalb County, on the 8th and was mustered on the 14th of November, 1862. He served faithfully in the field until August 10, 1863, when he resigned.

Rev. John A. Brouse, father of Captain Charles W. Brouse, of Company "K," entered the service from Indianapolis. He was commissioned September 18th and mustered on the 1st of November, 1863, and served faithfully with the Regiment in the field until the end of the war.

There was no more loyal or patriotic class of people in the United States service than the Regimental Chaplains; their voices all over the fields occupied by our armies, ascended daily as the voice of one man for the success of the Union cause and its Army. These officers were always found ready to aid and comfort the soldiers in camp, in the hospital or on the field of battle, for we had many fighting Chaplains in the army, and many of them were killed and wounded in the hottest of the fight.

The writer has seen Chaplain Brouse of the 100th Indiana, during an engagement, right in the front line of battle, perfectly oblivious to his own personal safety, aiding and encouraging the men to fight. He was beloved by the officers and men of his Regiment because he was a Christian and a patriot. He was brave and fearless, and knew no danger in the field, where he was always found during an engagement.

Eleven Chaplains were killed and many were wounded in battle during the war.

George W. Gore enlisted as a private soldier in Company "B," 100th Indiana, August 15, 1862. He was promoted to First Sergeant of Company "B," and was very severely wounded in the assault on Missionary Ridge. He served notwithstanding until the end of the war, and was mustered out as Sergeant Major of the Regiment, to which position he had been promoted for gallantry in battle.

Quartermasters.

Regimental Q. M. Alba M. Tucker entered the service from Goshen, Indiana, and was commissioned R. Q. M. September 9, 1862. He was promoted to Captain and A.Q. M., and mustered out by way of favor.

R. Q. M. German Brown enlisted as a private soldier in Company "B," at Orland, Indiana, August 15, 1862. He was promoted Regimental Quartermaster January 5, 1864, while we lay at Bellefont, and served until the end of the war.

John H. Broderick enlisted as a private soldier in Company "D," 100th Indiana, was mustered September 18, 1862. Mr. Broderick was a quick and correct business man, and the attention of his superior officers was for that reason soon attracted to him, and he was promoted to be Regimental Commissary Sergeant, a position of great responsibility which he filled to the entire satisfaction of the officers and with great credit to himself, although one of the hardest in the Regiment to fill. He served faithfully and

A. Devilbiss M. D.
Hospital Steward 100th Indiana Infantry.

creditably until the end of the war, and was mustered out with the Regiment.

Quartermaster Sergeant.

Frank J. Blaine enlisted as a private soldier in Company "D," 100th Indiana Regiment, August 22, 1862. He was soon after promoted to be Quartermaster Sergeant, and served as such to the satisfaction of the Regiment and was mustered out with it.

15th Army Corps Scouts--Known also as Hall's Scouts.

Hall's Scouts were organized by Henry J. Hall, of Company "C." He aided in recruiting that company. He was ambitious and the element of fear was not in him. He longed for an opportunity to distinguish himself by the performance of daring and reckless acts. Under the direction General Hurlbut he did scouting in the winter of 1862-3. During that time he performed such distinguished services that the General gave him an order to select men from any command he desired. He chose men from his own Company, "C," of the 100th—a number of as brave, reliable and intrepid men as could be found in the entire Federal Army, embracing among others, Theodore F. Upson, John Ryason, John Whitlock, James A. Taylor, Harlow J. Hearne, Milo B. Squires, William Sharp, and others. These men Hall knew would fight until they were dead when duty required it, and they performed such valuable services during the siege of Vicksburg and Jackson that General Sherman gave Hall permission to select 100 men for special duty as scouts. Nelson Austin, S. A. Albright, Thomas Legg and others, were taken from the 100th and added to these scouts, and many indeed are the daring exploits they performed. With only five men, near Florence, Alabama, Hall, captured a Confederate Lieutenant Colonel, a Major, a Captain, a Sergeant and thirteen privates and turned them over to General Sherman. He set out once with a few men on a most hazardous expedition. In the dusk of the evening he and his men were ambushed by a superior force with double barrelled shot guns and Hall was mortally wounded. After his death the scouts were divided up among the different army headquarters. Theodore F. Upson was captured twice during the battle of Atlanta, but escaped. Some of the scouts were killed, others wounded, but they left a name for the performance of deeds of daring, of which any soldier might be proud indeed.

Rev. John A Brouse,
Chaplain 100th Indiana Volunteers

John H. Broderick.
Com.-Sergeant 100th Indiana Infantry.

Theodore F. Upson.
One of the daring 15th A. C. Scouts.

Roster of Company A, 100th Indiana Infantry.

Captain Marquis L. Rhodes recruited Company "A" at Auburn. He enlisted August 6, 1862, and was commissioned August 13th. He died in Memphis, near Fort Pickering, December 10, 1862.

Ezra D. Hartman entered the service as Second Lieutenant on August 13, 1862. He was promoted to First Lieutenant October 4th, and to Captain on the 11th of December, 1862. He served in the field in Northern Mississippi and Southern Tennessee in the winter of 1862-3; was in active service along the line of the Memphis & Charleston Railroad during the winter and spring of 1863. He commanded his Company during the siege of Vicksburg and on the march to Jackson. During the siege of those places he was much exposed to the intense heat and dust during the summer of 1863, the effects of which broke down his health and almost destroyed his eyesight. He was honorably discharged by order of the war department November 6, 1863. Captain Hartman took with him the regrets of both officers and men when he left the service.

Lucius Barney entered the service as Orderly Sergeant. He was promoted to Second Lieutenant, then to First Lieutenant and then to Captain. He was honorably discharged for disability August 12, 1864.

John H. Moore entered the service as Second Sergeant. On the 11th of December, 1862, he was promoted to Second Lieutenant, and on the 7th of November to First Lieutenant, and was commissioned Captain, but was not mustered as such. He served faithfully in the field during 1862-3-4. He was mortally wounded by a cannon shot on the front line at the battle of Lovejoy, September 2, 1864, and died at Marietta, Georgia, October 1, 1864.

Eli J. Sherlock was promoted to Orderly Sergeant, was through the campaign in Northern Mississippi, the seige of Vicksburg and Jackson, the march from Vicksburg to Chattanooga; was wounded in the assault on Missionary Ridge, participated in the Atlanta campaign, was Assistant Provost Marshal of Marietta, Georgia, in July and part of August, 1864; was in the battles of Jonesboro and Lovejoy, the pursuit of Hood, the march to the sea; was wounded at Griswoldville, was at the siege of Savannah, was at the burning of Columbia, made the march through the Carolinas. Was promoted to First Lieutenant August 13th, 1864, and to Captain, October 2nd, 1864.

Lieut. H. E. Meeker entered the service August 13th, 1862. On October 2nd, 1864, he was promoted to First Lieutenant. He served through the sieges of Vicksburg and Jackson; was wounded at Missionary Ridge. He made the march to Knoxville and was in every engagement of the Atlanta campaign; was in the march to the sea and the siege of Savannah and took an active part in the march through the

Captain E. D. Hartman.
Company A, 100th Indiana.
(From an old photograph, 1867.)

Carolinas, being on detached service under special orders in charge of a forage detail. His men had many brushes with the Rebels. Lieut. Meeker was a good soldier and officer and had in him naturally all the elements of a dashing cavalry commander.

Lieutenant Albertus A. Waters was promoted on November 22nd, 1864, to Second Lieutenant. He served during the war and was honorably discharged at Washington, D. C., June 8th, 1865. Few men in the regiment were better known than Lieutenant Waters.

Fair, William H., was promoted to Sergeant for bravery in front of the enemy. Sergeant Fair was one of the solid men among the soldiers of Company "A" as every member of that Company will bear witness. His conduct as a soldier on all occasions was such as to merit the confidence and esteem of his superior officers, and he enjoyed the distinction of participating in every battle or skirmish in which the Regiment was engaged. He served faithfully during the war and was honorably discharged at Washington, D. C., June 8, 1865.

Kindell, John L., Sergeant—Died at Lagrange, Tenn., January 11, '63.

Lockhart, Wm. C., Sergeant—Discharged October 23, '63.

Klien, Cleveland A., Sergeant—Died at Collierville, Tenn., April 2, '63.

Dewitt, Daniel, Sergeant—Discharged October 24, '65.

Hall, John M., Sergeant—Mustered out June 8, '65.

Robbins, Albert—Discharged, Nov. 11, '62.

Davis, Oliver S.—Wounded at Jackson,

Mississippi, and at Missionary Ridge; died at Fayetteville, North Carolina, February, '65.

Walker, James P.—Died at Memphis, Tenn., October 24, '63.

Bodine, David C., Sergeant—Wounded severely at Missionary Ridge.

Shuman, George, Musician—Mustered out May 19, '65.

Durbin, Joseph C., Wagoner—Served faithfully during the war.

Anthony, Abraham—Died at Holly Springs January 8, '63.

Arthur, Martin—Promoted to Corporal for meritorious conduct in line of duty; served faithfully during the war; mustered out June 8, '65.

Beams, George—Died at Memphis, Tenn., November 24, '62.

Bolinger, Benjamin—Served faithfully during the war; mustered out June 8, '65.

Boren, John W.—Died at Atlanta, Georgia, Oct. 24, '64.

Butler, Irving—Died at Snyder's Bluff on Yazoo river, Miss., July 24, '63.

Boyles, Artemas—Died at Grand Junction, Tenn., Feb. 20, '63.

Buchanan, Reason—Died at Nashville, Tenn., Jan. 24, '64.

Buchanan, George—Wounded severely at Griswoldville, Georgia, Nov. 22nd, '64; mustered out, June 8, '65. He was a good soldier.

Buchanan, John A., Sergeant—Served during the war; discharged, June 8, '65.

Culver, Harrison—Died at Memphis, Tenn., Dec. 24, '63.

Critchet, Jonathan—Auburn. Served faithfully during the war; mustered out June 8, '65.

Captain E. J. Sherlock.
Company A, 100th Indiana.
(From an old war times photograph.)

Hanford E. Meeker.
First Lieutenant Company A, 100th Indiana.

Sergeant William H. Fair.
Company A, 100th Indiana.

Dimmit, William H.—Died at Abbeville, Miss., Dec. 24, '62.

Davis, James—Died at Jefferson Barracks, Mo., Dec. 22, '64.

Davis, John—Served during the war; mustered out June 8, '65.

Frees, Samuel—Served during the war; mustered out June 8, '65.

Frees, Hammond—Wounded, Mission Ridge. Served during the war; mustered out June 8, '65.

Fiant, John—Served during the war; mustered out June 8, '65.

Friedt, Henry—Discharged, disablity, January 30, '63.

Farver, Lemuel—Served during the war; mustered out June 8, '65.

Guthrie, Simeon—Served during the war; mustered out May 26, '65.

Goodenough, Abel R.—Discharged January 28, '63.

Grubb, John—Died at Collierville, Tenn., March 18, '63.

Haines, Napoleon A.—Wounded, Mission Ridge, and transferred to V. R. C.

Howser, Jonathan — Promoted Corporal; mustered out June 8, '65.

Howser, Gideon—Died at Collierville, Tenn., May 1, '63.

Hursh, John—Died at Memphis, Tenn., February 8, '63.

Hursh, Benjamin—Transferred to Company "F"; served during the war.

Hammond, James—Died at Grand Junction, Tenn., February 22, '63.

Holden, Samuel—Transferred to V. R. C., November 25, '63.

Jones, Wesley J.—Discharged for disability, May 26, '63.

Jones, Theodore—Killed, Dallas, Georgia, June 8, '64.

Long, Harrison—Wounded slightly on head battle Dallas, Georgia, June 8, '64; served during the war.

Likens, William—Discharged for disability August 21, '63.

McNabb, John—Died spotted fever at Holly Springs, Miss., Jan. 6, '63.

Maxwell, William B.—Wounded, Mission Ridge, November 25, '63; mustered out May 13, '65.

Melvin, George W.—Served during the war; discharged June 8th, '65.

Melvin, Wallace J.—Died at Holly Springs, Miss., December 2nd, '62.

Mohler, John R.—Wounded severely, Mission Ridge; discharged June 17th, '64.

McGoon, Benjamin P.—Wounded, Mission Ridge; mustered out June 8th, '65.

McConnel, John—Wounded, Mission Ridge; died at Auburn, Ind., Jan. 1st, '64.

Miller, Silas C.—Transferred to V. R. C.; discharged July 14th, '65.

Noel, George—Died at Memphis, Tennessee, Nov. 5th, '63.

Corporal Charles T. Rogers.

Company A, 100th Indiana.

Served faithfully during the war; was promoted for meritorious conduct as a soldier; was well known in the regiment, and had the respect of both officers and men.

William B. Graham, M. D.,
Company A.
Served faithfully during the war. He enjoyed the respect of his officers and the esteem of the men.

Osburn, Enos—Died at Nashville, Tennessee, June 3rd, '64.

Olinger, John S.—Honorably discharged May 26th, '63.

Olinger, Anthony—Killed at Battle of Lovejoy, Georgia, September 2nd, '64.

Olinger, Daniel—Served during the war; discharged June 8th, '65.

Penny, Lewis F.—Died at Memphis, Tenn., November 24th, '62.

Piffer, Daniel—Discharged for disabilty May 9th, '63.

Piffer, Joseph—Wounded at Mission Ridge; Honorably mustered out as Corporal June 8th, '65.

Powell, Levi B.—Wounded at Mission Ridge and at Griswoldville, Georgia, Nov. 22nd, '64.

Palmer, Hiram—Served during the war; mustered out June 8th, '65.

Prosser, Joseph—Promoted to Corporal, served faithfully during the war; honorably mustered out June 8th, '65.

Raub, John B.—Served during the war; mustered out June 10, '65.

Symonds, John C.—Wounded at Mission Ridge; mustered out July 7th, '65.

Swander, John Discharged for disability Nov. 11th, '62.

Squires, Asher—Died at Paducah, Kentucky, August 17th, '63.

Squires, Nathan—Wounded severely at

Mission Ridge, Nov. 25th, '63; mustered out June 8th, '65.

Shaw, Ansel M.—Served faithfully for three years. He was wounded at the battle of Missionary Ridge, having been placed on the skirmish line that day by the writer. He was promoted for bravery on the field.

Smith, Isaac—Served during the war, mustered out June 8, '65.

Skinner, Orlander—Died at Memphis, Tenn., November 17, '62.

Ulm, Jeremiah—Served faithfully during the war. Honorably mustered out June 8, ,65.

Vanlear, John D.—Served honorably until the close of the war. Mustered out June 8, '65. Was wounded in the battle of Resaca.

Wiltrout, Benjamin S.—Served until the close of the war. Ben was a good soldier.

Wearly, Calvin J.—Transferred to Marine Brigade.

Warner, John—Died at Collierville, Tenn., April 8, '63.

Wilson, Shipley—Discharged for disability May 26, '63.

Wolf, Henry—Wounded severely at Mission Ridge Nov. 25, '63. Captured at Cassville, Georgia. Mustered out June 22, '65. Promoted for bravery at the battle of Missionary Ridge.

Wyatt, Richard—Died at Memphis, Tenn., October 16, '63.

Cordray, Walter—Discharged for disability, March 23, '63.

Corporal A. M. Shaw.
Company A.

Campbell, Alvin—Transferred to 48th Indiana Infantry May 30, '65.

Carr, Cyrus—Transferred to 48th Indiana Infantry May 30, '65.

Kramer, Christian—Dropped out of ranks near Whiteside, Tenn., Dec. 19, '63; undoubtedly killed.

Moe, Lemuel—Transferred to 48th Indiana Infantry May 30, '65.

Nickerson, Alden—Died at Murfreesboro, Tenn., Nov. 24, '63.

New, Leopold—Discharged for disability, Department of Memphis, Jan. 16, '63. He afterward supplied the army with newspapers by permission from General Grant.

Olinger, Cyrus—Transferred to 48th Indiana May 30, '65.

Phelps, George S.—Mustered Dec. 6, '64; transferred to 48th Indiana May 30, '65.

Rawson, Thomas—Wounded, Dallas; transferred to 48th Indiana May 30, '65.

Roster of Company B, 100th Indiana Infantry.

Captain Orla J. Fast was mustered as First Lieutenant of Company "B," September 10th, 1862, and as Captain, March 15th, 1864. He resigned May 30th, 1865, to accept a promotion as A. A. G. U. S. Vols., having been commissioned as such by the President. Captain Fast was well known and highly respected throughout the whole army.

Captain Joseph W. Gillespie entered the service August 15th, 1862. He served until January 29th, 1864, when he resigned.

Capt. Marden Sabin enlisted August 15th, 1862. On May 1st, 1864, he was promoted to First Lieutenant, over the heads of several very good men, on account of his efficiency and meritorious conduct as a soldier. Lieut. Sabin served with credit and distinction through all of the engagements in the Atlanta campaign, the march to the sea and through the Carolinas. May 1st, 1865, he was promoted to the Captaincy of his company, an honor which was by him well deserved and honestly merited. He enjoyed the respect of the officers and men of the regiment. He was an intelligent, efficient and brave officer.

Walter R. Parker enlisted in Company "B" as a private soldier August 15th, 1862. He served as such until November 22nd, 1864, when he was promoted from the ranks to be Second

Captain Orla J. Fast.
100th Indiana Infantry.
Commissioned A. A. G. by the President.

Captain Marden Sabin.
Company B. 100th Indiana Infantry.

Lieutenant of his company for meritorious conduct in the line of his duty; and on May 1st, 1865, he was promoted to be First Lieutenant and was mustered out with the regiment.

Lieut. Samuel Blanchard entered the service as Fourth Sergeant of Company "B." He was promoted to be First Sergeant and on May 1st, 1865, to be Second Lieutenant. He served faithfully during the war.

Gillespie, David S.—Discharged for disability, Sept. 3rd, '63.

Conkey, Manning S.—Killed at Jonesboro, Georgia, Aug. 31st, '64, by shell.

Flint, Francis—Promoted to Sergeant Aug. 31st, '63.

Carver, Henry W.—Discharged for disability May 22nd, '63.

Rude, Charles—Died at Grand Junction, Tenn., Jan. 22nd, '63.

Sutherland, Andrew J.—Served during the war.

Chadwick, Samuel—Died August 26th, '64, at Marrietta, Georgia.

Brooks, Henry—Died September 19, '62, at Madison, Ind.

Wilder, Charles H.—Served during the war.

Bodley, Aaron—Served during the war.

Abbott, William—Served during the war.

Brockway, George—Died September 14, '63, at Camp Sherman.

Bodley, James—Served during the war.

Bodley, Philo—Died Dec. 30, '62, at Holly Springs.

Bradley, James—Mustered out, June 30, '65.

Bradley, Daniel—Mustered out June 30, '65.

Brock, Monroe—Served during the war.

Blass, Clarkson B.—Served during the war.

Blass, Jefferson—Died Feb. 20, '64, at Bellefonte Station, Ala.

Burton, John—Mustered out Aug. 9, '65.

Betzer, Peter—Died March 5, '63, at Grand Junction, Tenn.

Betzer, Adam—Discharged for disability at Memphis, Tenn.

Baily, Samuel—Promoted to Corporal June 25, '64.

Carpenter, Chauncey—Promoted to Corporal, June 6, '64.

Cole, Royal—Wounded severely in the battle of Missionary Ridge; discharged on account of wounds, June 6, '64.

Cook, George F.—Served faithfully during the war. He was promoted for meritorious conduct in line of duty. He possessed many soldierly qualities, was a good man and a brave and effecient soldier.

Casper, Levi—Promoted to Corporal Dec. 31, '64.

Casper, Lewis—Died Feb. 18, '63, at Grand Junction, Tenn.

Cluck, George—Died April 1, '63 at Collierville, Tenn.

Clark, John C.—Killed at siege of Atlanta, August 21, '64.

Cleveland, Addison—Served during the war.

George F. Cook.
Company B, 100th Indiana Infantry.

Gil. Rhoades.
Company B, 100th Indiana.

Dillingham, Jerome B.—Died April 9, '63, Collierville.

Dillingham, James—Served during the war.

Davis, William—Served during the war.

Dudley, Grove H.—Served during the war; was a good soldier.

Dimon, Henry—Discharged for disability June 3, '63.

Denman, Smith—Discharged for disability June 3, '63.

Ebert, James M.—Served during the war.

Ellis, Charles—Killed in a skirmish near Cave Springs, Georgia, November 1, '64, after he was a prisoner.

Emerich, Jonathan—Served during the war.

French, George—Wounded, Resaca, Ga., May 13, 1864; mustered out May 30, '65.

Goodrich, Silas—Served during the war.

Gillespie, Rufus R.—Promoted to Corporal Dec. 8, '62.

Green, David—Died April 28, '63, at Memphis, Tenn.

Hurd, Harvey M.—Discharged Sept. 3, '63, at Camp Sherman.

Haynes, Martin—Died July 22, '63, at Memphis, Tenn.

Haynes, John—Served during the war.

Haines, Monroe J.—Served during the war.

Hoover, Joseph—Served during the war.

Hilton, Lewis L.—Promoted Corporal; promoted Sergeant; served during the war.

Hoolihan, Joseph—Discharged June 9, '63, Memphis, Tenn.

Jarvis, Clement—Served during the war.

Johnson, Henry—Served during the war.

Jadwin, John P.—Promoted to Corporal Dec. 31, '64.

Kellogg, William—Discharged March 7, '63, at Cairo, Ill.

Kale, James—Died March 19, '63, at Collierville.

Keith, Lewis—Killed in the battle of Jonesboro, Georgia, August 31, '64, by fragment of shell.

Lee, Clark—Died Feb. 11, '63, at Grand Junction, Tenn.

Musser, John—Promoted Corporal; promoted Sergeant; served during the war.

McLane, Ambrose—Discharged June 9, '63, at Memphis, Tenn.

Northway, George F.—Died May 3, '64, at Memphis, Tenn.

Pulver, William O.—Mustered as Wagoner after Dec. 31, '63.

Parker, Samuel—Served during the war.

Powers, George W.—Promoted to Corporal; discharged Feb. 16, '63.

Root, Rodney H.—Died Nov. 7, '64, at Chattanooga, Tenn.

Rollins, George R.—Served during the war.

Rhoads, Gil—Everybody knew Gil—he was the life of his Company. A brave man and an honest, trustworthy and intrepid soldier. He served faithfully and efficiently during the war. He had the respect of all the officers and men of the Regiment, and never faltered when duty called.

Rodgers, Bradley—Promoted to Corporal; served during the war.

Shumway, Return U.—Was an exemplary man, an efficient soldier, brave and faithful in the

Return U. Shumway.
Company B. 100th Indiana Infantry.

discharge of all his duties. He was discharged for disability, September 8, '64.

Sutherland, Christopher Columbus—Wagoner.

Suppenough, Tuffle — Served during the war.

Sultz, Jacob—Served during the war.

Scott, Henry—Wounded mortally at Resaca.

Snyder, George—Died November 12, '63, as Memphis, Tenn.

Snyder, J. Andrew—Served with distinction during the war; a good soldier.

Soule, David—Killed at Atlanta, August 25, '64.

Sperry, Jackson E.—Discharged Feb. 12, '63, at Indianapolis, Ind.

Taylor, Cornelius—Discharged Feb. 25, '63, at Indianapolis.

Taylor, William J.—Served during the war.

Taylor, Warren—Drowned in Mill creek near Bentonville, N. C., March 22, '65.

Taylor, Orrin R.—Discharged for disability June 3, '63.

Welch, William J.—Died April 15, '63, at Memphis, Tenn.

Woodworth, Homer S.—Discharged Sept. 3, '63, for disability.

Wiggins, Nathan—Served during the war.

Young, Riley — Promoted to Corporal; served during the war.

Zimmerman, John—Served during the war.

Fanshaw, John H.—Transferred to 48th Indiana for further duty.

Van Allstin, Charles E.—Transferred to 48th Indiana for further duty.

Captain Harvey Crocker entered the service August 15, 1862. He made the campaign of 1862-3 in Northern Mississippi. He enjoyed the respect of his superior officers and the fullest confidence of his men. He became severely afflicted with rheumatism during the winter of 1863, to such an extent that he was wholly unfit for duty, and was forced to resign in 1863 to save his life.

Captain John K. Morrow entered the service August 15, 1862, as First Lieutenant. He was promoted to Captain June 3, 1863, and resigned February 20, 1864. He did service at Vicksburg, Jackson and Missionary Ridge.

Captain Edward Fobes entered the service as Fifth Corporal of Company "C." He was promoted to be First Lieutenant October 31, 1863, and March 1, 1864, was promoted to be Captain. January 8, 1865, he resigned on account of disability.

Captain John B. Pratt entered the service as Sergeant. He was slightly wounded at Mission Ridge. He was promoted to be First Lieutenant and on January 9, 1865, to be Captain of Company "C."

James Boyd was commissioned Second Lieu-

Captain H. Crocker,
Company C.

tenant August 15, 1862, and on June 3, 1863, he was made First Lieutenant. He died at Snyder's Bluffs on the Yazoo river, July 2, 1863.

Samuel W. Dille was promoted to First Lieutenant March 18, 1865. He served through the war and was honorably discharged with the Regiment. Wounded at Resaca May 14, 1864.

Samuel R. Miller was several times promoted, the last being to that of Second Lieutenant on November, 22, '64. He was honorably discharged with the Regiment.

Myers, Sandford W.—Wounded mortally, New Hope Church, Georgia.

Fuller, John W.—Sergeant, discharged January 10, '63.

Cook, Jarred—Sergeant, served with 15th Army Corps Scouts.

Butler, Charles—Mustered out June 8, '65.

Finney, Isaiah E.—Mustered out June 8, '65.

Legg, Peter—Died at Grand Junction, Tenn. Feb. 4, '63.

Spangler, George S.—Mustered out as Sergeant June 8, '65.

Beck, James—Discharged May 15, '65.

Hearn, Harlow J.—Served with distinction in Scouts 15th A. C. Severely wounded at Knoxville, Tenn.

Brown, Theodore—Served with 15th A. C. Scouts.

Collins, James—Served with 15th A. C Scouts.

Austin, Nelson M.—Served with 15th A. C. Scouts; an excellent soldier.

Atwater, Marcus L.—Captured on Atlanta Campaign, '64.

Alspaugh, Reuben—Died at La Grange, Tenn., Feb. 13, '63.

Albright, Samuel A.—Wounded at Resaca; an excellent soldier.

Bennett, David—Promoted to Captain 129th Regiment.

Brady, John—Discharged Sept. 1, '63.

Boocher, Robert—Wounded in battle of Dallas, Atlanta Campaign.

Brady, David—Discharged June 12, '64.

Bean, John—Mustered out June 8, '65.

Barks, John—Wounded at Jackson, Mississippi; was a good soldier.

Brower, Henry O.—Transferred to V. R. C. Oct. 2, '63.

Blackson, John J.—Died at Camp Sherman, Miss., Aug. 21, '63.

Bishop, C. Vancleve—An excellent soldier; promoted to Corporal.

Coomer, Justice—Discharged June 10, '63.

Coonrad, Jeremiah—An excellent soldier, always faithful.

Cook, Richard—Died at Grand Junction, Tenn., Feb. 23, '63.

Chaffee, Ezra A.—Mustered out as Corporal June 8, '65.

Clark, George M.—Died on Hospital Boat, Sept. 28, '63.

Clark, John H.—Transferred to V. R. C.; mustered out July 14, '65.

Eiman, Abraham—Served during the war; an excellent soldier.

Finley, Cyrus—Discharged June 16, '63.

Finney, Daniel A.—Discharged January 4, '64.

Gillett, Franklin—Killed on Ogeechee river December 6, '64.

Harding, Daniel—Promoted Corporal; an excellent soldier.

Harding, Mathias—Severely wounded Mission Ridge; an excellent soldier.

Harding, Henry—Mustered out June 8, '65.

Hall, Henry—Wounded mortally near Florence, Alabama, while in command of 15th A. C. Scouts; a good soldier; he was brave and fearless. (See Hall's Scouts.)

Himes, Henry—Mustered out as Corporal; a good soldier.

Hand, Charles E.—Served faithfully during the war.

Hulburt, George A.—Discharged January 22, '63.

Hunt, William P.—Died at Colliersville, Tenn., May 2, '63.

Hiestand, Samuel—Died at Colliersville, Tenn., April 15, '63.

Johnson, George—Died Grand Junction, Tenn, Feb. 4, '63.

Kingsley, James H.—Died Haines Bluff, Miss., July 18, '63.

Kimball, Omer A.—Detailed as Division Blacksmith.

Lazenby, Robert C.—Died at LaGrange, Ind; was color bearer.

Leib, Daniel M.—Promoted 1st. Lieut. 12th Cavalry.

Legg, Thomas E.—Served with the 15th A. C. Scouts; an excellent soldier.

Miller, William—Died at Memphis, Tenn., Oct. 12, '63.

Millnes, William—Mustered out June 8, '65.

Nichols, Thomas F.—An excellent soldier; complimented by Col. Heath for keeping cleanest gun in Regiment.

Oliver, Thomas—Mustered out May 30, '65.

Phillips, Aaron—Mustered out as Corporal June 8, '65.

Phillips, Solomon A.—An excellent soldier.

Phillips, John C.—Served during the war.

Pontius, Jacob—Wounded, Dallas, Ga., May 28, '64; was absolutely without fear in battle.

Powell, John F.—Died at Haines Bluff, Miss., September 28, '63.

Pickel, Joseph—Discharged May 2, '63.

Plumb, Henry—Died at Grand Junction, Tenn., Feb. 21, '63.

Ryason, John—Served with 15th A. C. Scouts; was personally complimented for bravery by General Harrow.

Rowe, Lewis—Discharged July 5, '64.

Royce, Joel W.—Died at Holly Springs, Miss., Jan 3, '63.

Ruff, William—Wounded mortally at Mission Ridge.

Richmond, Benjamin—Served 15th A. C. Scouts; an excellent soldier.

Reed, Amos—Died at Memphis, Tenn., May 1, '63.

Rhodes, Paul—Mustered out June 8, '65; a grand, good soldier.

Rassler, John—Mustered out as Corporal; was a good soldier.

Rathwell, John—Discharged Jan. 15, '63.

Sturgess, James H.—Was a good soldier.

Squires, Miles B.—Served with 15th A. C. Scouts; was captured and paroled near Fayetteville, N. C.

Starr, Hulburt—Died at St. Louis, Mo., Feb. 19, '63.

Sharp, William—Killed at Jonesboro, Georgia, while Orderly on General Harrow's Staff. Favorably mentioned in the General's official report of that battle.

Tippett, James—Discharged June 2, '63.

Todd, John W.—Discharged May 11, '63; a good soldier.

Taylor, James H.—Served Scouts 15th A. C.; an excellent soldier.

Thorn, Albert—Wounded, Mission Ridge; mustered out as Sergeant.

Whitney, Edward — Killed, Missionary Ridge, Nov. 25, '63.

Wolford, Aaron---Killed, Griswoldville, Ga.; a good soldier.

Woodruff, David—Killed by tree, Haines Bluff, July 8, '63.

Weaver, Samuel—Died at Lagrange, Tenn., March 13, '63.

Whitlock, John W.—Served with distinction in 15th A. C. Scouts.

Wicson, George S.—Died at Colliersville, Tenn., May 6, '63.

Zook, Joseph—Detailed as Wagoner in Ammunition train.

Phillips, Hector—Served during the war; an excellent soldier.

Roster of Company "D," 100th Indiana.

This Company was raised by Col. R. M. Johnson. He was its first Captain (see Col. R. M. Johnson in Field and Staff).

John W. Geisinger was promoted First Lieutenant August 22, and mustered October 16th. On May 1, 1864, he was commissioned as Captain of that Company.

Lieutenant William J. Myers — Mustered September 10, 1862; resigned August 10, 1863.

Asa A. Norton was commissioned as Second Lieutenant November 22, 1864, and as First Lietenant May 1, 1865, and mustered out with the Regiment.

James L. Winans was commissioned Second Lieutenant May 1, 1865, and was mustered out with the Regiment at the close of the war. Lieutenant Winans was a brave and faithful soldier.

Sergeant Luke L. Sawyer was a good and faithful soldier. He enjoyed the respect and esteem of the officers and men of his Company in the highest degree. The hardships of the war were more than he had the power to bear, and he was discharged for disability, contracted in his line of duty, January 18, 1863.

Firestone, Emanuel—Died at Madison, Ind., April 6,'65.

Reed, William C. — Wounded, Mission Ridge; transferred to V. R. C.

Sergeant Luke L. Sawyer,
Company D, 100th Indiana.

Sergeant Corneleus Coleman.
Company D, 100th Indiana.
Promoted for bravery.

Terwilliger, Calvin S.—Served during the war.

Jones, William B.—Wounded December, '63, near Lookout Mountain.

Blaine, Henry C.—Mustered out June 8, '65.

Grubb, John F.—Mustered out June 8, '65, as Sergeant.

Compton, Samuel R.—Served during the war.

Spiker, Jefferson—Discharged May 13, '63.

Mishler, Henry—Discharged Dec. 30, '64.

Arney, George—Mustered out June 8, '65.

Swartz, Jonas—Drowned in Mississippi river at Memphis, June 9, '63.

Alvine, Jacob—Transferred to Co. "K," October 3, '63.

Bowers, Isaac—Discharged Dec. 12, '63.

Brubaker, Amos—Killed, Missionary Ridge, Nov. 25, '63.

Bickle, Thomas—Transferred to Co. "K," October 3, '63.

Bender, Urias—Drowned at Beaufort, S. C., Jan. 26, '65.

Brondage, Jacob—Died Feb. 2, '63; he was a model soldier and enjoyed the respect of all his comrades in arms.

Black, John—Died March 9, '63.

Coleman, Cornelius—Was a messenger on Brigade Division and Corps Staff and performed many feats of daring during the progress of the severest battles of the war. He was at the Headquarters of Generals Corse, Logan and Sherman much of his time and also General Hugh Ewing. He was shot through the body in an engagement with the Confederates at Turkey Town Valley, Alabama October 25, 1863, but recovered. He was promoted to Sergeant for bravery.

Crull, Jacob—Wounded at Mission Ridge Nov. 25, 1863. Mustered out June 8, 1865. This man was a brave and fearless soldier.

Carr, Lafayette—Discharged January, 1863.

Compton, William A.—Wounded at Missionary Ridge while in the act of throwing a six pound shell back of our lines; the shell having stopped and the fuse still burning within 12 inches of his head.

Carr, Lewis J.—Was one of the best men in Company "D", was always ready to do his duty and had the respect and confidence of his officers. He served three years faithfully and was promoted for meritorious conduct in front of the enemy.

Clay, Thomas—Wounded in the thigh at Dallas. Mustered out June 8, 1865.

Chivington, Phillip—Served through the war; was a true man and soldier; was mustered out at Washington, D. C., June 8, 1865.

Every, William—Killed in battle of Jackson, Miss., June 15, '63. He was the first man of the Regiment killed in battle.

Eyer, Isaac—Mustered out June 8, 1865. Served three years.

Eversole Simon P.—Mustered out June 8, '65. Served three years.

Finch, Elias S.—Served during the war. Mustered out June 8, '65.

Firestone, Isaac—Served during the war. Mustered out June 8, '65; was a good soldier.

Gore, Charles H—Served during the war.

Gift, William—Served during the war.

Hall, Lucius—Died Dec. 7, '62.

Corporal Lewis J. Carr.
Company D, 100th Indiana.
(Promoted for meritorious conduct.)

Charles R. Kingsley.
Company D, 100th Indiana.

Harring, James—Discharged Jan. 16, '63.

Johnston, Samuel — Drowned, Beaufort, South Carolina, Jan. 26, '65.

Johnson, Frederick W.—Mustered out June 8, '65.

Keyport, John L.—Discharged April 3, '63.

Charles R. Kingsley—Served faithfully for three years. He was well known and respected by every man in the Regiment, and had the respect and confidence of his superior officers. He served his country well and was honorably discharged June 8, '65.

Keller, Richard—Mustered out June 8, '65, as Corporal.

Lusher, Eli—Served during the war.

Longsdorff, Henry — Wounded mortally, Mission Ridge, Nov. 25, '63.

Leedy, Jacob—Killed, Missionary Ridge, Nov. 25, '63.

Myers, Anthony—Mustered out June 8, '65.

Mishler, John—Died March 9, '63.

Mills, Jacob—Served during the war; mustered out June 8, '65.

Mott, George W.—Died April 16, '63, at Colliersville, Tenn.

Mott, Silas—Served during the war; mustered out June 8, '65; was a true soldier and a good man.

Miller, Alonzo—Served during the war.

Myers, Isaac—Severely wounded at Resaca through right arm.

McDowell, William—Transferred to V.R.C.

Mann, Christian—Mustered out June 8, '65.

Neigle, Jacob—Wounded through wrist at Missionary Ridge.

Newman, Daniel E.—Mustered out June 8, '65.

Neikart, John W.—Taken prisoner at Atlanta, Ga. Died.

Overholt, Isaac—Mustered out June 8, '65.

Oaks, John W.—Killed, Missionary Ridge, Nov. 25, '63.

Ott, Alaway—Discharged Feb. 19, '63.

Ott, Levi—Mustered out June 8, '65.

Pletcher, Jacob—Died Nov. 11, '63.

Palmer, Noah E.—Transferred Company "K," Oct. 3, '63.

Thomas Price was a model man in the army. He was always brave and fearless, and was at all times and under all circumstances dignified and honorable. His moral character in the army would have been an ornament to any officer or man. He faithfully performed his duty with punctuality and efficiency.

Pippenger, David—Mustered out June 8, '65.

Peoples, George W.—Discharged May 13, '63.

Prickett, Nimrod—Discharged; date unknown.

Rapp, William G.—Wounded mortally, Missionary Ridge, Nov. 25, '63.

Rodsbaugh, Samuel—Transferred to Company "K" Oct. 3, '62.

Rowell, Wesley W.—Mustered out June 8, '65.

Russell, Samuel N.—Transferred to Company "K," October 3, '62.

Rookstool, Joseph—Died March 19, '63.

Rookstool, Adam—Died March 26, '63.

Thomas Price.
Company D.

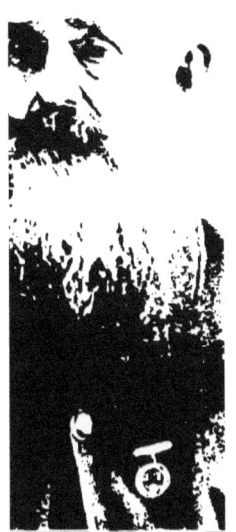

William Stadler.

Rookstool, John—Mustered out June 9, '63.

Reinbold, Solomon — Wounded through wrist at New Hope Church; served faithfully during the war; was a good man and soldier.

Ruple, Jonas—Mustered out June 8, '65, as Corporal.

Shultz, Isaiah—Served faithfully during the war; was a good soldier and an excellent man.

Streely, Frederick—Served faithfully three years; mustered out June 8, '65. He always performed his duties as a true soldier.

Stebbens, Henry E.—Transferred to V. R. C.

Sheldon, Hiram H.—Severely wounded at Bentonville.

William Stadler—Served faithfully and well for three years. His military history may be written thus:—"He was brave, intrepid, faithful and reliable;" a moral man and a model soldier of whom his descendants may well be proud.

Skinner, Azel—Discharged May 9, '63.

Swartz, Henry—Died March 10, '63.

Tallerday, Andrew J.—Mustered out June 8, '65.

Twiford, William—Discharged Dec. 12, '63.

Trump, William H.—Was as brave a soldier as ever carried a gun. He was very severely wounded in the face and head on the skirmish line at the railroad at Missionary Ridge. After fighting until he was unable to stand alone from loss of blood he fell to the ground and crawled away from the line of battle to escape capture.

True, Jeremiah P.—Jaw broken by kick of a battery horse at Beaufort.

Voorhees, Isaac—Discharged Jan. '63.

Vallance, William—Mustered out Aug. 12, '63.

Vannote, George W.—Transferred to V. R. C. Jan. 23, '64.

Wilson, Marion—Died Sept. 14, '63, at Black River.

Williams, Enoch S.—Mustered out June 8, '65.

Walters, Henry W.—Transferred to V. R. C.

Andrews, David—Transferred 48th Regiment May 30, '65.

Geisinger, Samuel—Transferred to 48th Regiment May 30, '65.

Gephart, Jackson—Transferred to 48th Regiment May 30, '65.

Spade, Joel—Transferred to 48th Regiment May 30, '65.

Roster of Company "E" 100th Indiana Infantry.

Captain William M. Barney recruited Company "E"; was commissioned Captain September 1st and mustered September 10, 1862. He served with distinction through the sieges of Vicksburg and Jackson, Mississippi, and resigned August 8, 1863.

Captain Merwin F. Collier entered the service as First Lieutenant, September 1, 1862; he was promoted to the captaincy and on June 9, 1864, he was honorably discharged. He enjoyed the respect of the officers and men of the Regiment.

Captain Henry H. Nelson was promoted to Second Lieutenant June 15, 1863. August 9 he was promoted to First Lieutenant and on June 30, 1864, to the captaincy of his Company. He possessed the confidence of the men of his Company and the respect of the officers of the Regiment. He discharged the duties of his office with fidelity and was esteemed as a gentleman and a soldier. He was wounded in the hip during the assault on Mission Ridge, November 25, 1863.

Lieutenant John C. Vaught was promoted from the ranks to Second Lieutenant, August 9, 1863, for efficiency and meritorious conduct in the line of his duty. On June 30, 1864, he was promoted to be First Lieutenant. He enjoyed the respect and confidence of the officers and soldiers of the Regiment. He served until the end of the war and was honorably mustered out in June, 1865.

Ichabod Jones was mustered Second Lieutenant of Company "E" September 10, 1862, and was afterward promoted to be Major of the 1st Tennessee Artillery.

Lieutenant Charles C. Pierce was promoted to Second Lieutenant November 22, 1864. He served during the war.

Groff, Charles F.—Discharged Sept. 3, 63.

Crane, Samuel C.—Discharged May 16,'63.

Butts, Anson W.—Transferred to V. R. C.; mustered out July 27, '65.

Shattuck, Ira H.—Served during the war; mustered out June 8, '65.

Wylde, Charles—Died, Memphis, December 7, '62.

Bennett, Andrew J.—Mustered out as private June 8, '65.

Cumming, Alfred J.—Died at Indianapolis Sept. 15, '62.

Locker, Edmund A.—Captured at the battle of Missionary Ridge, November, 25, '63; served during the war and was mustered out June 8, '65.

John W. Miller served faithfully and efficiently for three years, and deserved and enjoyed the respect and confidence of the officers of the Regiment. He performed many acts during his term of service which entitled him to distinction. He was promoted for meritorious con-

Captain Henry H. Nelson.

duct and was honorably mustered out as Sergeant June 8, '65.

Sweet, Jerome—Discharged June 27, '63.

Young, Abraham—Died at Memphis Dec. 11, '62.

Miller, John—Served during the war; mustered out June 8, '65.

Gorpe, Emerson—Served during the war.

Shaw, Joseph—Served during the war.

Bailey, William H.—Died at St. Louis, Dec. 24, '62.

Bearrup, John W.—Discharged Sept. 18, '63.

Cuppitt, John—Wounded severely; discharged Feb. 25, '65.

Cox, Thomas J.—Promoted to Corporal. Served in the field during the war; mustered out June 8, '65, as Corporal; was a model soldier; was promoted for bravery on the field of battle and for soldierly conduct.

Calkins, William W.—Killed, Missionary Ridge, Nov. 25, '63.

Corbin, Nathan H.—Served during the war.

Chilson, Nathan—Served during the war.

Drake, James L.—Died from a shock received, Mission Ridge, Nov. 25, '63.

Drake, Christopher C.—Served during the war.

Drake, Daniel T.—Wounded severely at the battle of Lovejoy, Ga., Sept. 3, '64; honorably discharged Feb. 25, '65.

Davis, Moses H.—Discharged for disability June 23, '63.

Dallas, George T.—Promoted to Corporal; mustered out June 8, '65.

Evans, Frank C.—Served during the war; mustered out June 8, '65.

Easterday, Sylvester—Served during the war; mustered out June 8, '65.

Engle, John—Died in Camp Sherman, Mississippi, Aug. 23, '63.

Elder, Abner—Died at Madison, Ind., Oct. 6, '62.

Eley, John H.—Wounded at Dallas, Ga., May 28, '64; served faithfully during the war; was honorably mustered out June 8, '65, at Washington, D. C. He was taken prisoner in the assault on Missionary Ridge; he was brave, intrepid and fearless in battle.

Folk, Charles—Died at Nashville, Jan. 20, '64.

Grubb, Allen—Discharged Nov. 23, '63.

Gretzinger, Frederick—Served during the war.

Grimm, John J.—Mustered out June 8,'65.

Graham, Peter F.—Discharged April 16, '63.

Gunnett, Michael—Served during the war.

Gunnett, Samuel—Wounded at Dallas, Ga., May 28, '64.

Hoffman, Peter—Served during the war.

Hooper, James—Served during the war.

Hoover, Elias W.—Discharged Feb. 16, '63.

Hoffman, John—Died at Hickory Valley, Tenn., Feb. 5, '63.

Hall, Jesse—Killed in battle of Dallas, Ga., May 28, '64.

Harris, Daniel—Captured, Mission Ridge.

Himes, George W. — Killed Missionary Ridge, Nov. 25, '63.

Sergeant John W. Miller.
Company E.

Harris, William—Died at Bellefonte, Alabama, Jan. 31, '64.

Haines, Bartley E.—Died at Memphis, Nov. 16, '63.

Harris, Joseph — Wounded, Griswoldville, Ga., Nov. 22, '64.

Harting, Ephraim—Discharged March 11, '63.

Knapp, Lucius H. — Killed, Missionary Ridge, Nov. 25, '63.

Kirkpatrick, Henry W.—Discharged March 11, '63.

King, Joseph—Killed at battle of Dallas, Ga., May 28, '64.

King, Michael D.—Killed, Dallas, Ga., May 28, '64.

Kinsey, Cornelius—Served during the war.

Linsey, Hiram—Died at Scotsboro, Alabama, Jan. 13, '64.

Myers, Henry—Served during the war. Mustered out June 8, '65.

Monroe, Charles A—Died Nov. 12; buried Cumberland Mountain.

Monroe, Robert L—Transferred to V. R. C.

McFarland, James—Served during the war.

Noble, Franklin—Served during the war.

Orr, Charles—Discharged March 5, '64.

Ogle, Charles H.—Discharged September 15, '64.

Orr, Samuel W.—Died at Keokuk, Iowa, January 10, '63.

Parker, Daniel—Died at Camp Sherman, Miss., August 22, '63.

Prouty, William—Served during the war.

Penn, George—Served faithfully three

years. Honorably mustered out June 8, '65; he was a good man and a brave soldier.

Rowell, Samuel—Served three years. Mustered out June 8, '65.

Rice, Harvey—Served during the war, discharged June 8, '65.

Rimmel, Aaron J.—Served in the field three years; was honorably mustered out at the close of the war as Corporal.

Rodman, Uriah B.—Transferred to V. R. C.

Rodgers, Wilford J.—Mustered out June 8, '65.

Rawson, Oliver P.—Wounded Mission Ridge, Nov. 25, '63.

Richards, George—Mustered out as Corporal June 8, '65.

Sowers, Phillip—Served during the war.

Sanborn, Edward O.—Died at Chattanooga, Tenn., Dec. 22, '63.

Simon, Charles—Discharged Sept. 18, '63.

Snider, Augustus—Discharged March 2,'64.

Tryon, Christopher—Served during the war. Mustered out June 8, '65.

Thomas, Franklin—Died at Memphis, Nov. 29, '62.

West, Robert—Wounded in leg at Mission Ridge.

West, Joseph—Wounded in heel at Mission Ridge. Mustered out June 8, '65.

Weaver, William S.—Wounded severely at Mission Ridge.

Warner, John D.—Died at Grand Junction, Tenn., January 30, '63.

Whitcomb, Moses—Served during the war. Mustered out June 8, '65.

John W. Trowbridge.
Company E, 100th Indiana Infantry.

Waltburn, Robert—Served during the war. Mustered out June 8, '65.

Warren, George W.—Wounded mortally at Battle of Dallas May 28, '64.

Waldren, Wesley—Transferred to V. R. C. August 10, '64.

Wyrick, Henry—Honorably mustered out June 8, '65.

Wainright, John W.—Mustered out at the end of the war.

Young, Josiah—Mustered out June, '65.

Axtell, Daniel M.—Died at Marietta, Ga., July 14, '64.

Burrows, Jeremiah—Transferred to 48th Indiana.

Browand, Christopher—Transferred to 48th Indiana Infantry.

Gardener, George—Transferred to V. R. C. April 22, '64.

Trowbridge, John M.—Served faithfully in the field until the end of the war when he was transferred to the 48th Indiana May 30, '65. Honorably mustered out under orders. He was a good man and brave soldier and was respected by all who knew him and had the confidence and esteem of his officers.

Roster of Company "F," 100th Indiana Infantry.

Captain Abram W. Myers entered the service September 2, 1862, from Columbia City. He served until January 27, 1863, when he resigned on account of failing health.

Captain Daniel T. Smith entered the service as First Lieutenant September 2, 1862. On January 28, 1863, he was promoted to Captain. He lost an arm in the assault on Mission Ridge, and was honorably discharged July 28, 1864.

Captain Leonard Akers entered the service as Second Lieutenant of Company "F" September 2, 1862. On the 28th of June, 1863, he was promoted to First Lieutenant, and on July 29, 1864, to Captain. He commanded part of the skirmish line in the assault on Mission Ridge and drove the enemy from the railroad. He took part in every campaign and in every engagement from that time until the end of the war. He was an efficient, brave and daring officer. He had the esteem of the officers of the regiment and was highly regarded by the men. During the war he led Company "F" into and out of many deadly and dangerous places.

Israel Biers entered the service as Third Sergeant of Company "F" August 18, 1863.

Captain Leonard Akers.
Company F, 100th Indiana.

On July 29, 1864, he was promoted to First Lieutenant and served in the field until the end of the war.

Adam Swihart was promoted from First Sergeant to Second Lieutenant of Company "F" Jan. 28, 1863. He resigned June 10, 1864.

Fletcher B. Harris was promoted to First Sergeant, and on November 22, 1864, he was commissioned Second Lieutenant and served until the end of the war.

Snider, David—Discharged January 26, '63, as Sergeant.

Heaton, Chauncey L.—Mustered out as Sergeant.

Stoler, Jacob—Promoted to Sergeant; was a gallant soldier.

Cole, Seymour—Mustered out as Sergeant June 8, '65.

Graves, Elijah—Died at Memphis, Nov. 12, '63.

Mossman, John—Died at St. Louis, Mo., December, '63.

Cole, Samuel—Died at Scotsboro, Ala., January 1, '64.

Schrader, Isaac—Mustered out as Sergeant; was a gallant soldier.

Plummer, Joseph—Wounded at battle of Mission Ridge.

Bills, James—Transferred to 44th Indiana, September 27, '62.

Bennett, John—Died at Camp Sherman, Miss., Aug. 1, '63.

Lamb, David J.—Died at Memphis, Tenn., Nov. 10, '63.

Hawkins, Reuben—Discharged, May 11, '65.

Acker, Washington—Died at Memphis, Tenn., Nov. 1, '63.

Arnold, Henry W.—Discharged Nov. 28, '62.

Bugbee, Nelson—Died at Scotsboro, January 21, '64.

Butler, Asa—Transferred to V. R. C.; mustered out Aug. 5, '65.

Bell, Albert—Discharged Dec. 28, '62.

Brown, Henry—Mustered out June 8, '65.

Burkholder, Hiram—Mustered out June 8, '65.

Crawford, Davis—Mustered out June 8, '65.

Clark, William A.—Mustered out June 8, '65.

Croy, Abraham A.—Discharged Nov. 10, '62.

Cleland, James—Mustered out June 8, '65.

Deems, Samuel—Discharged Dec. 28, '62.

Doag, Jacob—Transferred to V. R. C. March 27, '65.

Decker, Daniel—Mustered out June 8, '65.

Finch, Joseph—Mustered out July 3, '65.

Falk, John W.—Discharged May 8, '63.

Falk, Isaac W.—Mustered out June 8, '65, as Corporal.

Fullerton, James—Mustered out June 8, '65.

Finch, David—Mustered out June 8, '65.

Forsythe, Andrew J.—Wounded at Mission Ridge.

Goble, Isaac H.—Mustered out June 8, '65.

German, Daniel—Mustered out June 8, '65.

Harrington, Dennis—Mustered out June 8, '65.

Hettinger, John—Enlisted Sept. 1, '63. He served faithfully until Aug. 31, '64, when he was killed in the battle of Jonesboro, Georgia, while acting as an Orderly on Harrow's Staff.

Helms, J. B.—Discharged. Date unknown.

Hills, George—Mustered out as Corporal June 8, '65.

Johnson, William R.—Shot near Jonesboro. Mustered out June 8, '65.

Jacquay, Lawrence P.—Discharged Dec., '62.

Kenaga, Mathias—Mustered out June 8,'65.

Kearns, Adam N.—Discharged Nov. '62.

Kearns, William S. — Killed Missionary Ridge Nov. 25, '63.

Lindle, William W. — Died at Memphis Tenn., '63.

Litehiser, George—Transferred to 48th Indiana May 30, '65.

Miller, George—Mustered out June 8, '65.

McCoy, Josiah—Mustered out June 8, '65, as Corporal.

Minier, Aaron — Discharged January 25, '63.

Mellet, Calvin—Died Memphis, Tenn., Nov. 4, '62.

Malone, Andrew—Wounded severely. Discharged March 7, '65.

McNabb, John—Died at Holly Springs, Miss. Jan. 15, '63.

Mack, Henry—Mustered out June 8, '65.

Nobles, Charles—Mustered out June 8, '65

North, Edward—Died at Columbus, Ohio.

Owens, John—Died, Indianapolis, Nov. '62.

Pumphrey, Reason W.—Died, Pigeon Roost, Nov. 28, '62.

Price, Jonathan—Mustered out June 8, '65.

Plough, John H.—Mustered out June 8, '65.

Pittman, Boyer—Killed, Missionary Ridge, Nov. 25, '63.

Quinn, Othaina—Discharged Dec. 28, '62.

Samuels, James—Killed, Missionary Ridge, Nov. 25, '63.

Scott, McArthur—Mustered out June 8, '65.

Sterling, William—Discharged Oct. 28, '64.

Swindle, Charles—Died at Grand Junction, Tenn., April 8, '63, from injuries received while in the discharge of his duty.

Shaffner, Franklin—Mustered out June 8, '65.

Simpkins, George—Discharged Dec. 28, '62.

Tuttle, Henry C.—Discharged September 6, '63.

Thrasher, Thomas—Mustered out June 8, '65.

Whiteleather, David—Color Bearer; mustered out as Corporal, '65.

Winegardner, Joseph—Mustered out June 8, '65, as Corporal.

Walker, William T.—A gallant soldier; mustered out as Corporal.

Weil, John—Killed, Missionary Ridge, Nov. 25, '63.

Young, Hiram—Mustered out January 8, '65.

Butler, Asa—Transferred to 48th Indiana.

Groves, Isaac—Died at Chattanooga, Nov. 7, '64.

Ginger, Philander H.—Transferred to 48th Indiana.

Hinman, James—Transferred to 48th Indiana.

Kenaga, Benjamin F.—Transferred to 48th Indiana.

Newcomb, Henry J.—Transferred to 48th Indiana.

Richards, Daniel—Transferred to 48th Indiana.

Simpkins, George—Died in the field Nov. 16, '63.

Taylor, Samuel—Died at Camp Sherman, Miss., Aug. '63.

Roster of Company "G," 100th Indiana Infantry.

Captain Godlove O. Behm entered the army from Lafayette September 9, '62. He was promoted to Lieutenant Colonel of the 116th Indiana Aug. 28, '63.

Captain John M. Carr entered the army Aug. 3, '62. On Nov. 8, '62, he was promoted to First Lieutenant and on Aug. 30, '63, to Captain, and mustered out May 15, '65.

William Burnside entered the service as First Lieutenant. He resigned Nov. 1, '62.

Elijah Young was made Second Lieutenant Sept. 24, '62. Aug. 30, '63, he was promoted to be First Lieutenant, and was discharged Sept. 20, '64.

Harvey J. Sawyer was promoted to First Lieutenant Oct. 1, '64, and served until the end of the war.

Asa J. Fisher was promoted to Second Lieutenant and served until the end of the war.

William G. Kiger was one of the solid men of Company "G." He was promoted for meritorious conduct in front of the enemy. He served three years, and was honorably mustered out with the Regiment.

Hunt, Cornelius—Died at Calhoun, Tenn., January 30, '64.

Holloway, Thomas N.—Wounded at Griswoldville, Georgia.

Freeman, William—Promoted to Sergeant; mustered out June 8, '65.

Ridgway, James T.—Mustered out June 8, '65, having served faithfully during the war; was a brave soldier.

Timmons, David—Mustered out May 24, '65.

Bohen, Con.—Mustered out June 8, '65.

Williamson, Noah—Mustered out June 8, '65.

Williams, Lewis — Mustered out June 8, '65.

Stedman, Harrison—Wounded at Mission Ridge; mustered out June 8, '65.

Fenton, Daniel M.—Served during the war; mustered out June 8, '65. He was a brave soldier and enjoyed the respect of his superior officers and all who knew him.

Cook, Ulysses—Discharged; date unknown.

Alexander, John—Badly wounded Nov. 25, '63.

Ashba, Abram—Discharged May 8, '65.

Ayers, John R.—Transferred to V. R. C., July 1, '64.

Barry, Lawrence—Discharged, date not known.

Belew, Isaac N.—Severely wounded Nov.

Sergeant William G. Kiger,
Company G.

25, '63; mustered out June 8, '65. He was a good man and a brave soldier.

Brada, William — Discharged May 11, '65.

Burns, Michael—Wounded severely; sabre cut, November, '64.

Campbell, George N.—Died June 19, '64.

Carey, John—Served during the war; mustered out June 8, '65.

Doty, George—Killed at Missionary Ridge.

Drummond, William—Promoted to Corporal; mustered out June 8, '65.

Erickson, John—Discharged October '62.

Fairchild, Henry—Wounded severely at Griswoldville, Ga.

Fairchild, John L.—Mustered out June 8, '65.

Fardin, Joseph—Wounded by shell in battle of Jackson, Miss., and gunshot wound through the left arm at Mission Ridge. Rendered three years of faithful service and was honorably discharged June 8, '65.

Gattis, Andrew—Discharged.

Garrard, Alfred—Died at Collierville April 23, '63.

Garrard, Samuel—Wounded on Atlanta campaign; mustered out as Corporal.

Gaskill, Amos—Died at LaGrange, Tenn., January 25, '63.

Gillett, Joab—Mustered out June 8, '65; served during the war.

Golat, Frederick A.—Mustered out June 8, '65.

Henry, John—Died at Collierville, April 23, '65.

Hight, Abram—Killed Mission Ridge.

Jessup, Levi—Wounded. Mustered out as Corporal.

Jones, James W—Mustered out June 14, '65.

Kilroy, Anthony—Mustered out June 8,'65.

Kirk, Timothy—Killed. Dallas, Georgia, May 30, '64.

Lewis, Samuel—Mustered out June 8, '65.

Little, William D.—Killed Missionary Ridge.

Ludy, William—Died at Memphis, October 4, '63.

Meadows, Robert D—Wounded in battle. Mustered out '65.

Metsker, Abraham—Discharged May 1, '63.

Minicar, Nelson—Mustered out June 8, '65.

Minicar, Allen—Died at Camp Sherman August 4. '63.

Mitcham, Henry—Transferred to V. R. C. July 1, '64.

Nelson, James H—Killed at Atlanta, Aug. 23, '64.

Pike, Thomas—Mustered out June 8, '65.

Powell, Thomas W—Died at Indianapolis, May 6, '65.

Powell, Uriah D—Mustered out June 8,'65.

Sanson, John—Mustered out June 8, '65.

Sewall, Thomas G—Wounded. Discharged December 20, '64.

Sewall, Amos R—Discharged June 17, '64.

Shipp, Albert—Discharged.

Small, Caleb—Mustered out June 8, '65.

Smith, James W—Promoted to Corporal.

Smith, Nathan—Mustered out June 8, '65.

Snider, Nathan—Shot Nov. 25, '65; died from wound at Nashville.

St. John, William—Died between Chattanooga and Bridgeport.

Stebbins, Henry—Killed South Carolina near Peays' Ferry Feb. 22, '65.

Stanfield, John—Died in hospital Memphis, October 11, '63.

Street, Hiram C.—Mustered out June 8, 65.

Swadley, Nicholas A.—Served faithfully in the war until the end, was a good man and a brave and intrepid soldier.

Swanson, Andrew—Mustered out June 8, '65.

Tabor, Stephens C.—Died at Hilton Head, Feb. 10, '65.

Timmons, William—Mustered out June 8, '65.

Tolson, John—Discharged.

Tounsley, Robert—Wounded. Mission Ridge.

Watkins, James W.—Discharged.

Wakeman, Charles—Died at Scottsboro, Alabama, January 12, '64.

Watkins, Benjamin—Transferred to V. R. C. July 1, '64.

Williams, John—Wounded Missionary Ridge; discharged.

Wood, Edward B.—Died at Mound City, Illinois, August 20, '63.

Doudican John—Transferred to 48th Indiana.

Kent, Redmond—Transferred to 48th Indiana May 30, '65.

Myers, Jacob K.—Transferred to 48th Indiana.

Norris, Benjamin—Transferred to 48th Indiana.

Roster of Company "H" 100th Indiana Infantry.

Captain John W. Headington organized Company "H". He was promoted to Major and Lieutenant Colonel. (See Field and Staff.)

Captain Isaac N. Frazee was promoted to First Lieutenant January 9, '65, and to Captain May 1, '65. Captain Frazee did active service in the field during his entire term of service; he was severely injured by being run over by an artillery wagon in the engagement near Turkeytown, Alabama.

Lieutenant Gideon Rathbun served with distinction on the Campaigns in Northern Mississippi, and through the sieges of Vicksburg and Jackson, Miss.; he was severely wounded by a grape shot in the assault on Missionary Ridge; being unable for active field duty after he was

Lieutenant Gideon Rathbun.
Company H, 100th Indiana.

wounded, he acted as A. R. Q. M. for some time; he had the good opinion of all of the officers and the respect and confidence of the men of his Command; he was brave and intrepid on the field of battle.

Eli Vore was promoted to Second Lieutenant Jan. 24, '65, and to First Lieutenant May 1, '65, and mustered out with the Regiment.

Stephen B. H. Shanks entered the service as Second Lieutenant of Company "H" Sept. 11, '62, and was honorably discharged Jan. 23, '65, for disability; he was in active service in the field during that time.

Edwin Rowlett was promoted to First Sergeant and to Second Lieutenant, for meritorious services in the field, May 1, '65.

Ware, William F.—Died at Collierville, April 4, '63.

Moore, David J.—Wounded, Missionary Ridge.

Koons, Thomas—Died at Grand Junction, Tenn., Feb. 1, '63.

Havaland, Jacob—Wounded, Mission Ridge; promoted to Sergeant; served during the war.

Barnes, Solomon M.—Promoted to Sergeant; mustered out June 8, '65.

Coldron, Sanford B.—Promoted to Sergeant; mustered out June 8, '65.

Patterson, Liberty—Mustered out June 8, '65.

Thomas, Andrew J.—Discharged May 7, '65.

Bosworth, Jacob—Discharged March 22, '63.

Fifer, William—Served during the war.

Hammons, Henry—Mustered out June 8, '65.

Mills, Aquilla K.—Promoted to Corporal.

Wiley, William —Mustered out June 8, '65.

Antles, Joseph—Mustered out June 8, '65.

Allman, Samuel—Wounded at Missionary Ridge; mustered out June 8, '65.

Bowden, John F.—Promoted to Lieutenant in 12th Indiana Cavalry.

Burd, Evan—Died at home August 24, '63.

Baker, James—Mustered out June 8, '65.

Borden, George D.—Mustered out June 8, '65.

Bronner, William—Promoted to Corporal; mustered out June 8, '65.

Bickel, Daniel—Died at Memphis, Oct. 23, '63.

Bubmire, Nathan—Mustered out, June 8, '65.

George H. Bonnell served faithfully until the end of the war and was mustered out June 8, '65. He had the respect and confidence of the men and his superior officers.

Bair, James M.—Mustered out June 8, '65.

Blake, Samuel A.—Died at Memphis, Jan. 8, '63.

Cain, Jonathan—Discharged May 26, '63.

Castar, Charles W.—Died at Bellefonte, Ala. Feb. 19, '64.

John M. Collett was one of the men who never shirked the performance of a duty, whether in camp, on the march or in battle. He was faithful, efficient and reliable.

Carl, Joseph L.—Mustered out May 13, '65.

Cartwright, James—Died at Memphis Nov. 29, '65.

Dehoff, Joseph—Died at St. Louis, Dec. 20, '62.

George H. Bonnell.
(From a war times picture.)

Ducket, Amos—Mustered out June 8, '65.

Fritzenger, George—Mustered out June 8, '65.

Fitzgerald, Richard—Transferred to V. R. C. Dec. 28, '63.

Flauding, John—Killed in battle of Missionary Ridge, Nov. 25, '63.

Flood, Joshua W.—Served faithfully in the field during the war; was a brave soldier always ready to do his duty. He was severely wounded at Griswoldville, Ga., Nov. 22, '64. He enjoyed the respect and confidence of his superior officers. Mustered out June 8, '65.

Frazee, Abner—Mustered out June 8, '65.

Gibson, Obed—Died at La Grange, Tenn., Jan. 15, '63.

Ginger, Daniel D.—Mustered out June 8, '65.

Giger, Abram—Severely wounded by gunshot through the wrist joint while bearing the Regimental flag at Missionary Ridge, November 25, '63.

Hughs, Stephen W.—Mustered out June 8, '65.

Hilton, Levi P.—Died at Vicksburg, Sept. 20, '63.

Holtstapple, Henry C.—Died at Bellefonte, Ala., Feb. 28, '64.

Hawkins, Joseph C.—In the battle of Missionary Ridge the colors of the regiment fell from the hand of Abram Giger, who was severely wounded. Hawkins took them up and bore them along with the Regiment, accompanied by Lieut. Col. John W. Headington, for which he was complimented by the presentation of a fine suit by the officers of the Regiment.

Hardy, James—Died at La Grange, Tenn., March 9, '63.

Horner William W.—Promoted to Corporal; mustered out June 8, '65.

Iliff, Thomas H.—Died, St. Louis, Aug. '63.

Kunce, Noah—Died at Memphis, November 26, '62.

Lafollett, Joseph W.—Died at La Grange, Feb. 26, '63.

Morris, John C.—Died at Nashville, Dec. 18, '63.

McCroskey, Jacob W. Mustered out as wagoner June 8, '65.

Mills, David—Transferred to V. R. C. Jan. 28, '65.

Mason, James A.—Severely wounded Missionary Ridge; mustered out June 8, '65.

Mills, Cassius B.—Discharged May 20, '63.

Merchant, John—Died at Collierville, May 7, '63.

Mills, John M—Died at La Grange, Tenn., Feb. 8, '63.

Morgan, Lafayette — Died at Scottsboro, Ala., Dec. 27, '63.

Nichols, Edward—Mustered out June 8, '65.

Porter, Elias A.—Mustered out June 8, '65.

Poling, Joshua—Mustered out June 8, '65.

Plummer, Charles—Transferred to V.R.C.

Parkinson, Isaiah—Mustered out June 8, '65.

Rowlett, Ezekiel—Discharged Aug. 25, '63.

Rathburn, John J. — Mustered out June 8, '65.

Ruhl, Noah—Promoted to Corporal; mustered out June 8, '65.

Ruhl, Alexander W.—Mustered out June 8, '65.

John M. Collett.

Joshua W. Flood, Esq.
Company H, 100th Indiana Infantry.

Rarrick, Charles W.—Mustered out June 8, '65.

Rines, Eli—Promoted to Corporal; mustered out June 8, '65.

Schultz, Adam—Mustered out June 8, '65.

Staley, Henry C.—Promoted to Corporal; mustered out June 8, '65.

Sutton, Jacob—Discharged March 11, '63.

Spahr, Henry—Died on Big Black River Aug. 18, '63.

Stratton, Solon C.—Died, Tallahatchie River Dec. 2, '62.

Towle, Taylor—Mustered out June 8, '65.

Tucker, Alva J.—Mustered out June 8, '65.

Tucker, Granville C.—Mustered out June 8, '65.

Wilkison, Samuel—Wounded in battle at Jonesboro, Ga., Sept. 3, 64.

Whitenack, Joseph B.—Mustered out June 8, '65.

Walker, James G.—Killed, Missionary Ridge, Nov. 25, '63.

Wilson, Cyrus L.—Died at Snyder's Bluff, Miss., June 30, '63.

Westfall, John—Mustered out June 8, '65.

Armantrout, Jonathan—Mustered out Aug. 22, '65.

Bonnell, Lewis B.—Mustered out Aug. 15, '63.

Carl, Mulford—Transferred to 48th Ind.; wounded in skirmish, Atlanta, Ga. '64.

Collins, Jesse—Transferred to 48th Ind., May 30, '65.

Cherry, William—Died at Chattanooga, Sept. 21, '64.

Flauding, Henry—Transferred to 48th Ind.

Graves, Henderson—Wounded in battle at Dallas, Georgia.

Hood, James—Died at Rome, Ga., July 15, '64.

Haffner, George B.—Transferred to 48th Ind.

Hester, William H.—Transferred to 48th Ind. Infantry.

Horner, Joseph—Transferred to 48th Ind.

Jones, James—Wounded in battle at Atlanta, Ga.

Towel, Robin M.—Transferred to 48th Ind.

Thompson, Jesse—Transferred to 48th Ind. Infantry.

Wolfe, David—Transferred to 48th Ind., May 30, '65.

West, Jacob—Wounded in battle of Mission Ridge, Nov. 25, '63; transferred to 48th Ind. for further services.

Charles W. Rarrick.

Charles W. Rarrick was a model soldier. He was strong, brave and fearless, always ready to do more than his duty. He repeatedly declined a promotion in his company. He was on special duty during the campaign in the Carolinas, and had many brushes with the enemy. He loved the excitement of tthe skirmish line, where he was nearly always to be found. His country can never pay the debt it owes him. He was widely known and highly respected.

Roster of Company "I," 100th Indiana Infantry.

James N. Sims entered the service as Captain of Company "I" September 12, '62. He served with distinction through the campaigns of 1862-3 in Mississippi and through the sieges of Vicksburg and Jackson. He resigned on account of bad health Aug. 20, '63.

Captain James M. Harland entered the service as First Lieutenant of Company "I" September 12, '62; was made Captain, August 12, '63. He was killed at the head of Company "I," on the front line, in the assault on Missionary Ridge. He had seen active service in the Mexican war in 1848-9. He was beloved by the men and honored and respected by the officers.

Thomas C. Dalbey entered the army as Second Lieutenant of Company "I" September 12, '62. He was promoted to Captain, November 26, '63. He served in the field during the entire term of his enlistment; was through the campaigns in Northern Mississippi in 1862-3, the sieges of Vicksburg and Jackson. He took command of his company in the front line of battle during the hottest of the fight in the assault on Missionary Ridge. He participated in every action in which the Regiment was engaged. In

March, '65, he was promoted to Lieutenant-Colonel of the 150th Indiana Infantry. Captain Dalbey enjoyed the esteem and confidence of all who knew him.

Noah T. Catterlin was promoted to First Lieutenant of Company "I," November 26, '63, and to Captain April 1, '65.

James M. Gentry was promoted to First Lieutenant April 1, '65. He served through the war and was mustered out with the Regiment. He was highly esteemed by the officers and men of the Regiment and enjoyed their respect.

Lieut. Isaac D. Hockman took part in the Sieges of Vicksburg and Jackson. The Knoxville and Atlanta Campaigns, including the siege of Atlanta and the battle of Jonesboro.

He was wounded with canister in the shoulder in front of a Rebel battery at Jonesboro August 31,'64. He was well known by every officer and man in the Regiment and enjoyed their esteem. He was promoted to Lieutenant November 22, '64.

Robinson, Andrew M.—Sergeant; enlisted August 29, '62; was made orderly sergeant of his Company; was unable physically to bear the hardships of the field and was discharged for disability Dec. 28, '62. He re-enlisted in the Company February 26, '64, and served until the end of the war. He was a brave and patriotic man.

Hockman, William W.—Discharged September 6, '64.

Thompson, Craven—Served during the war.

Spray, Henry N.—Served during the war.

Young, John W.—Served during the war; mustered out June 29, '65.

Thomas C. Dalbey.
Captain Company I, 100th Indiana and Lieutenant-Colonel 150th Indiana.
(From a war times photograph).

Aldridge, Willian T.—Discharged November 13, '62.

Walters, Harrison—Wounded in arm in action at Kenesaw Mountain June, '64; served during the war.

Parvis, John W.—Wounded in hand by gunshot at Jonesboro, Ga.

Gillespie, John—Discharged.

Keys, Thomas P.—Served during the war.

Pierce, John H.—Served during the war; mustered out June 8, '65.

Cook, John M.—Wounded in the head and shoulders at Griswoldville, Ga., November 22, '64; served during the war.

Gaddis, George P.—Served during the war.

Baum, Henry M.—Discharged.

Allen, Moses R.—Served during the war.

Aughe, Darlington—Wounded in side and on head by bursting shell at Missionary Ridge, Nov. 25, '63, from effects of which he died at Marietta, Ga., Sept. 13, '64.

Butler, Henry—Served during the war.

Baumgarten, Jacob—Killed, Griswoldville, Ga.

Cresan, William—Discharged May 27, '63.

Carmaney, Joseph—Served during the war.

Coonrad, Josephus—Died at Nashville, March 12, '64, from the effects of a wound received at the battle of Missionary Ridge.

Christman, Levi—Died, Grand Junction, Tenn., Feb. 10, '63.

Cook, Henry—Missing at Missionary Ridge; probably killed.

Douglass, John—Discharged.

Davids, Allen J.—Died at Indianapolis, Nov. 27, '62.

Doctor, Charles H.—Honorably discharged June 8, '65.
Davis, Isaac M.—Discharged.
Enright, John—Was wounded in battle and discharged June 8, '65.
Fudge, George—Mustered out June 8, '65.
Fragar, Milo—Died at Grand Junction, Tenn., Feb. 10, '62.
Fisher, Samuel P.—Transferred to V. R. C., Jan. 10, '65.
Goble, Samuel—Served during the war; mustered out June 8, '65.
Gray, John—Served during the war; discharged June 8, '65.
Ghere, Samuel—Discharged April 25, '63.
Goldsberry, Thomas B.—Discharged.
Hancock, Cyrus E.—Served during the war; mustered out June 8, '65.
Hoover, Thomas J.—Served during the war; mustered out May 11, '65.
Hendrickson, Isaac—Promoted to Sergeant; wounded in arm at Missionary Ridge.
Hindman, Samuel—Honorably discharged; served during the war.
Hillis, James—Mustered out June 8, '65.
Jones, Benajah—Mustered out June 8, '65.
Jones, Elias H.—Killed in the battle of Griswoldville.
Johnson, John W.—Mustered out June 8, '65.
Johnson, James C.—Mustered out June 8, '65.
Kelley, William—Wounded in thigh and shoulder, Griswoldville, Ga.
Kelley, David S.—Discharged March 6, '63.
Kelley, John R.—Promoted to Corporal; mustered out June 8, '65.
Kane, John—Mustered out June 8, '65.

Lieutenant Isaac D. Hockman,
Company I, 100th Indiana.

Keneday, Milton H.—Promoted to Sergeant.
Leach, Thomas—Mustered out June 8, '65.
Lyons, Samuel—Mustered out as Corporal June 8, '65.
Lee, Robert—Died Dec. 2, '62.
Louck, Simon L.—Mustered out June 8, '65.
Lucas, George W.—Wounded near Dallas, Ga.
Lewis, Andrew—Died at Nashville, March 11, '64.
Martin, Simpson H.—Died at Indianapolis, Nov. 26, '62.
Messler, James W.—Mustered out June 8,
Messler, Cornelius J.—Transferred to 3rd Cavalry at Indianapolis.
Messler, John R.—Died at Memphis, July 24, '63.
Mann, John—Killed near Columbia, South Carolina, Feb. 15, '65.
Marley, John M.—Discharged.
Murphy, John—Mustered out June 8, '65.
McCarty, Thomas F.—Mustered out as Corporal, June 8, '65.
Ostler, Robert—Wounded in head at Griswoldville.
Price, Wallace F.—Mustered out as Corporal June 8, '65.
Price, William M.—Mustered out as Corporal June 8, '65.
Sheets, Jacob S.—Discharged Dec. 27, '62.
Senft, Adam L.—Wounded in head in front of Kenesaw Mountain.
Steele, Robert M.—Mortally wounded in head by canister shot at Jonesboro, Ga.

Strouse, William P.—Died at Collierville, April 13, '63.

Scott, Samuel—Wounded near Nashville, Tenn., and discharged.

Thompson, William—Transferred to V. R. C.

Turney, James W.—Mustered out June 8, '65.

Thatcher, John—Mustered out June 8, '65.

Trout, Daniel—Wounded in head severely at Griswoldville.

Waterbury, John J.—Wounded in cheek at Mission Ridge.

Wolfe, Joseph—Mustered out June 8, '65.

York, Jessie—Mustered out June 8, '65.

Roster of Company "K" 100th Indiana Infantry.

Captain Charles W. Brouse, recruited Company "K." He was the youngest Captain in the Regiment. He served in the Seiges of Vicksburg and Jackson. He was on detached duty when the assault on Missionary Ridge was begun—but he hastened his Company to the battle field and was soon in the very whirlpool of the carnage which took place in that engagement, at one time a confederate line had passed around our left over the tunnel, Captain Brouse requested permission of Col. Loomis to engage them, which being granted, he attacked the enemy furiously and was shot through an arm and a lung. For twenty-four hours he received no attention, having been laid among those whom the surgeons regarded as beyond hope. Men

Captain Charles W. Brouse.
Company K, 100th Indiana.

Captain James Bollinger.

died on each side of him, but he revived and lived though terribly wounded. He was specially mentioned for bravery in the Official Reports of the Brigade Commander.

Captain James Bolinger was promoted to Second Lieutenant May 1, '64, to First Lieutenant September 25, 64, and to be Captain of his Company January 17, '65. He was severely wounded at the battle of Griswoldville November 22, '64. He served until the end of the war. Captain Bollinger was an unostentatious officer, but he was resolute, firm and brave.

Jeremiah M. Wise was commissioned First Lieutenant September 24, '62, and resigned February 29, '64.

Henry G. Collis entered the service as Second Lieutenant of Company "K" September 24, '62. He was promoted to First Lieutenant of his Company; was detailed as an Aide on the staff of Col. Loomis, commanding the Brigade and served in that capacity with much credit. He was specially referred to and mentioned in the official reports of the Brigade Commander for bravery and entrepidity.

Lieutenant Cornelius List was several times promoted for bravery and efficient service; and on the 17th day of January, 1865, he was promoted to be First Lieutenant of his Company. He was a faithful soldier, was brave and generous to a fault. He was loved by all who knew him and was esteemed and respected by the officials of his Regiment.

Lieutenant B. Burch was promoted often. On the 22nd day of November, 1864, he was promoted to Second Lieutenant. He served in the field until the war ended.

Henry, William—Sergeant; transferred to V. R. C. June 18, '63.

Burch, Leonard B.—Promoted Sergeant for meritorious conduct.

Cherry, William—Sergeant; killed by cannon shot at Congaree Creek near Columbia, South Carolina, Feb. 15, '65.

Stirling, Robert D.—Mustered out June 29. '65, as Sergeant.

Parkhill, Samuel—Mustered out June 8, '65, as Sergeant.

Norwood, Dayton T.—Wounded in battle; mustered out June 29, '65.

Batts, Richard A.—Killed in battle of Jonesboro, Georgia, Aug. 31, while bringing ammunition to the line of battle during the Confederate Assault.

Irons, James H.—Mustered out Aug. 25, '65.

Pollard, Zachariah—Mustered out June 29, '65.

Toon, John M.—Discharged Feb. 5, '63.

Beals, Malvin M.—Mustard out, June, '65.

Martin, Ragsdale S.—Discharged Dec. 25, '62.

Eaton, Morgan H.—Discharged April 31, '63.

Allwine, Jacob—Mustered out June 14, '65.

Armstrong, John P.—Severely wounded, Missionary Ridge; discharged May 5, '65.

Anderson, David L.—Discharged Dec. 31, '64.

Beals, Malvin M.—Mustered out June 29, '65.

Lieutenant Henry G. Collis.
Company K, 100th Indiana Infantry; A. A, G. on Loomis' staff.

Lieutenant Cornelius List.
Company K. 100th Indiana Infantry.

Bennett, David O.—Wounded, Mission Ridge; mustered out June 29, '65.

Bogg, John—Mustered out June 29, '65.

Binder, John W.—Wounded, Missionary Ridge; mustered out June 29, '65.

Burdick, Louis B.—Discharged May 16, '65.

Borntrager, George—Wounded in battle of Griswoldville; mustered out July 15, '65.

Bickle, Thomas—Mustered out June 14, '65.

Colclazer, Joseph—Died at Memphis, Dec. 5, '62.

Crum, Michael E.—Wounded at Dallas, Georgia; mustered out June, '65.

Cash, Alfred A.—Discharged Dec. 31, '64.

Casteel, Calvin—Died at Keokuk, Iowa, June 20, '63.

Cramer, Mathias—Mustered out June 29, '65.

Duke, Columbus—Killed, Missionary Ridge, Nov. 25, '63.

Dearmin, James M.—Transferred to V. R. C. May 31, '64.

Everson, Jacob M.—Discharged May 3, '65.

Foster, Henderson—Honorably discharged June 29, '65.

Gratner, Henry—Discharged May 3, '65.

Gearing, Dennis—Mustered out June 29, '65.

Hoag, John—Died at Holly Springs, Dec. 31, '62.

Heady, James W.—Mustered out at the end of the war.

Hays, Samuel J.—Mustered out June 29, '65.

Hastings, Thomas A.—Mustered out June 29, '65.

Haswell, George J. — Mustered out May 30, '65.

Haynes, Andrew—Mustered out as Corporal June 29,'65.

Haynes, Frank—Mustered out June 29, '65.

Jackson, Wm.—Mustered out June 29, '65.

Jackson, Jacob—Mustered out June 29, '65.

Kennedy, Levi M. — Mustered out June 29, '65.

Kepler, John.—Died at Memphis, October 15, '63.

Logan, William A.—Mustered out June 29, '65.

McClelland, Edward M.—Wounded at Missionary Ridge.

Mullis, Ennis P.—Taken prisoner in North Carolina, April, '65, and shot while trying to escape.

Morgan, George W.—Mustered out June 29, '65.

Moore, Jesse W.—Mustered out June 29, '65.

Moore, James M. — Mustered out June 29, '65.

Nerhood, John K.—Killed in battle of Missionary Ridge.

Pollard, William H.—Wounded in battle of Griswoldville, Ga., Nov. 22, '64.

Pratt, Josiah.—Discharged April 16, '63.

Phillips, Benjamin. — Died at home Dec. 24, '64.

Pugh, David N.—Wounded at Missionary Ridge Nov. 25, '63; wounded at Griswoldville Nov. 22, '64; served faithfully during the war, was a brave soldier and a great favorite with his brave little Captain, who was standing by him when he was shot.

B. F. Smith.
Company K. 100th Indiana Infantry.

Pugh, Moses N.—Was one of those quiet soldiers who always managed to do all of his duty at all times and under all circumstances, whether on the march or in battle. The country owes a duty to Moses N. Pugh. He was wounded at Bentonville, March 21, '65, while on the picket line with the writer.

Palmer, Noah E.—Discharged Dec. 31,'64.

Richardson, Ethelbert.---Discharged May 11, '63.

Rouse, George W.—Mustered out June 29, '65.

Rapp, Michael.—Mustered out June 29, '65.

Russell, Samuel N.—Died at Jackson, Tenn., Jan. 26, '63.

Rodebaugh, Samuel.—Mustered out May 18, '65.

Spratt, John E.—Enjoys the distinction of being the youngest soldier in the 100th Indiana, being less than fourteen years old when he enlisted; mustered out as Corporal June 29, '65.

Smith, William—Died at Grand Junction Feb. 23, '63.

Stouffer, John T.—Mustered out June 29, '65.

Smith, B. F.—Enlisted August 13, 1862, when a mere boy, and with a single exception he was the youngest soldier in the Regiment; a frail little fellow but he had a great big man's heart in his breast. He soon became a favorite with the men and officers. He was fearless, boy as he was, but he performed a soldier's whole duty from the date of his enlistment to the end of the war. When the war ended he was yet a boy. He was a high-minded, moral, brave little soldier. He was wounded severely in battle of Griswoldville.

Stabler, Christian—Discharged April 16, '63.

Swisher, Solomon—Mustered out June 29, '65.

Snyder, Murray—Mustered out June 29, '65.

Tucker, David—Killed at Missionary Ridge Nov. 25, '63.

Vanwarmer, William A.—Mustered out as Corporal June 29, '64.

Ward, Levan—Mustered out June 29, '65.

Williamson, William J.—Discharged Dec. 31, '64.

West, John W.—Mustered out June 29, '65.

Zook, Jacob A.—Mustered out June 29, '65.

Baker, Solomon—Mustered out June 29, '65.

Cordray, Walter—Served with Company "A."

Destiger, Emanuel—Taken prisoner in North Carolina, and shot while trying to escape April, '65; same time as E. P. Mullis.

Eagle, John D.—Transferred to 48th Indiana June 29, '65.

Frank, Andrew J.—Transferred to 48th Indiana June 29, '65.

Gallazio, Charles G.—Mustered out July 3, '65.

Gullion, George W.—Discharged.

Hilbert, Thomas J.—Died at Nashville, Sept. 28, '64.

Haswell, Lewis R.—Transferred to 48th Regiment June 27, '65.

Lower, Israel—Died at Keokuk, Iowa, March 14, '63.

Moses N. Pugh,
Company K, 100th Indiana Infantry.
(From an old time tin-type).

George Wert.
Company K, 100th Indiana Infantry.

Charles Sims.
Company K. 100th Indiana Infantry.

Leavitt, Philander C., Jr.—Transferred for further service.

Norwood, Isaac N.—Wounded severely at Griswoldville.

Obert, Frederick—Transferred to 48th Indiana June 27, '65.

Robinson, Henry—Died at Marietta, Ga., Aug. 10, '64.

Sherman, John Q. A.—Transferred to 48th Indiana June 27, '65.

Simons, George—Discharged Oct. 29, '64.

Wert, George—Entered the army August 21, '62; he was one of the many faithful and reliable soldiers in Company "K"; he served faithfully and efficiently until the war closed, and made a clean, enviable and noble record.

Sims, Charles—Was another man who did noble service during the war; when duty called he was always there to answer; he served faithfully, and had the esteem and respect of the men and officers of his Company; he deserves to be remembered well by those who come after him.

Sharpnack, Charles—Transferred to 48th Indiana, June 27, '65.

Tupper, Frank—Transferred to 48th Indiana June 27, '65.

OUR REGIMENTAL ASSOCIATION.

To perpetuate memories and friendships formed under the pressure of common danger and in many instances bathed in and cemented by the blood of the parties, the survivors of the Hundredth Regiment have organized an association which holds a reunion each year, which has served to keep alive these memories and has been the cause of great good. The first Reunion was held Nov. 25, 1886, at Kendallville. Ten of these Reunions have been held and the 11th is to be held at Kendallville in 1896. They are well attended and the body of men who were members of the 100th compare favorably with those of any society socially and intellectually.

At these reunions the utmost good feeling and fellowship prevails. The wives of the soldiers, who as a body of womanly matrons have no superior socially or patriotically, aided by the Woman's Relief Corps and the good people where the reunions are held, always have prepared a bountiful repast where all are welcome to the refreshments provided.

The talented and refined sons and daughters of the old Veterans always have an interesting program for the evening's exercises embracing vocal and instrumental music, patriotic songs, set to National airs and humorous and dramatic recitations.

Miss Isa Lloyd Upson.
The daughter of the regiment, adopted November 25th, 1886.

At the first reunion Miss Upson was adopted as the daughter of the Regiment at the age of six years. She possesses dramatic talent and with the assistance of the sons and daughters of the old soldiers, many of whom also possess rare talent, the entertainments are rendered first class. These exercises are usually interspersed with an address by some member which renders the reunions beneficial and highly entertaining. It is to be hoped that when the last gray haired Veteran has gone the way of all the earth that these reunions will be perpetuated by their sons and daughters and their descendants.

The following table shows the death and other losses by Companies of the 100th Indiana during its term of service:

CO.	DEATHS.	DISCHARGED.	TRANSFERRED.	RESGD.	TOTAL.
"A"	34	15	9	3	61
"B"	25	15	2	3	45
"C"	26	13	2	4	45
"D"	22	12	13	2	49
"E"	26	14	7	3	50
"F"	23	16	11	2	52
"G"	19	13	7	2	41
"H"	24	12	11	0	47
"I"	16	14	4	2	36
"K"	15	16	8	2	41
Total...	230	140	74	23	467
Fld. Staff	1	1	0	5	7
Totals...	231	141	74	28	474

The following table shows the number of deaths during the War in each Regiment of the Second Brigade, First Division, Fifteenth Army Corps:

NAME OF REGIMENT.	KILLED. OFF.	MEN.	DIED. OFF.	MEN.	TOTAL. DEATHS.	REMARKS.
100th Ind. Vol. In.	3	62	3	166	234	(Error of 3.)
97th Ind. Vol. In..	3	51	6	172	232	Maj. Genl. Chas. R. Wood, Com. Div.
26th Ill. In.........	2	88	2	194	286	
40th Ill. In.........	6	119	4	117	246	
103d Ill. In........	8	87	1	153	249	Col. Charles C. Wolcott, Com. Brig.
46th Ohio In ...	10	124	7	149	290	
6th Iowa In........	8	144	2	126	280	
	39	676	25	1077	1817	

A group of the 100th who attended the 6th Reunion at Auburn, Indiana, October 14th, 1891.

A group of the 100th who attended the 6th Reunion at Auburn, Indiana, October 14th 1891.

The following table shows the total death losses during the War in the Four Army Corps and the Cavalry which marched to the sea.

	KILLED.		DIED.		
	OFF.	MEN.	OFF.	MEN.	TOTAL.
14th Army Corps....	196	3,903	93	7,613	11,858
20th Army Corps....	238	4,364	70	5,797	10,489
17th Army Corps....	165	2,920	89	6,912	10,096
15th Army Corps....	293	4,756	170	11,166	16,385
7th Cavalry Corps...	42	646	26	2,232	2,946
TOTAL DEATH LOSS.	934	16,589	448	33,720	51,774

TOTAL DEATH LOSSES—ALL CAUSES.

The following table is an approximate statement of the total deaths in the Union army from all causes during the war:

	OFFICERS.	MEN.	TOTAL.
Killed and mortally wounded.....	6,365	103,705	110,070
Died of various diseases..........	2,712	197,008	199,720
Disease and starvation in prison..	83	24,783	24,866
Accidental	248	8,810	9,058
Murders and sunstrokes..........	42	791	833
Prisoners murdered..............	14	90	104
Self destruction (suicides)	26	365	391
Executed under sentence	..	267	267
Executed by rebels	4	60	64
Unknown causes.................	90	14,065	14,155
TOTALS,	9,584	349,944	359,528

The Confederate total losses were doubtless about the same. During the last year of the war their reports were very incomplete and the true losses sustained cannot be ascertained.

The following table shows the strength of the four Army Corps and Kilpatrick's Cavalry Division on the march through the Carolinas in 1865:

	INFANTRY.	CAVALRY.	ARTILLERY.	TOTAL.
15 Army Corps	15,244	23	403	15,670
17 Army Corps	12,873	30	261	13,164
Total Army Tenn	28,117	53	664	28,834
14 Army Corps	14,653	....	445	15,098
20 Army Corps	12,471	....	494	12,965
Total Army Georgia	27,124	....	939	28,063
Total Both Armies	....	....	....	56,097
Cavalry Division	....	5,484	175	5,659
Total on March through the Carolinas	....	....	....	61,756

The following table shows the strength of the Union army at different times during the war. The figures to the right of any particular date in the column will give the number of troops in the service of the United States at that time:

```
January 1, 1861........................    16,367
July 1, 1861..........................   186,751
June 1, 1862..........................   575,917
March 31, 1862........................   918,191
June 1, 1863..........................   860,737
January 1, 1865.......................   959,460
March 31, 1865........................   980,086
May 1, 1865 .........................  1,000,516
```

At the close of the war the Unionists had more than a million men in the service, many thousands of whom never reached the seat of war.

THE END.

www.ingramcontent.com/pod-product-compliance
Lightning Source LLC
Chambersburg PA
CBHW020541300426
44111CB00008B/747